THOMSON
COURSE TECHNOLOGY
Professional ■ Technical ■ Reference

Web Downloads Available

PICTURE YOURSELF

Planning Your
Perfect Wedding

Step-by-Step Instruction for Planning, Organizing, and Personalizing Your Wedding

Sandy Doell

Cover photograph credits: Stewart Pinsky, Adlam Herod, Abbie DeLeers, Tad Denson, Melissa Roland, and Eric Limon, Waldek Photography, Aaron Lockwood Photography, Cameron H Photography, Mick Pederson.

Interior photograph credits: Autumn Azure, Cameron H Photography, Holly Istas Photography, James Karney, Aaron Lockwood Photography, Stewart Pinsky Photography, Mark Ridout, Amber Sisson, TriCoast Photography, Waldek Photography, Kim Benbow, Abbie DeLeers, Sally Emory, Elizabeth Furbish, Ted Herod, Mick Pederson, Melissa Roland, Tahlia Vaccarella, Elizabeth Woodhouse.

ISBN-10: 1-59863-439-9

ISBN-13: 978-1-59863-439-6

Library of Congress Catalog Card Number: 2007931842

Printed in the United States of America

08 09 10 11 12 BU 10 9 8 7 6 5 4 3 2 1

Publisher and General Manager, Thomson Course Technology PTR:
Stacy L. Hiquet

Associate Director of Marketing:
Sarah O'Donnell

Manager of Editorial Services:
Heather Talbot

Marketing Manager:
Jordan Casey

Acquisitions Editor:
Mitzi Koontz

PTR Editorial Services Coordinator:
Erin Johnson

Copy Editor:
Heather Urschel

Interior Layout:
Shawn Morningstar

Cover Designer:
Mike Tanamachi

Indexer:
Sharon Shock

Proofreader:
Sandi Wilson

Thomson Course Technology PTR,
a division of Thomson Learning Inc.
25 Thomson Place
Boston, MA 02210
http://www.courseptr.com

THOMSON
COURSE TECHNOLOGY
Professional ■ Technical ■ Reference

*To Dave, who patiently agreed when I had to postpone
our 20th wedding anniversary trip to finish writing this book,
demonstrating once again the meaning of "for better or worse."*

Acknowledgments

MANY PEOPLE HAD A HAND in the creation of this book, and it would take more space than is available here to thank each of them properly. Some are especially deserving of my personal appreciation though. Among them:

Mitzi Koontz, who took a personal interest in this book and its development, much more so than was her duty as the acquisitions editor, and who is one of the brides featured here.

Heather Urschel, who also helped develop the text and added many suggestions that didn't occur to me. She, too, is a featured bride in the book.

Shawn Morningstar put together all the puzzle pieces of text, notes, and photographs. And then she did it again when I asked her to rearrange entire chapters. Shawn also selected the beautiful color palette of the book and perfected the design to create an elegant interior—her changes made a tremendous difference. Sandi Wilson was also rushed, but she stayed focused on detail, and the book is much better for her involvement. Sharon Shock patiently waited as the deadline loomed and then did a week's worth of work in two days. All three maintained their professionalism and perseverance throughout the layout process. Jordan Casey was cheerfully helpful when I asked her to help me acquire impossible interviews and images, and Mike Tanamachi created just the look I hoped for on the cover and created accurate and beautiful illustrations of diamonds as well.

My mother-in-law, Judy Doell, family historian, took an interest as soon as I shared with her what my next project would be, digging out pictures from albums, taking them out of frames hanging on her walls, and entrusting me to take these family keepsakes away to be reproduced for the book.

Those family wedding pictures from the Doell, Abney, Alexander, and York families add a personal touch I couldn't have found anywhere else.

And then there were the brides. Many friends, family members, and co-workers responded to my plea for wedding pictures and stories, but one in particular took a personal interest in the book; Cathleen Small's responses to my original questionnaire were detailed and informative about many things; her wedding was a recent memory, and she shared with me how she went about planning the day in unique ways that suited her and her husband Chris's characters and beliefs. Cathleen also knew I'd need permission from subjects and photographers, so she set about to gather those for me before I even asked. Not only did Cathleen share her own extensive collection of wedding photographs, she then recruited her friends to share theirs and was just as diligent in seeking out permission for their use from both photographers and subjects.

All the couples who contributed stories, photographs, or both: Jennifer & Ryan, Heather & Mark, Mitzi & John, Jackie & Joni, Reneé & Scott, Lisa & Chris, Cathleen & Chris, Lisa & Joe, Sarah & Jay, Maria & George, Rhea & Gil, Nancy & Ray, Nicole & Will, Theresa & Randy, Kristin & Scott, Priscilla & Josh, Tiffany & Chad, Tiffany & Priscilla's mother Michie, Karen & Joe, Michael & Marni, Sandy & Dave, Shawn & Eli and all the others whose names I never knew.

Finally, many people went to great lengths to dig out details of their own weddings, complete my questionnaires, and tell me their stories—not all of them made the final cut. What to leave in and what to leave out is a difficult decision. The stories I left out are just as deserving as the ones I included; I still have them though, and I hope to make use of them in other ways in the future.

The idea behind the *Picture Yourself* series is, of course, pictures. Central to the theme of this book is the photography. All of it is good; some of it is art. If a photograph has "Courtesy of Shutterstock" and then the author's name listed in the credit, you can find information about him or her at Shutterstock.com. The others are listed below with web addresses if available:

Autumn Azure	http://www.artwanted.com/artist.cfm?ArtID=24224&SubGal=People
Cameron H Photography	www.cameronhphotography.com
Holly Istas Photography	www.hollyistasphotography.com
James Karney	www.capaphoto.com
Aaron Lockwood Photography	www.aaronlockwoodphotography.com
Stewart Pinsky Photography	mauiweddinggallery.com
Mark Ridout	www.ridoutphotography.com
Amber Sisson of Amber James Photography	http://web.mac.com/amberjamesphoto/iWeb/AmberJames/
TriCoast Photography	www.tricoastphoto.com
Waldek Photography	www.waldekphoto.com
Melissa Roland	
Mick Pederson	
Sally Emory	
Tahlia Vaccarella	
Elizabeth Furbish	
Kim Benbow	
Elizabeth Woodhouse	
Abbie DeLeers	
Ted Herod	

Several companies were gracious enough to allow me to use images of their product or to interview designers and executives; their contributions were central to making this book current and helpful, and I appreciate their cooperation, insight, and advice: Dan Scott of Scott Kay Jewelry Design, Caroline Flagler of David's Bridal, Matthew Swart of 1st Class Wedding Invitations, Lauren Curmi of Lippe/Taylor, Linda Shonk of Sweet Art Galleries—their input on topics in which they are specialists gives the book added credibility.

My grandsons, Jonathon, Jimmy, and Timothy, started college, scored touchdowns, and learned how to walk, respectively, while I worked long hours to put this book together. We missed some fun times, and I can't wait to go shopping, see some movies, and play video games again.

About the Author

BEFORE EMBARKING ON A CAREER in publishing nearly 20 years ago, Sandy Doell had another career as a caterer in both a country club and a hotel setting. One of her main responsibilities was to serve as the reception coordinator for hundreds of brides. Sandy guided bride, groom, and the rest of the bridal party through the cake cutting ceremony, toasting, the first dance, and bouquet and garter tossing—she has personally cut and served hundreds of wedding cakes. She has firsthand experience with countless wedding receptions where she worked to coordinate activities with photographers, chefs, and wedding planners. She learned how to be a calming influence on nervous brides and grooms as she skillfully guided them through their first social duties as a married couple.

Sandy currently works as a freelance book editor and writer, and is the editor of award-winning computer workshop materials for the Indiana University IT Training Department. She has served in many roles in publishing and has edited hundreds of books, most recently *301 Inkjet Tips and Techniques: An Essential Printing Resource for Photographers* by Andrew Darlow. In *Picture Yourself Planning Your Perfect Wedding*, Sandy brings together skills from both her careers (not to mention her natural proclivity for storytelling) to share with you the stories and pictures of dozens of brides on their most perfect day.

She is the author of *Mom's Field Guide: What You Need to Know to Make It Through Your Loved One's Military Deployment*, published in 2006 by Warrior Angel Press. That book is based on her experiences when her son, David, was deployed to Iraq with the U.S. Army in 2004. She has been interviewed by dozens of radio hosts around the country, discussing the needs of the troops and their families, and, along with Warrior Angel Press, she maintains two web sites (momsfieldguide.com and whileourchildrenserve.com) in support of the families of deployed military personnel.

Table of Contents

Introduction xiii

Part I   *Engaged!* 1

Chapter 1   Wedding Trends and Fashions 3

Every Little Girl's Dream 7
The Proposal 9
        Creative Ways to Propose 9
        Which Comes First? The Ring or the Question? 11
Arranged Marriages from Long Ago 12
The Betrothal 14
A Note of Caution 15

Chapter 2   Choosing the Rings 17

Wedding Ring History and Traditions 19
        Why a Ring? 19
The Diamond 21
        Why a Diamond? 21
        How to Choose a Diamond 21
The Band 27
        Gold 28
        White Gold 28
        Platinum 28
The Setting 29

Chapter 3   **Telling Everyone** **31**

Keep It in the Family First 33
    Visit, Call, Write, E-Mail. 34
If You Have Children 35
Introducing the Families. 37
Telling the Rest of the World 38
    Newspaper Announcements 38
    Alumni Magazines. 40
The Engagement Party 41

Chapter 4   **Dream, Plan, Realize** **43**

Budget Meets Dream 45
    Plan. 46
Getting Organized 48
    Start Early and Stay Organized 49
    Keeping Records. 51
Choosing the Date and Time 52
    Season 52
    Day of Week 53
    Time of Day. 54
    Religious Restrictions. 55
A Vision of Your Big Day 56

Part II   *Serious Planning* *57*

Chapter 5   **Strictly Business** **59**

The Budget, or Who Should Pay for What 61
    Today's Fiscal Responsibility 62
Worksheets and Calculators 64
    Head Count. 66
Prenuptial Agreements 67
    Community Property vs. Common Law States 68
Other Business Concerns 70
Wrapping Up the Business Aspects 71

Chapter 6 **Choosing the Sites, the Theme, the Tone of Your Wedding** **73**

The Ceremony 75
    Get Specific and Ask the Right Questions 79
    Changing Religions to Get Married 80
    Reserve Musicians for the Ceremony 81
Coordination 82
The Reception 83
    Space Concerns 85
    Concern for All Your Guests 86
    Consider the Work That Must Be Done 87
    Reserve Musicians or DJ for Reception 88
    Smart Moves 89

Chapter 7 **Getting Down to Some Details** **91**

Color Scheme 94
    Emotions Associated with Color 94
    Some Facts about Color 95
    Consult a Florist 96
Invitations 97
    Save the Date Cards 99
    Other Stationery Items 100
    Speaking of Favors 101
Attendants 102
    How Many? 102
    How to Choose Them 103
    Responsibilities of the Attendants 104

Chapter 8 **Shopping for The Dress...and More** **107**

Wedding Gown Vocabulary 109
Making the Choice 113
Accessories 118
    Trains 118
    Veils 119
    Tiaras 120
    Gloves 120

Undergarments 121

Other Accessories 121

Shoes 122

Still More Shopping to Do 124

Bridesmaids' Dresses 124

Mothers of the Bride and Groom. 126

Groom's and Groomsmen's Attire. 126

The Tuxedo, the Suit Itself 127

Fit 128

Fathers of the Bride and Groom 129

Chapter 9   Florists, Cakes, Photographers, and More . 131

Flowers 133

The Bride's and Bridesmaids' Bouquets. 133

Centerpieces, Altar Flowers, Pew Pieces 135

Corsages and Boutonnières 135

Other Decorative Items 136

The Cake 138

Choosing a Photographer. 144

Videographer 148

Transportation 149

Part III   *All the Revelry That Comes Before. . . 151*

Chapter 10   Pre-Wedding Parties 153

Showers 155

Bachelor and Bachelorette Parties. 157

Special Gatherings. 158

Rehearsal and Rehearsal Dinner 159

Post Wedding Brunches 161

Chapter 11   Gifts: Giving and Getting 163

Gift Registries 165

Other Gifts. 167

Wedding Favors and Goody Bags 168

Chapter 12   **Legal Considerations** **171**

License to Marry.. 173

Changing Your Name... 175

Insurance 177

Checking Accounts, Credit Cards, and Taxes.................... 178

Chapter 13   **Planning the Honeymoon** **181**

Destination Wedding and Honeymoon........................ 184

Part IV   *The Wedding Day................... 187*

Chapter 14   **Getting Ready for the Big Day** **189**

Preparing Yourself for the Event of a Lifetime 191

Pre-Marital Counseling 192

Dancing Lessons 193

Hair Styles.. 194

Toning Your Body...................................... 195

The Day Before the Wedding.............................. 196

The Morning of the Wedding.............................. 197

Chapter 15   **The Ceremony.......................... 201**

Music for the Ceremony...................................... 203

The Wedding as Entertainment 204

The Vows 205

After the Vows 205

Photo Sessions 214

Chapter 16   **The Reception.......................... 219**

Food and Drink.. 222

Music... 230

Lighting.. 232

Afterword   The Honeymoon and Beyond 233

Appendix   Sample Forms and Checklists 235

       Budget Sample 236
       Discussion Questions for Couples 237
       The Master To Do List 246
       Sample Verification Letter/Fax 250
       Event Manager Master To-Do List—Rehearsal 251
       Event Manager Master To-Do List—Wedding Day 252
       Ceremony Music Outline for Musicians 253
       A Sample Wedding Program 254
       Photographer's Guide 258
       Master List for Reception DJ 260

       Index 261

Introduction

THE GOALS OF A COUPLE for their wedding day are of two varieties. If you ask any couple—okay, let's be honest here...any bride-to-be planning her wedding—what she wants her special day to be like, she will answer either, "I want a traditional wedding with all the trimmings, white dress, bridesmaids, flowers, walking down the aisle, and seeing tears stream down my groom's face as he awaits me at the altar," or she will say, "I want our wedding to be uniquely about us. We'll write our own vows, keep the ceremony simple and meaningful, have a party, and ignore tradition entirely."

The wedding has, throughout history, been a day when women are "traditionally" entirely in charge. The groom waits patiently at the altar with his supporters by his side. It is the bride, the bride's mother, and all the lovely bridesmaids who are the center of attention at a wedding and the real force behind planning the day. Whether a bride wants a traditional wedding or has a more modern idea of entering into a partnership, there's always that word that creeps into any conversation when weddings are being discussed: perfect.

Many of the brides interviewed for this book describe their very different wedding days as "perfect." And many brides planning their wedding use that word. Their goal is often stated as wanting to plan the "perfect wedding."

There are many guide books available that cover every aspect of wedding planning and tell you how to do it, some on literally a day-to-day basis. It seemed intimidating to try to add to that body of work something that would be both unique and useful, perhaps even inspirational. But those words kept coming up again and again: perfect, traditional, unique, and so I began to think about what those words mean.

The Meaning of Traditional

When a bride says she wants a traditional ceremony, what does she picture? Certainly, she's not thinking of the oldest of weddings, when our distant ancestors roamed in tribes and a wedding was much more like a kidnapping. There's even a term for kidnapping a bride in such a way—it's called a Danish wedding because it is reputedly the way the Vikings acquired their wives. No...rape, murder, and pillage are pretty much out of favor these days, so we need to look for the meaning of tradition a bit farther along in history.

The Victorian Age brought us much closer to the romantic notion we have today of a traditional wedding, and Queen Victoria herself, being adamant about the way she wanted her wedding to Prince Albert to proceed, is truly responsible for many of the traditions we think of today when we think of weddings. She wore a veil (and wore it off her face so that the reporters and others gathered for the occasion could see her face). She wore white and thereby set a standard still in effect nearly 170 years later. Now we're getting somewhere. This is tradition.

So it began with Queen Victoria and moved steadily forward to today's five-tiered wedding cake, sumptuous reception menu for 200, and a dress that takes your breath away when you see it, not to mention a year-long engagement because it takes that long to put the whole affair together. Well, not quite. There were a few bumps in the history of wedding tradition.

Two world wars dictated that couples speed things up a bit. The World War II bride had no time for planning an event that would be the talk of the town for months to come. Her groom was about to be sent to war, perhaps not to return, and all either of them wanted was to be married first. These brides put on their best suits, went to stand before a judge and be married, spent a hurried two-day honeymoon, and then said good-bye to their new husbands and went home to start the letter writing campaigns that would sustain their relationship for the next few months.

Here's a memory of one such bride, my mother, describing her wedding day:

> We took the #9 train into Birmingham, went to the courthouse and got our license and then went across the street to a judge's house where we were married. Clyde and Corene stood up with us. We went back home, and Mama had fixed a really nice supper. Mrs. Cooper baked a cake. We had supper and got on the bus to go to Tallahassee where your father was stationed at the time.

It was difficult to maintain traditional weddings during World War II, but the 1950s saw a return to the church wedding with all the trimmings. Another English princess was married, Princess Elizabeth to Prince Philip, and a new standard was set.

We do tend to borrow tradition from royalty, and since royalty is somewhat rare these days, we settle for celebrity and pay close attention to the weddings of movie stars and famous musicians and sports stars.

Tradition, it seems, changes a bit with each generation, not just adding to or building upon, but sometimes reverting to an earlier time. Our current definition of tradition is more akin to the Victorian wedding than it is to the more recent pragmatic unions of the 1940s.

Even the weddings of the post-war years pale in comparison to today's lavish blowouts where no detail is too small for a bride to have an anxiety attack over. The 1950s saw us having a big church wedding and then either retiring to the church basement for cake and punch or having a reception in the bride's family home. That seems rather tame compared to today's cathedral weddings with the reception in a ballroom or country club featuring an extensive menu with ice sculptures and floral arrangements bedecking every nook and cranny of the hall, creating a fairy tale-like space.

So tradition means what we want it to mean. To some brides, it means honoring her ethnic and cultural roots; to others it simply means as lavish as possible, while others emphasize the religious traditions associated with weddings. Today's bride can afford to indulge her dreams too; as both women and men are older, well employed, and independent at the time of their wedding, they tend to take more of the financial burden on themselves. And they demand the best for every aspect of what has turned into an event.

Perfection

But what about perfection? Why do so many brides use that word? And why do some suffer so much anxiety over the shade of white that is the icing on their wedding cake? What is it about this day that makes us say we want it to be perfect, when the complications and details involved almost ensure that perfection in all aspects of the day is impossible? With so much going on, no matter how many guidebooks and planning guides, checklists and comparison studies, even with the assistance of professional wedding planners...no matter how hard we try, we are bound to fail at some small overlooked detail.

Still, perfect is what we aim for, and this definition gets interesting—because even if it rained all day, even if the limo got lost on the way to the church, or a bridesmaid lost her heel...all those things contribute to the story of the wedding that will be told ever afterward. And the bride, to a woman, will say that her wedding was perfect. She'll laugh over the things that went wrong and rhapsodize over the beauty of it all.

So perfection, it seems, isn't quite what the dictionary says it is, at least not in the case of weddings.

Unique and Personal

So how do you reconcile all these ideas associated with weddings: traditional, perfect, unique, personal? And how do you tell a bride-to-be the very best way to go about attaining the wedding day she wants? Having given the history and the definitions and the individual stories much thought, it seems to me that the secret to perfection lies in the title of this book: *Picture Yourself Planning Your Perfect Wedding.* The key word is *your.* It's your wedding, so it should be a personal statement, a reflection of who you are, your values, character, and personality. Traditional, trendy, vintage...the weddings featured in this book in stories and in pictures are real-life weddings with real-life brides and grooms who all say that their wedding was perfect.

Your wedding is perfect because it's your wedding, so read this book with that thought in mind. The couples who share their stories here all had perfect weddings. Things went wrong. Spills occurred. All the weddings were perfect though because they expressed the personalities and lifestyles of the people being joined together for a lifetime.

Turn the page, and

Picture Yourself Planning Your Perfect Wedding.

Part I
Engaged!

I F THERE'S ONE WORD ASSOCIATED *with weddings, it's perfect. Each detail must be perfect, and there are hundreds, nay, thousands, of details. So how do you keep track of all those details, each of which must be perfect? It might rain on your big day, or it might be unseasonably cold or hot. The flowers may be delivered a few minutes late, the photographs take too long, or the ring bearer might decide to stop and say "Hi" to his uncle on the way down the aisle. Anything might happen, but still your day will be perfect because it reflects who you are as a couple within your circle of family and friends and because it's all about one thing: love.*

You do need a bit of organization and planning to get to that day, though, and this book will help keep you on track. Your plans should be a guideline, a plan to work from. Plan...and then relax and go with the flow a bit. In the end, it will all be perfect because it's about your love for each other and about your friends and family showing their love for you both. Whether you are planning an extravaganza with ice sculptures on the hors d'oeuvres table, eight attendants, and a 20-piece band playing at the reception; a backyard wedding with a pitch-in dinner and CDs of your favorite dance tunes; or a destination wedding for 50 people...there are as many ways to celebrate your uniting as there are couples, and all of them are perfect.

Courtesy of The Foster Family

Wedding Trends and Fashions

Marry in haste; repent at leisure.

EVERY GENERATION IS ENAMORED, it seems, of at least one big, stupendous celebrity or royal wedding, which then becomes the model for weddings around the world. Most recently, we all watched in awe as Eva Longoria and Tony Parker tied the knot in a simple civil ceremony followed by an elaborate and unbelievably expensive ceremony in Saint-Germain-l'Auxerroix Church in Paris, followed by an even more elaborate reception at Vaux-le-Vicomte, a 17th-Century chateau outside the city. And it all took place on the luckiest day ever: July 7, 2007 (7/7/07).

A generation ago, half the world stayed awake all night or woke up early to watch as Prince Charles of England wed Diana Spencer on July 29, 1981. Long before that, little girls poured over fashion magazines and news stories as Grace Kelly literally became a princess when she answered "I do" (in two ceremonies, one civil on April 18, the other religious the following day) and became the wife of Prince Rainier of Monaco in 1956. In 1906 the celebrity wedding of the decade was celebrated when Alice Roosevelt became the bride of Nicholas Longworth in a White House ceremony. And, believe it or not, Queen Victoria and Prince Albert sparked a whole raft of wedding traditions in 1840 that we still honor and adhere to today.

Alice Roosevelt's wedding to Nicholas Longworth, a Representative to Congress from Ohio, set the style for this early 20th Century wedding couple to emulate.

Queen Victoria set the trend for white wedding gowns, but it took a few years for the trend to become a tradition.

Perhaps this bride and groom had Elizabeth Taylor's and Conrad "Nicky" Hilton's wedding in mind as they chose their attire.

Senator John F. Kennedy and Jacqueline Lee Bouvier wed in a ceremony that is still talked about today in Newport; this couple, wed in 1957, used some of the same ideas for their ceremony, although their cake only had to serve about 100 guests, not the 1200 who showed up for JFK and Jackie's reception.

The weddings of John F. Kennedy and Jacqueline Bouvier and, later, of JFK, Jr. and Carolyn Bessette are examples of what American "royalty" can achieve in terms of grace and style. Jack and Jackie were married September 12, 1953 after an engagement that lasted only three months. Their reception at Hammersmith Farms in Newport, Rhode Island, included a two-hour receiving line followed by dancing and champagne for 1,200 guests. They had a motorcycle escort from St. Mary's Church in Newport, where they were married by Cardinal Cushing and where a papal blessing was read. Four decades later, in the age of paparazzi, JFK, Jr. and Carolyn Bessette chose to keep their wedding as secret as possible and opted for the tiny African Baptist Church in Cumberland Island, Georgia. They were married on September 21, 1996 and managed to keep their nuptials a very private affair, which may have required more effort than the extravaganza that was the wedding of Jack and Jackie.

These and other weddings of the high and mighty, the famous, the beautiful, the "hot," set the tone for the rest of us. We aspire to look as blushing and innocent as Diana did on her wedding day or to wear a dress as stylish and flattering as Grace Kelly's still looks, even though she wore it more than 50 years ago. Never mind that some of these marriages ended in divorce or early death or wore on through adultery, unhappiness, and difficulties of various sorts. The marriage and the wedding seem to be two very different things, and it is the wedding with which we will concern ourselves in the pages of this book, although we'll bear in mind that the marriage is the important thing and that perfection is almost never totally possible. Still, happiness is, and that is what you should hope for on your wedding day.

On April 19, 1956, Grace Kelly became Princess
Grace of Monaco, in a high-necked, long-sleeved
gown, fitted over the torso with a billowing skirt
and composed of hundreds of yards of silk taffeta,
peau de soie, tulle, and lace. She wore a Juliet cap
decorated with seed pearls and a veil made from
90 yards of tulle. The gown was designed by MGM's
costume designer, Helen Rose. Brides today still
emulate her style and grace.

*This bride wore a dress whose bodice is strikingly similar to the
one worn by Grace Kelly in 1956.*

From the collection of Judy Doell

Courtesy of Ryan and Jennifer O'Donnell
© Stewart Pinsky

*Unlike his parents, JFK, Jr. and Carolyn opted for a
private wedding on a remote barrier island far
from prying eyes and cameras. This couple was
able to achieve the same tone in Hawaii.*

The wedding is one day; the marriage is for a lifetime. So before you begin to plan the
wedding, make sure of one or two things. Most important, make sure you have chosen the
right person. Consider well, and if you have any doubts whatsoever, don't do it. Marriage wasn't
meant to be an undertaking that we enter into "until someone better comes along" or "as long as I still
enjoy spending time with you." The vows you take on your wedding day are pretty clear about "'til death
us do part." So don't do it unless you really mean it. The wedding is a big deal, a happy day to celebrate
the beginning of your life together, but it's not an end; it's a beginning. The rest of your life follows.

Every Little Girl's Dream

BEFORE THE MIDDLE OF THE LAST century, little girls grew up creating needlework to fill hope chests, being gifted with fine furniture in anticipation of the homes they would one day manage, and looking forward to shopping for a trousseau in the months before their weddings. In those pre-Betty Friedan days, marriage was the best career choice available to a woman. She should go to college and get an education, but the truth was that women went to college in those days because that's where the most promising marriageable men were to be found. Her education would be used to make her a better conversationalist and life partner for her professional husband, a better help-mate.

Her career would always center on home management and rearing children, and that's what she was brought up to do. A woman went from living with her parents to living in a dorm, back home for a summer to plan a wedding, and from then on she was best known as Mrs. Somebody. Through all this, her big day, her one day to be a princess, came on the occasion of her wedding. It was the day she looked forward to all her life and the day she spent the rest of her life looking back on. The only thing that might possibly outshine it would come about 20 years later when she planned her daughter's wedding.

Courtesy Shutterstock © Brian Chase

Courtesy Shutterstock © Kathryn Bell

Courtesy Shutterstock © Brian Chase

Courtesy Shutterstock © Pattie Steib

Fine needlework, grace, good taste, and beauty were the talents a bride brought to her wedding day before the social changes that began after the end of World War II. Women were admired for their homemaking abilities, their frugality, their cooking, and skill in the domestic arts. Only in the past few decades have women been valued as equal wage earners.

These days, we've all opted for careers and independence. We are free thinkers, we have our own homes complete with mortgage, our own retirement accounts, and our own credit cards. We live on our own and become quite successful before we entertain the idea of marriage and children. Times change. So with all this independence, what has become of the extravagance, the white dress, the three-tiered cake, the thousands spent on one day that was the culmination of a dream and signaled the beginning of life as an adult woman? One might assume we are less romantic than our predecessors, less inclined to indulge in the almost exclusively feminine excitement of a big wedding. But that isn't the case. The fact is, we spend more, stress more, and our weddings these days are more opulent than our parents, grandparents, and even Queen Victoria ever dreamed possible. Maybe we do it because now we can afford it. Maybe it's a chance, in the midst of a life that consists of corporate sameness and ambition in the world of business, to just be that princess for a day that we still read about in the pages of *People* and *Us* magazines. Maybe it's a chance to show off our project management skills rather than all those almost forgotten homemaking skills our ancestors were so proud of.

Nowadays, instead of working to create the hope chest and dreaming of knights in shining armor, while planning careers as veterinarians or astronauts, girls between the ages of 3 and 10 focus on Barbie dolls and Disney fairy tales. They have pink bedrooms and, if not glass slippers, then surely at least one pair of acrylic ones. We're still focused on the princess life, and the culmination of that is the fairy tale perfect wedding when we walk down the aisle to be joined to the man of our dreams.

It is appropriate that we indulge that little girl dream and give ourselves one special day when we are the absolute center of attention, so go ahead and do it exactly as you want (or at least as close to what you want as you can reasonably, or even somewhat unreasonably, afford) without pangs of guilt or remorse over the cost. Let's also keep it in perspective. You don't have to actually *be* a princess to spend one day living the life. You can be a nurse from Denver, a college student in Kentucky, a librarian in Des Moines, or an executive assistant from Minneapolis; your wedding can be very formal with morning coats and a dress with a train in a 200-year-old cathedral, or you can do it outside and barefoot. No matter the style, place, and level of formality, you can give yourself that one day of being the princess you've always dreamed of being. You can do it without doubling your current debt load or asking your parents to take out a second mortgage; you can do it with style and grace and beauty. Or you can go for broke, even take out a second mortgage yourself, and pull out all the stops for a blast that rivals any movie star's castle wedding or the ones sponsored by the morning news shows on TV—and still do it with style and grace and beauty. You can do it any way you want and at any level of expense. All you need is to get organized and start planning.

Today dolls have careers as business executives, fashion models, veterinarians, and even presidential candidates, but it is as brides that they truly shine.

The Proposal

B EFORE THERE CAN BE A MARRIAGE, before there can be a wedding, there must be a proposal. Some men are better at this than others. If you have not yet been given an engagement ring, if all you've done so far is talk about "someday" when you're married and have children, if you're just exploring the idea and questions have yet to be asked, that's great! You have time to plan this major turning point in your life, too.

A friend once told her significant other that she wanted the proposal to come as a surprise when she would least expect it. So he proposed to her one morning in the bathroom, between the tub and the toilet. It's likely that wasn't quite what she had in mind, but it certainly was what she asked for—a surprise. If nothing else, she probably learned to be a bit more clear when making requests in the future for any kind of gift or celebration.

Here are a few ideas for more romantic proposals.

Creative Ways to Propose

Of course, the traditional way to propose is on bended knee, perhaps in a restaurant or with the woman seated on a park bench among strangers on the beach or in a city park. Or privately, with the woman sitting on her couch and the man getting down on one knee to beg for her hand in marriage.

It's okay to ask the question first and shop for the ring later.

There are as many ways to propose as there are couples. Men, know your woman and know what she will appreciate. Don't propose to her during the seventh inning stretch at a White Sox game unless you know she'll be impressed by your public declaration of love. Don't rent a billboard that she passes every morning on her way to work unless you are quite certain she'll be amused and excited and flattered by the expense and the audacity of such a stunt. And do we even have to tell you: Don't propose in public unless you are 100 percent certain of the answer. Remember the scene in *Crocodile Dundee* where the longtime boyfriend makes an elaborate proposal in front of friends and family at the dinner table? He had lots of confidence...he just didn't know his woman as well as he thought he did.

Mitzi & John

Grand, romantic proposals in Paris aren't only for Tom and Katie! Slip the ring on her finger as you kiss in the New Year under the lights of the Eiffel Tower in Paris. That is the most memorable, most perfect proposal we can imagine, and it actually happened to Mitzi, one of the editors of this book, when John proposed to her while vacationing in Europe. He planned in advance and brought the ring with him from the U.S. all the way through the rain-kissed streets of Paris to the foot of the Eiffel Tower, just to create a moment. What drama and style!

Nancy & Ray

A few decades ago another prospective groom, Ray, gave Nancy a box of chocolates. They were all wrapped in foil a la Godiva. He suggested that she try the one in the center first because he'd tried one of those and they were really good. She unwrapped the paper to find that it contained, instead of a chocolate truffle, her engagement ring. Ray and Nancy celebrated their golden wedding anniversary a few years ago, and she's still wearing that same ring, so his inventiveness went over quite well.

A proposal can be done in many different ways. It isn't always even the man who gets down on one knee; it could be the woman who does the asking. And, of course, in gay unions, it doesn't even have to be one of each gender participating in this ritual. And, as we mentioned earlier, asking may not even be the way it's done. But presenting the ring is what we are thinking of when we use the word "proposal," and as with all presentations, it should be done with some flair.

Beware of your surroundings as well. Proposals on snow covered mountains and in the middle of quiet lakes are beautiful but excited hands can easily drop engagement rings never to be found again. A friend became engaged during a ski trip in Colorado only to spend the next four hours hauling hot water from their cabin to the spot of the proposal because the ring had slipped from her nervous fingers into several feet of snow! While the persistent couple eventually found the ring, it was not the romantic moment either of them had in mind. (Although it does make an entertaining story!)

We have some suggestions for how not to give someone an engagement ring, though. Presenting a ring by wrapping it in foil and placing it in a box of chocolates is a romantic gesture. Hiding it in the mashed potatoes, ice cream, or chocolate pudding is less so. Think about it: If your idea for presenting the ring in a surprising way involves putting it in food and having to rinse the ring off before your beloved puts it on her finger, maybe you should reconsider. Freezing it in an ice cube isn't a very good idea either. Three words come to mind: tacky, tacky, tacky.

There is also the story of a man who placed his beloved's engagement ring in a box of Cracker Jacks—you know, a prize comes in those anyway. That might be sufficiently romantic, but it comes with some security concerns. You need to watch closely to make sure she doesn't throw the "junk toy" away with the empty box. Just think carefully about your chosen method if it is going to be anything that veers too far from tradition.

Which Comes First?
The Ring or the Question?

This dilemma requires some thought, and the answer, of course, varies from couple to couple. What could be more romantic than proposing and immediately slipping the perfect ring on the finger of your beloved? What could be more intimidating than choosing the ring she will be showing off to her friends and family and presumably wearing for the rest of her life without her input on matters of style, cut, and setting...not to mention size? Of course, if you have limitless money to spend on this purchase, you'll probably be able to make the choice and impress her with carat size alone. But if you're a regular guy, you might not feel so secure in making this choice on your own.

Consider making your plans to be married and then setting a time to go choose rings together. Then you can just find a way to present the ring that you already know is one she will adore, not to mention one that fits her finger. Another delicate matter is cost. The diamond ads in magazines say that you should plan on spending two and a half months' salary on this purchase, so at nearly a quarter of your annual income, this is something you'll want to give a lot of consideration. When you determine just how much you are comfortable spending on this purchase, you might consider asking the jeweler ahead of time to show rings in your price range and then choose the one your prospective bride likes best from among those shown. We'll go into more detail about the ring—more detail than you might imagine possible—in Chapter 2, "Choosing the Rings."

Heather & Mark

Mark asked Heather to marry him one morning before they headed off for a weekend camping trip. They took a detour on the way out of town to learn about diamonds and ring styles at a jeweler, picked one, got the sizing taken care of, and picked the ring up Monday evening. This also gives you a bit of time to get used to the idea of marrying this person before you start telling people, making announcements, and showing off the ring. You need to take a moment to savor your new status anyway, just the two of you, before you start telling parents and friends and being asked a million questions you probably haven't even considered yet yourselves.

Courtesy of Lisa Boyadjian and Chris Duval

This bride-to-be just proposed to her groom on a camping trip by presenting him with flowers; they chose their rings later on.

11

Arranged Marriages from Long Ago

WHY DO WE HAVE SO MANY traditions regarding proposals and length of engagement and announcements and all the details that go into this time in your life? Many of our traditions originated in European medieval times when marriages were not considered religious sacraments at all, but rather business arrangements, meant to join together the property and fortune of two families as much as they were meant to join two loving people for life. Nor were marriages associated with the idea of romantic love. In fact, marriageable children of the upper classes were often little more than pawns in someone's scheme to garner more property and wealth. Marriage for love actually originated with the lower classes, who apparently had less to lose by following their hearts.

Courtesy Shutterstock © Kanwarjit Singh Boparai

Early weddings were more business arrangement than romantic alliance.

The Victorians added to the list of wedding rituals with their prim and proper behavior and their ideas about etiquette. Social behavior in those days, especially as it pertained to young people in search of a mate, was all about making sure young ladies of gentle birth found husbands who could support them. Otherwise, they were destined to a lifetime as a governess or a poor aunt who lived as well as her better off relatives allowed her to. Jane Austen understood the society of her day, and making a good marriage is the overriding subject of her novels. For some insight into some of our wedding rituals, read *Pride and Prejudice*. Better yet, see the BBC mini-series with Colin Firth and Jennifer Ehle. The 2005 movie with Keira Knightly and Matthew Macfadyen is good too, but nobody broods and smolders like Colin Firth.

We no longer arrange marriages as a business transaction between one family and another, and only rarely does a young man maintain the tradition of asking the bride's father for her hand in marriage before the proposal. This is almost never done now for obvious reasons—brides are no longer considered property whose ownership is to be passed from one man, her father, to another, her husband, although in many cultures, including the more genteel among us in modern society, it is considered a very polite and gentlemanly thing to do (see Chapter 3, "Telling Everyone").

A chapel in the English countryside where Jane Austen might have attended a wedding.

The remaining bit of etiquette from that period of "marriage as business arrangement" that we should honor today is this: After the two of you have agreed to marry, after the ring has been bought, and after you've had time to savor your new status privately, the next people who should hear of your plans are the bride's parents. After that, the groom's parents should be notified. Of course, if either of you have children, they take precedence over everyone, since, presumably, they will be a part of the new nuclear family you are about to create. See Chapter 3 for more about telling your parents (and children if you have them), but give some thought to the reaction you expect when you make your announcement. Don't take your prospective partner along if you think your parents or other close family members will initially disapprove. You'll have an opportunity then to reassure them without anyone feeling too uncomfortable. Then when they do meet your proposed mate, they will have had time to adjust. At this point, you might also want to arrange for a dinner party where the two families can get together. Making the public announcements to other family members, friends, and the community will also be covered in Chapter 3.

Bring your families together to share in the joy of your engagement.

We do still observe the tradition of having the father give the bride away at the wedding, so it is not really so difficult to imagine asking him to perform that function ahead of time. What does remain of that tradition for all of us is the equally nerve-wracking ritual of telling the parents, introducing the prospective spouse to the parents if they haven't had the opportunity to meet yet, and arranging a way for both families to come together to form a friendship and new family structure based on the alliance of their children.

The Betrothal

YOUR ENGAGEMENT BEGINS WITH the acceptance of the ring, the introduction of the parents, and the announcement of the upcoming nuptials. This was once the time when such things as dowries and bride prices were settled. Often, the bride had no say in these business matters; in fact, she might not have met her fiancé until after the business side of things had been arranged between the two families. The betrothal was a time when the two principals could get to know each other. Later, during Victorian times, it gave the upper class bride time to shop for a trousseau and attend a round of parties and dances, all designed to give the couple a chance to spend time together without actually being left alone together (although it still lasted only about three months). It also marked their graduation into the world of adulthood and community responsibility, and the round of betrothal and engagement parties helped serve to introduce the happy couple to society.

This engagement period is now used to plan the wedding. The average length of an engagement in the United States these days is 17 months[1]. Sometimes the most popular reception halls, the most wonderful caterers, the florists, the bakeries, the churches and halls, and even the minister or priest you have your heart set on are booked up a year or more in advance. The sooner you start planning and making phone calls to book these places and people, the more smoothly the whole affair will go and the more likely it will turn out just as you wish.

Why does the bride wear a veil? This modest custom has its roots in the past. When marriages were arranged as business deals between families, intended as a means to make both families more prosperous and secure in their holdings, it was not necessary for the bride and groom to meet before the ceremony. In fact, if the bride was perhaps not as agreeable in appearance as might be hoped, it was considered in the best interests of all that the groom not get a good look at her. So she was veiled until after the vows had been made and there was no chance that he could back out of the deal.

The story of Jacob and Rachel (and Leah) in the Old Testament is one such story. Jacob offers to work seven years for the hand of Rachel in marriage. After seven years, he arrives to claim his prize. The wedding takes place with the bride properly veiled, and when Jacob lifts the veil, he finds Rachel's older sister Leah—because the older sister has to be married first. Then Jacob is required to work seven more years for Rachel. Quite a horse (er, daughter) trader was Laban, the father of Rachel and Leah. I might add that he was also Jacob's mother's brother, making both Rachel and Leah Jacob's first cousins—but let's just leave the story there.

[1] The Wedding Report at weddingreport.com.

A Note of Caution

EARLY IN THE ENGAGEMENT is the time also to start thinking of some of the practical aspects of marriage today. Given that early marriages were more business affair than romantic interlude, you should not feel guilty about broaching the subject of a prenuptial agreement. In the past century, people tended to get married early without much fortune on either side. Dowries were a thing of the past, and women worked almost exclusively in the home raising children. Still, it turned out that later in life (and as society's expectations of women and their roles changed), women could be left in the lurch, aging and alone while their middle-aged husbands flew to Jamaica with younger women. Those wives did not often think to protect themselves, and the lack of community property laws in some states left them alone and penniless after years of investing all their efforts in a marriage they thought would continue to support them "until death us do part." The reality is that 50 percent of all marriages end in divorce. That number may be going down a bit in recent years, but you need to get those stars out of your eyes just long enough to understand what you're getting into in pure financial terms.

In these days of later marriage and longer periods of time spent working and amassing property as a single person or bringing property from a prior marriage with you to the new relationship, both parties would be well advised to at least discuss the idea at this point in the proceedings. Marriage is a contract, and you should know what the laws in your state view that contract to be. Each of you likely has assets of your own and you should protect those assets.

Because we marry later, not only do we both bring assets to the marriage, we also are likely to bring children from previous relationships whose interests must be protected. If you have children, even if they are grown and independent, or if you own property, then you must have some agreement in place to protect those children and their rightful inheritance.

Think about the financial agreement you are entering into with this other person, talk it over, and if you both agree, sign a prenuptial agreement. This will be discussed in more detail in Chapter 5, "Strictly Business," but consider this: From this point on, you'll be entering into all sorts of debt and business agreements together. If nothing else, a prenuptial agreement is just practice for all the business deals you'll make as a couple in the future.

Discussing the prenuptial agreement?

Choosing the Rings

Opportunity knocks for every man; but you have to give a woman a ring.

—Mae West

You'll MAKE MANY BIG PURCHASES over the next several months and spend a lot of money; the average engaged couple spends about $28,000 on the festivities that surround their wedding vows; some will spend as much as $80,000 and about 2% will spend even more than that. You'll occupy whole days trying on wedding gowns looking for just the right one that creates the best look for you. You'll interview florists and caterers, taste food for the reception, and shop for invitations. In the end, the gown will be worn for several hours at best. The flowers will wilt the next day and be trashed a few days later; the food will be eaten; even the beautifully created work of art that is the wedding cake will be demolished and the top layer stored in someone's freezer for you to eat, if you dare, on your first anniversary; most of the invitations will eventually end up in someone's wastebasket. But 50 years from now, at your golden wedding anniversary celebration, you will still treasure the diamond you choose at this time. The wedding day will come and go, and years from now all you'll have from your wedding day will be memories and photographs. The rings, though, will still be worn every day, almost becoming a part of your body, and now is the time to choose this jewelry that will be with you for the rest of your life.

The proposal is the first of many joyful occasions on your way to wedded bliss.

Deciding which ring to buy is, therefore, going to be the choice you make that has the greatest long-term impact on your life, other than the one you've already made, of course: your prospective spouse. Of all the choices you make over the next few months, this is the one you need to be most informed about.

Throughout history, a wedding ring has been a part of the marriage rite, but it wasn't always placed on the third finger of the left hand. First one finger and then another has been the digit chosen to be encased by the wedding ring, and with a few exceptions, throughout history it was only the bride who wore a wedding ring. Although it is currently the trend for husbands as well as wives to wear wedding bands, this has only rarely been the case in the past. Occasionally, a powerful Roman Catholic or Church of England leader spoke out on the matter and insisted that men and women both wear wedding rings, but the practice for men soon fell away as that leader's influence waned. Today, more men than ever wear wedding rings, perhaps because we've changed as a society and women have gained more economic and social power than they ever had before in history.

The ancient Greeks were convinced that a vein ran from the third finger of the left hand directly to a woman's heart (no mention of whether there was a similar vein in men), and that placing a ring there was symbolic of a direct link to her heart. The medieval bride was often gifted with rings, but they didn't always come from her groom. His female relatives often gave the bride rings as a gift to welcome her to the family—and perhaps to impart to her some of the wealth of the family.

Rings today symbolize love and commitment, fidelity and honor on the part of both husband and wife, but the truth of their origin is a bit less romantic. Their original intent was most likely as a sign of ownership. The woman wore the engagement ring to show that she was spoken for and the wedding ring simply sealed the deal.

Wedding Ring History and Traditions

TRENDS IN WEDDING RING FASHION have been around for ages—literally—with change happening most frequently during periods of great wealth. The Renaissance saw an increase in trade and wealth and, along with it, greater style and delicacy in wedding rings. This was the time when jewelers were growing more skilled and could inscribe the inside of wedding and engagement rings with the names of the couple, their wedding date, or even whole lines of poetry.

After that trendsetter Queen Victoria married her Prince Albert, ring styles changed because of her choice, as did much of the fashion during the 19th century. She opted for a wedding ring that was a bit more pretentious than the plain band that had been common until then, one shaped like a serpent with diamonds for eyes, and soon brides everywhere were following the trend and having rings created that matched their own personal tastes.

No one knows when the custom of wearing an engagement ring began. Certainly the ancient Greeks and Egyptians followed the practice. Probably it was simply a matter of placing a man's mark upon his chosen woman. Nevertheless, the custom today means something entirely different to us all, so the choice of rings is not just a huge monetary decision; it's also one that proclaims your love for each other. You should learn as much as possible about diamonds, other precious stones, and the whole art and practice of wedding jewelry.

Cathleen & Chris

Cathleen: "Ah, the ring. Well, I love mine! I didn't pick it out—I wanted to be surprised. And in fact, Chris didn't even really pick it out. We have a family friend who is into gems and jewelry and such, so he does the gem buying whenever there's occasion in their family. So my oh-so-subtle husband, when he got in his mind that he wanted to propose, let Jeff (the diamond guy) know, and Jeff took it upon himself to quiz me at another family event. 'Cathleen, my wife wants a new diamond ring for our anniversary. If you were her, what would you want? What kind of diamond? What size? What color gold? Or platinum?' It was very subtle, let me tell you.... Anyway, mine is not overly huge, but I love it because it doesn't look like any one I've ever seen. Jeff and his wife picked it because it looked antique-y, and they thought I'd like it. They sent it to Chris for approval, and he loved it."

Why a Ring?

The tradition of exchanging jewelry during the wedding ceremony is as old as at least as the early Egyptians. The gift of a ring or bracelet might have its origins in the tradition of *handfasting*, a Celtic joining ceremony in which a bride and groom join hands and then the wedding guests bind their hands together with ribbons and bows.

This tradition actually originated in a betrothal ceremony in which a couple agreed to be bound for a year and a day. At the end of that time, if they chose to stay together, they could marry; if not, their bonds could be broken and no harm was considered to be done. Somehow the two traditions came together—from the Greek and Roman tradition, the gift of rings to the bride during the wedding, and from the Celtic tradition, the binding of wrists together to form a semi-permanent bond. Now we simply consider the engagement ring to be a sign of undying love and devotion, a commitment to join couples together and their intention to form a new family. The wedding ring is a sign that the deed is done. With the exchange of vows and the gift of rings, two people join together and are one, a new family, leaving the old family behind and pledging allegiance to the new one.

The circular shape of the engagement and wedding rings is symbolic in itself. The circle represents eternity, wholeness, and perfection. It also represents the sun, moon, and stars, which presumably you find in each other. So a circle made of precious metal holding a diamond, that hardest of precious gems, represents not just a historic tradition dating back at least to 1477 when Archduke Maximillian gave a ring to his betrothed Mary of Burgandy (and probably even farther back to the Ancient Greeks), but perhaps an even older tradition stemming from prehistoric times. We have no record of this, of course, but we do know that the circle has represented unbroken love throughout man's history, and we can know that by presenting and exchanging rings during the reciting of wedding vows, we are using a symbol perhaps as old as mankind.

Courtesy Will and Nicole Robertson © Mick Pederson Photography

This couple, honoring their Scottish background, included Tartan shawls and handfasting in their ceremony. The almost forgotten tradition of handfasting is enjoying a comeback.

The Diamond

T HE HEART OF YOUR BRIDAL RINGS
will be the diamond engagement ring. It's the
most noticeable, and it's the ring you will be
showing off to everyone you meet for the next few
months and even into later years of marriage.

Why a Diamond?

Other gems have been and continue to be used
in engagement rings and wedding bands. The
diamond is the most popular gem for wedding
and engagement sets, however, because of all it
symbolizes: clarity, purity, and value. Diamonds are
hard enough to scratch glass and have long been
traded as precious stones. Diamonds, in fact, are
useful as more than just something pretty to wear
on your finger, neck, or toe. Because of their hard-
ness (they are the hardest known natural mineral),
diamonds are used in industry to cut other surfaces,
such as limestone or glass. An early test used to
make sure the gem in a piece of jewelry was
actually a diamond was to try to cut a mirror
with the gem. If it cut the mirror, it was indeed
a diamond. A diamond can be scratched only by
another diamond. It is interesting to note that fully
80% of all diamonds mined in the world today are
used for industrial purposes and aren't ever seen
by a jeweler.

In recent years, a few brides have chosen anything
but a diamond for their engagement and wedding
rings. There is controversy over what is referred to
as *conflict diamonds*, those mined in Sierra Leone
and Angola (and now in other parts of Africa),
which may be used to fund rebellions in those

countries. This is an ever-changing scenario, with
the diamond industry making efforts to block the
sale of illicit "blood" diamonds and peace organizations speaking out against the sale of all diamonds.
If you want to investigate the political ramifications
of your planned diamond purchase before you buy,
do a bit of research. The best place to get current
information is online.

The diamond industry's explanation of the problem
is available at:

www.diamondfacts.org

Read what the United Nations has to say about the
issue at:

www.un.org/peace/africa/diamond.html

How to Choose a Diamond

You've heard of the Four C's: cut, color, clarity, and
carat. We'll just define them here and explain what
each word means as it pertains to the diamond
industry. We'll also add a fifth C to the list: certifi-
cation. And we'll explain the most noticeable
attribute of your new diamond, its shape. What
you want to be sure of is that you get a good value:
You want to get as much brilliance and beauty for
your buck as possible, and the information in this
section will help guide you to making a wise purchase. We also suggest a visit to the following web
sites before you buy:

www.adiamondisforever.com

www.tiffany.com

www.bluenile.com

No matter when or where you do it, the presentation of the ring is one of the most romantic moments in life.

Steep yourselves in the knowledge of diamond buying and shop around. You wouldn't go car shopping and buy from the first dealer you talked to or just pick a computer without investigating its features, would you? You'll probably pay as much for this ring as you did for the first car you bought and more than you did for your laptop, so be just as careful when choosing it. Check out different diamond dealers and learn all you can before you buy.

Cut

The cut of a diamond determines its brilliance. The diamond can have great clarity and color and be as big as a house, but if it isn't cut correctly, it won't shine on your finger. Cut is what determines how light bounces off your rock. Light enters the diamond, bounces around inside, and shines back at you. The depth of the diamond determines whether all that shine comes back to you through the top of the stone or bounces around inside and goes straight through the bottom in a too shallow diamond or bounced back out the side in one that's too deep.

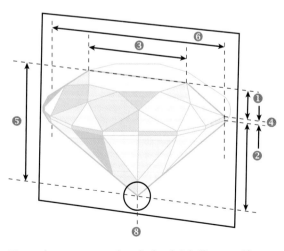

Diamonds are cut so as to best display their brilliance and beauty.

❶ Crown: The top part of the diamond, measured from the girdle to the table.

❷ Pavilion: The bottom part of the diamond, below the girdle.

❸ Table: The largest facet of the diamond.

❹ Girdle: The broadest part of the diamond where the crown and the pavilion come together.

❺ Depth: The length from the top of the diamond to the bottom.

❻ Width or Diameter: The measurement from one side to the other of the diamond, taken at the girdle.

❼ Facet: A facet is simply one of the flat surfaces of the diamond.

❽ Culet: The culet is the tiny point (actually another facet) at the very bottom of the diamond. The smaller it is the better.

Cutting a diamond is an exacting, nowadays often computer-controlled, art. The better the symmetry amongst all the facets of the diamond, the better the shine and sparkle. Each surface must also be polished to bring out the beauty of the stone.

Color

The following table lists the grades for a white diamond. We'll limit our discussion here to white diamonds, but they do also come in colors, such as blue, pink, green, and many other shades. These, of course, are graded a bit differently for color.

Grade	Definition	Description	Value
D	Completely colorless	Highest color value	Most expensive
E	Colorless	Minute traces of color that can be detected only by an expert	Rare and expensive
F	Colorless	Slight color can be detected but only by an expert	Still considered a quality diamond and still expensive
G – H	Near colorless	Color can be detected when viewed alongside a diamond of a higher grade	A good buy
I – J	Near colorless	Slightly noticeable color	A good buy
K – M	Noticeable color		
N – Z	Noticeable color		

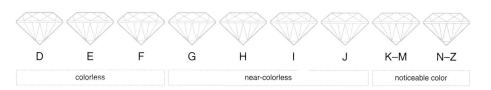

Diamond color is measured from colorless through noticeable color. The less color, the higher the value.

Clarity

Clarity is a measure of the imperfections contained in the diamond. Flawless diamonds, of course, are the most rare and the most valuable. Clarity is important in the value of a diamond, but a diamond does not have to be completely flawless to be valuable and certainly not to be beautiful.

The following table lists the levels of clarity to be found in diamonds. Most jewelers probably will not show you an I1, I2, or I3 diamond, and FL or IF are beyond the price range of most of us. You'll probably want to choose from among diamonds whose clarity falls in the middle of this table.

Ask your jeweler to show you several different grades of diamonds under the microscope. Yours should be happy to show you the difference between an obviously flawed diamond and one that has a high clarity rating.

Courtesy of Shutterstock
© Christina Tisi-Kramer

The diamond solitaire is a classic engagement ring.

Grade	Definition	Description	Value
FL	Flawless	Rare	Very expensive
IF	Internally Flawless	Rare	Still very expensive because any flaws are on the outside and can be polished away
VVS1, VVS2	Very, very slightly included:	Imperfections barely able to be detected with a 10x microscope	A quality diamond
VS1, VS2	Very slightly included	A bit less expensive, but any flaws are not visible to the naked eye	A bit less expensive
S1, S2	Slightly included	Inclusions are visible with a 10x microscope but not to the naked eye	Still a good value diamond
I1, I2, I3	Flawed diamonds	You will be able to detect the flaws in these diamonds at a glance	These are a bargain; you might get a much larger I1 diamond for your money than if you go for a higher clarity grade. After all, who is going to look at it that closely?

Carat Weight

Carat is a measurement of weight (not size), but diamonds are not priced "per carat"—not exactly—not, ahem, the way carrots are. Larger diamonds are more rare than small ones, so the larger a diamond, the greater its value. In other words, a two-carat diamond is worth more than two one-carat diamonds, affected of course by color, clarity, and cut. The following illustration provides a relative idea of what a carat actually looks like. Keep in mind that the size of your hands, the size of your fingers, and the setting will affect what looks "big" on your hand. If you wear a size 4 ring, a two-carat diamond is going to look huge, but if you wear a size 8, it will look more proportionate. A delicate setting will make a diamond look larger, but it will also be a bit more fragile for daily wear.

Value

Value: getting something for your money. What is it you want from this diamond? Do you want a flawless gem that can be handed down to future generations and treasured? Or do you want something splashy to flash around and make your friends and co-workers envious? It's okay to go for the bling if that's your goal. The idea is to use the amount you can afford to spend to satisfy your desires for this ring. If you want a large diamond, say, a 3-carat rock in a solitaire setting, then choose one that is not rated as Very fine or Flawless, and choose one with a bit of color; you will stay within your budget and still get something showy. If you're the more conservative type who thinks of this ring as representing your undying perfect love and you simply want the satisfaction of knowing that you bought a near perfect ring, size won't matter so much to you. You should buy a flawless or near flawless gem.

| 0.25 Carat | 0.33 Carat | 0.5 Carat | 0.75 Carat | 1 Carat | 1.25 Carats | 1.5 Carats | 1.75 Carats | 2 Carats | 2.5 Carats | 3 Carats | 3.5 Carats | 4 Carats |

An approximation of the size stone you'll get at each carat weight.

Heather & Mark

Heather says, "daily wear is an extremely important consideration: my sister demanded that her fiancé take her ring back and get a 'cleaner' setting because she's a nurse. Daily wear, and especially washing, can really grunge a ring, not to mention the variety of occupational hazards. I stopped wearing mine when I started changing diapers, mostly because I kept scratching the kids with it, but also because of the ick factor."

A pear-shaped or marquis diamond in a solitaire setting might appeal now, but consider the rest of your life. Keep in mind too, that you can still indulge that desire for the most delicate of settings now and later you can have the setting changed. Your diamond purchase is not necessarily a static one.

Shape

Shape is not the same thing as cut. Shape is a description of the form the diamond is cut into. The shapes of a diamond are

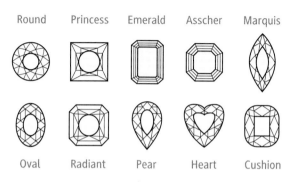

Round   Princess   Emerald   Asscher   Marquis

Oval   Radiant   Pear   Heart   Cushion

Diamonds can be cut into many shapes and sizes to suit your taste. Some are more practical than others.

Certifications

Your diamond, like your AKC registered standard poodle, will come with "papers." All reputable diamond dealers will provide you with a certificate showing that the diamond in your ring has been checked, described, and registered by diamond professionals. The Gemological Institute of America (GIA) issues a diamond grading report. This document provides a clear and detailed description of every diamond sold. The GIA offers several grading reports to its clients, including a complete description of the diamond on the report: cut, color, clarity, shape, carat weight, and even more details.

At the GIA web site (www.gia.edu) there's a helpful tutorial called "How to Buy a Diamond." You wouldn't buy a car without looking under the hood, and you wouldn't look under the hood unless you knew the difference between the spark plugs and the battery. Learn all you can about how diamonds are graded and valued before you visit the jeweler. You'll feel much more confident as you bargain for your rock.

The American Gem Society Laboratories issues a Diamond Quality Document, which is accepted as an authentication of a diamond's quality.

You should receive at least one of these documents when you purchase your diamond. If one isn't offered, ask, but if one isn't offered you might want to consider shopping at another jeweler anyway. It is advisable to buy the diamond and then purchase the ring. Pick out your diamond and then choose the setting that will show it off. You'll be able to view the stone from all sides and truly understand the quality of the diamond you are buying.

The Band

YOU WILL GO TO A JEWELER to choose your diamond, but then you'll be faced with choosing a ring design and style. Most jewelers carry designs by a few different designers, so it does pay to shop around a bit. Choosing the band is no longer just a choice between metals. There are many different settings and jewelry designers for you to choose from, some of whom create unique and stunning pieces of jewelry. Your wedding band and the band you choose for the setting of your diamond engagement ring can be made of several different metals, can be engraved or not, and can have side stones or not. Through the years, gold, platinum, silver, and even pewter have been used. Currently, the most popular metals for this jewelry are gold, white gold, and platinum.

Here are some samples of men's and women's styles by Scott Kay, whose designs are available in many exclusive jewelry stores.

A crown setting with vintage hand engraving.

The man's ring: Javlin and javlin bolted.

This engagement ring features a crown setting in a contemporary design with no engraving.

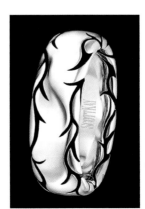

From the Sparta collection with vintage engraved detail by Scott Kay.

27

Gold

Gold is the most widely used and traditional look-ing band to show off your beautiful diamond. Pure gold is 24 karat; pure 24 karat gold is expensive and less durable than lesser karat gold. The lower the karat number, the more other metal alloys are mixed in, but the more durable the jewelry is. The total is always 24, so 10 karat gold is 10 parts gold and 14 parts a metal alloy; 14 karat is 14 parts gold and 10 alloy; and 18 karat gold is 18 parts gold to 6 parts alloy.

Another way to look at this is to consider that 18 karat gold is 75% gold, 14 karat gold is about 60% pure, and 10 karat gold is about 40%.

Gold bands of the same karat weight can be slightly different colors, depending on the other alloys mixed with the gold. So we have what is called rose, green, and other colors of gold, but in fact, the gold content depends simply on the karat weight measurement.

Karat and carat are two entirely different things. *Karat* is a measure of the purity of gold. *Carat* is a measure of the weight of a diamond.

White Gold

White gold jewelry is measured in the same way as yellow gold, anywhere from 10 to 18 karat gold. However, the other metal used to mix with the gold to create white gold is silver, nickel, palladium or an alloy containing more than one of these. The same rules apply in measuring purity as apply to yellow gold: the higher the karat weight, the greater the percentage of gold in the piece.

Platinum

Platinum is used in almost its pure state in jewelry: most platinum bands are 95% or more platinum. This is the most durable, longest lasting metal that is used in making wedding jewelry, and it requires very little maintenance. It is also the most expensive and feels heaviest on your finger. Platinum needs infrequent maintenance, but when it does need repair, the cost is greater than with a gold ring.

The Setting

AFTER YOU'VE DECIDED which metal you'd like your wedding bands to be made of, there's one other decision to make regarding the metal part of the ring: how you want the stone to be displayed in the metal. Here we have listed some common settings for diamond engagement rings.

- Solitaire: The most popular setting for a diamond engagement ring is the solitaire. One diamond is held aloft by four or six prongs. The more prongs, the greater security for your diamond.

- Solitaire with Side Stones: There is one large center diamond and several smaller diamonds around the perimeter of the ring. These can be set in a channel to protect them from damage or wear.

You should check your ring monthly or more often for prong damage or loose diamonds, but with the solitaire setting, you'll need to be even more careful, especially if the prongs are extra long. A yearly inspection by a jeweler is a must too.

- Engagement Rings with Matching Bands: Wedding bands can be either simple gold bands or they can be designed with diamonds to match the setting of the engagement ring. Engagement rings with matching wedding bands are more elaborate, use more diamonds, and are, of course, more expensive than a solitaire with a plain gold wedding band, depending upon the size of the center diamond.

- Three Stone Settings: These rings are made up of a row of three diamonds, although the middle one is often slightly larger than the side stones. These symbolize the past, present, and future. Three stone rings are also known as trinity or trilogy rings and are popular as anniversary rings as well as engagement rings.

Craig, our diamond importer friend, suggests that if you want to choose a diamond for your fiancée and surprise her with it, choose the diamond and have it placed in a simple solitaire setting in a white gold band, which costs about $150 to $200. Then she can take it back to the jeweler and choose her own setting for the diamond. You've pulled off your surprise proposal, gotten the diamond you know you can afford, and given her the opportunity to then help choose the design for her own ring.

Telling Everyone

We are family...da da da da da da do wee.

*—Gene Hackman as
Sen. Kevin Keeley in* The Birdcage

—also The Pointer Sisters

A WEDDING JOINS MANY MORE people than just the two who exchange vows. When you are married, you join your lives together, and that means your wedding affects all the friends, family, and co-workers (and more particularly, children, ex-spouses, and former love interests) that you both bring to the union. It's likely that many of these people have already had occasion to meet and they only need to be told now that you two are making your relationship permanent. If not, you have some work to do. In any case, you have some announcements to make.

We will discuss other organizations and entities that will need to know of your marriage (the post office, your health insurance plan at work, and the Department of Motor Vehicles, for example) in Chapter 12, "Legal Considerations," but for now you need to tell your community—starting with your parents and any children either of you might already have.

Perhaps you've been living together for some time now; everyone already thinks of you as a couple and wouldn't dream of asking you to a family gathering without issuing the invitation to both of you. Still, choosing your life partner is big news, and you'll want to share it with everyone you know. There are a few rules governing this step in the proceedings; some set by established etiquette guides and others just based on common sense and general good manners.

After you tell your parents and children, a family dinner is a good place to share your news with the rest of the family.

Keep It in the Family First

ELLING THE BRIDE'S FAMILY first has long been considered the proper thing to do. This practice stems from the days when asking a woman's father for her hand in marriage was considered part of the business deal that a marriage essentially was back then, so the bride's family were naturally the first people to know. In fact, during the Middle Ages where this tradition has its roots, the bride's father and male relatives would know she had a suitor even before she knew herself. Those days are long gone, but the tradition of telling the bride's family first remains. Although it's rarely done these days, it is not unheard of for a prospective groom to pay a special visit to the bride's father and formally ask his blessing on the union (or even his permission) before proposing. In some cultures, this is still practiced regularly, but it usually takes about one generation of exposure to modern society for this nicety to fall by the wayside. If you want to observe this tradition and the bride's father is no longer alive or no longer a part of her life, it's acceptable to ask her mother or another close relative. Strictly speaking, this isn't often done any more, but making a formal request might earn the prospective groom some really good respectability points with the future in-laws, even if you are far removed from the influence of any cultural background that would dictate a formal request.

After the bride's family gets the news, the groom's family should be next on your list to hear that you're planning a wedding and you would like their support and encouragement.

Why Do We Do That

Why do we say that a man asks for a woman's "hand in marriage"? There are a couple of theories. One story dates from Roman times when a prospective groom would purchase his bride (symbolically, of course) by handing her father a coin. The father would respond by placing the bride's hand in the groom's, thereby transferring custody of the woman from her father to her husband.

A Celtic tradition, which is experiencing a comeback, is called *handfasting*. In this ritual, the bride and groom clasp hands and then their two hands are tied together with ribbons and bows by the guests at the wedding. In this way, perhaps, her hand was literally "given" to him.

Today, asking for the bride's hand in marriage is simply a courtesy, and a quaint one at that, but it does show a young man to be a thoughtful person who values the daughter of the family and respects her parents for their contribution in creating the graceful, beautiful creature he wants to make his own.

Of course, who you tell first and how you tell them might be affected by geography, by the reactions you expect from each family, and just by your own needs and whims. There are no longer any hard and fast rules for this phase of the "getting married" process, but there are some courteous things you can do for family and friends.

If you can't be there in person, the next best thing is a phone call.

Of course, a picture—even via email or camera phone—is worth a thousand words.

If it's possible to tell your parents in person, then you should do so. If you know they will be delighted and pleased at the announcement, both of you should visit together and share in the hugs and good tidings and toasts. If your parents aren't so well acquainted with your intended or if you know they will have some doubts about your plans, perhaps you should break the news to them gently and then arrange for everyone to meet for dinner or some other social occasion. Give them a little time to get used to the idea of their new son- or daughter-in-law.

If your planned announcement falls near a holiday when everyone will be getting together (and assuming that you know the nuptials will be well received), you might want to take advantage of the festive atmosphere to share your good news. Perhaps you might want to do it quietly during a family dinner, or even schedule a time when you call ahead and ask both parents to be present because you have something important to tell them. You know your family best, you probably have a pretty good idea how they will react, and you know what works and what doesn't. Some people do not like public surprises at all; know your parents and know how best to present your good tidings to them.

Visit, Call, Write, E-Mail

That's pretty much the order in which you should consider methods for making your announcement. Most guides discourage sending an e-mail. We think it's definitely a last choice, but if you are skilled with the written word, there might be circumstances where it's acceptable to e-mail your news—maybe if you are both stationed somewhere near the North Pole with no access to a telephone or post office...maybe then.

If you live within driving distance, go share your news in person. If you are sure of a positive response, both of you should go together, maybe even showing off the rock on your finger. If you aren't living close by and don't have plans for a visit any time soon, then by all means, make your news known in a telephone call. If you regularly correspond with your folks, write the news in a letter.

Make sure you tell everyone yourselves. Personally speak to as many parents as you have. If they are divorced, call each one separately. Don't depend on Mom to let Dad know because you know they talk often and she'd be happy to share your news. This is big, and you need to make sure you tell it to everyone who cares about you yourself. There will be ample opportunity for everyone to get miffed or jealous over something in the coming months, there is no need to provide them with a reason this early in the game.

If You Have Children

O F COURSE, IF EITHER OR BOTH of you have children from previous relationships, then without question, those children deserve to know your plans first. Telling your children trumps all other concerns. They come ahead of parents, friends, employers, and other family members. Do not let them hear this news from anyone other than yourself. It's also a good idea for you to tell your ex-spouse or significant other yourself as well. Don't let the kids go back to their other home and say "Guess what, Dad. Mom's getting married!"

Seriously, if the other parent of your child doesn't know you're in a serious relationship, you have a problem. Make sure your previous partner, the other parent of your children, knows about your plans before anyone else. It is not the children's responsibility to tell their other parent. Your children should be your first concern, and they should not be made to feel that they are burdened with the task of telling one parent what the other one is doing. If you have problems with any of this, you definitely need to see a family therapist to make sure everyone close to you is as happy as you are with the upcoming wedding. It might not be apparent to you, but children are extremely sensitive to your actions now. They need to be reassured that they are your prime concern. Make it clear to them, whatever their age, that they are loved above all and that you will make sure their interests always come first.

You are already responsible adults who don't need your parents' permission to marry. What you do need is to make your children as comfortable with the decision as possible. You really need their acceptance because they will presumably be living in the same home with you and your new spouse at least some of the time. In effect, they're getting married too, and the very best second weddings where children are concerned always make them a central part of the planning and the ceremony itself. They matter. They matter even more than you and your fiancée.

Have a positive attitude when you talk to your children about your impending nuptials.

Courtesy Shutterstock © Fred Sweet

You should talk to your children about this big change in their lives as soon as you know it's a possibility. Ask how they feel about the proposed arrangement. That's not the same thing as asking their permission to get married; you're the adult in your relationship with them. What they think should matter and should be paid attention to, but this is your decision, not theirs. Reassure them that they come first no matter what and then show them that you mean that. You might be getting married, but not without them. And remember as time passes and the plans get overwhelming, your children still come first. Try to include them in the plans, ask how they're feeling about all the new developments. Make an extra effort to spend time with them and have lots of heart-to-heart talks about the upcoming changes. If you think they are having a problem dealing with the new life situation, don't hesitate to call in a therapist or family counselor.

Of course, if you have adult children, you'll want to include them in your plans, but presumably you have raised them to respect you and your decisions, so you'll not need to be quite so careful to explain matters to them. Do include them and do reassure them that you have made provisions for their inheritance. And then do that. I'll cover more about such matters in Chapter 12.

Courtesy Shutterstock ©Darren Baker

Let your children know that they'll always come first.

Introducing the Families

TRADITIONALLY, IT IS THE GROOM'S family's responsibility to make the first effort to contact the bride's family, perhaps inviting them to a "get to know you" dinner. Today we aren't so strict about where that first meeting is held or who the host is or even who calls whom, but if you are the groom's parents and you wonder what happens now, there's your cue: Call the bride's parents. If you are the bride's parents, though, and an effort isn't forthcoming, go ahead and make the initial move yourselves. If you are the bride or groom and no one is mentioning a meeting, schedule it yourself.

It's perfectly acceptable these days to have the introductions take place in the shared home of the couple about to be married, in the bride's family home, in the groom's parents' home, or even in a restaurant. You might also consider a weekend gathering at a resort or country house near one or the other family or a weekend camping trip for the new relatives to get to know each other, assuming that everyone is comfortable with those activities.

Telling your parents is probably one of the most nerve-wracking things you'll do. Not only have books been written about this ritual, many movies have also been made that center on disparate families coming together when their children are joined in wedlock. Usually these are comedies—for good reason. Think *The Birdcage* with Robin Williams. Think *Meet the Parents*. If you want to relieve some of your own anxiety over this meeting, rent either of those movies and just remind yourselves as you watch: It could be worse...much worse.

If you opt to host a dinner for both sets of parents in a restaurant, decide ahead of time who will pay and how that will be handled. If the groom will be paying, just quietly make payment arrangements with the waitstaff in advance. This is not a good time for awkwardness over who will be paying for what. If one of your parents will be paying the bill, know which one is doing the honors ahead of time and make sure the check is discreetly handed over. This is not the time to discuss who had the prawns and who had the lobster thermidor or to show off your math skills by dividing the check into two or three equal amounts. Be gracious. Be stylish. Be hospitable. If one of your parents pays for dinner, don't forget to say thank you.

Why do we have so many comedic movies about this ritual? Maybe it's because of the universal fear that it might turn into a tragedy. Romeo and Juliet had more to be concerned with than who would pick up the check if they had gotten so far as to bring their parents together—Mr. and Mrs. Capulet were not about to sit down to dine with Mr. and Mrs. Montague...not ever.

Telling the Rest of the World

AFTER YOUR CLOSE FAMILY members have been informed of your plans (and have oohed and aahed over the engagement ring and gotten a chance to ask questions about when and where and all the details you probably haven't thought about yet yourselves) and after your families have met, it's time to tell the rest of the world. Start spreading the news.

Newspaper Announcements

Make the announcement to the general public (and your ex-boyfriend from high school) by placing it in your hometown newspaper, the newspaper(s) where your parents live now, and the one where you live now. If they're all the same, that's good, but take into consideration who lives where when choosing the newspaper in which you'll publish your announcement. Small local papers are more than happy to publish engagement and wedding news (not to mention the weekly arrest record), but the big dailies also usually have one day a week when they publish engagement and wedding announcements (along with silver and golden anniversary news).

Most newspapers have forms for you to fill out and someone on staff who knows how the announcement should be worded and who will elicit the necessary information from you. Generally, your announcement should follow along these lines:

> *Mr. and Mrs. John Jones of Carmel announce the engagement of their daughter, Cassandra Sue, to Charles Alexander, son of Mr. and Mrs. Daniel Alexander of Indianapolis. Miss Jones is a graduate of Central High School and Graceland University. She received her master's degree from Iowa State University and is employed as a second grade teacher in Kalamazoo, Michigan.*

> *The future bridegroom graduated from Pike High School in Indianapolis and Graceland University. He is employed as a business analyst in Kalamazoo.*

> *The wedding is set for June 16 at St. John's Catholic Church in Kalamazoo.*

Cassandra and Charles would probably want to place this article in newspapers in Indianapolis, Des Moines, and Kalamazoo.

Mentioning the date is optional; you may not have been able to schedule all the players (church, minister, reception hall, caterers, band, or DJ) at this point, so leaving that part out is quite okay.

Of course, if a parent is deceased or are divorced, the announcement should reflect that. The wording would be more like:

> *...daughter of Mrs. Emily Jones and the late John Jones of Carmel...*

> or

> *...son of Mr. Daniel Alexander of Indianapolis and Susan Smith of Bloomington...*

Finally, if you have stepparents who played a big part in your upbringing or who you just want to recognize in the announcement, of course you should include their names as well.

> *...daughter of Mr. and Mrs. David Johnson and the late John Jones of Carmel...*

> or

> *...son of Mr. Daniel Alexander of Indianapolis and Dr. and Mrs. Joshua Smith of Bloomington...*

You should probably read a few engagement announcements in your own newspaper to get a feel for how you'd like yours to appear and what you want to tell the world about yourselves. A picture of the couple often accompanies the engagement announcement but is not strictly necessary. You should plan to pose for an engagement picture shortly after you become engaged. It's a picture that will come in handy for newspaper announcements and any that you mail to far flung friends

and family. It's also one you'll look back at fondly in years to come. If you want to include a picture of the two of you in the newspaper article but haven't posed for a formal one yet, it is possible to use a very good snapshot. The newspaper will crop out everything but the two of you if you ask them nicely.

Reading the Banns

In the history of both the Catholic and Anglican Churches, it has long been the practice to do something called reading the banns. In three successive Sunday morning services, an announcement is read by the priest or vicar informing the congregation of a couple's intention to marry. In the early days of the Church, this was the equivalent of informing the entire community of the upcoming nuptials. It gave anyone who had an objection to the marriage the opportunity to speak up. In those days of smaller communities, everyone who had an interest probably lived within three miles of the church, so making the announcement from the pulpit effectively informed everyone who needed to know.

If this is not the first marriage for either of you and it would seem awkward at this point in your lives to have your parents announce a change in your status, you would, of course, reword your announcement to reflect your station in life. Then you would just say:

> *Cassandra Sue Jones and Charles Alexander announce their engagement. She is the daughter of Mrs. Emily Jones and the late John Jones of Carmel.*

And then carry on with whatever pertinent information you care to share with the world. You might want to say "Mr. Alexander is the father of Brent Alexander of Kokomo and Mrs. Carolyn Speers of Lebanon." Whatever fits your situation is appropriate.

Contact the newspaper well ahead of the time you want the announcement to be placed. Remember, many set aside only one day a week to run these articles. Make sure too that there's no fee involved. Usually there isn't, but it doesn't hurt to ask.

Alumni Magazines

The alumni magazine is something you may not think of until you get the next edition in the mail, and since most of them are published quarterly, you need to think ahead and let them know you're getting married if you want college chums you're no longer close with to hear the news in a timely manner.

This charmingly phrased newspaper wedding announcement proclaimed the January 27, 1945 wedding of the couple pictured on page 2 of this book. Note the mention of gifts, which although proper during that period, would be very much out of place today.

Mr. R. Foster Weds Miss L. Kirkconnell

Two prominent families in Grand Cayman were united with the marriage on Saturday afternoon last, of Mr. Ritchie Ashlin Foster, son of Captain A. A. Foster and Mrs. Foster, and Miss Lilly Kirkconnell, daughter of Mr. Reginald Kirkconnell, a well-known shipowner of Grand Cayman, and Mrs. Kirkconnell.

The ceremony was performed in the St. Paul's Church by the Rev. C. M. Watler, in the presence of a large gathering of relatives and friends of the two families. The church was beautifully decorated for the occasion. Shortly after 5 o'clock, the bride, who was charmingly gowned, walked up the aisle escorted by her father, who gave her away in marriage. She wore a dress of eggshell taffeta, fashioned with a basque waist and buffon skirt from which flowed a veil of tulle. Her headdress was of orange blossoms.

The bridal party, which was also attractively attired, was constituted by Miss Denise Bodden, chief bridesmaid, and the little Misses Parkinson and Elemeire, flower girls. Best man was Mr. Duval Tibbetts, while Messrs Cleo and Clinton Foster were ushers.

The reception was held later that evening at 17 Pembroke Road.

Presents were many and costly.

The Engagement Party

AFTER BOTH SETS OF PARENTS and any children involved have met and broken bread together, it's time to let others in on the festive affair you're planning. This is an optional but enjoyable informal gathering of friends and family. You might host it yourself or the new "in-laws" might host it jointly. This is the time for a lawn party with croquet and badminton, a party in the back room of your favorite neighborhood watering hole, or a backyard barbeque: It should just be a casual gathering of family and friends for no other purpose than to hear your news, admire your ring, and bask in your joy.

Everyone will have questions, some will have concerns, and a few might even voice their disapproval. But that's not likely. Your family and friends love you, and you've chosen wisely, so just enjoy. And flash that rock for everyone to admire.

Now that everyone has been made aware of your plans, it's time to start work on the details. In Chapter 4, "Dream, Plan, Realize," we'll start to talk about the business at hand—your wedding day.

Courtesy Cathleen and Chris Small © Sally Emory

A casual gathering is usually best for introducing your two families.

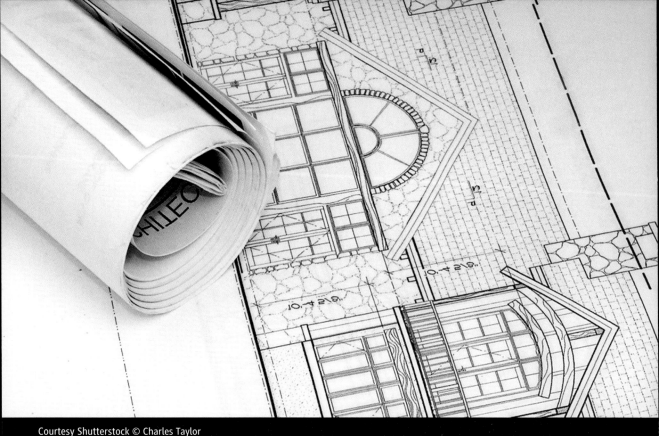

Dream, Plan, Realize

To achieve great things, two things are needed: a plan, and not quite enough time.

—Leonard Bernstein

TURNING ANY DREAM INTO REALITY requires a few things: work, money, and most important, a plan. You wouldn't begin to build a house without first having blueprints drawn, and you shouldn't just start booking caterers and hiring musicians without a plan either. Now, months before your wedding day, is the time to begin budgeting and planning to create the day of your dreams and to do it without causing bankruptcy, physical exhaustion, or frazzled nerves. You are preparing for the biggest celebration of your life. Those big events of your past—prom, Sweet Sixteen party, getting your driver's license, graduating from college—all pale in comparison to the one that's now looming on your horizon. Even if you are at the pinnacle of success in your chosen profession, hold a Ph.D. in anthropology, can speak multiple languages, and have traveled around the world, the idea of planning your wedding day can paralyze you with thoughts of "Where do I begin? What do I do first when faced with planning such an event?"

There is a wealth of information available about just what you're going to have to do over the next few months. It's called event planning, wedding planning, and wedding coordination, and you can do it yourself (with a few helpful hints, tips, checklists, and handy forms that we've provided in the appendix of this book, or you can hire a wedding planner who knows the ropes and has the inside track on all the vendors you'll need to hire over the coming months and just seems to know intuitively where to find three pounds of fresh pink rose petals and can feed 250 people without wrinkling a brow or even seeming to hurry. (In either case, whether you do it by yourself or with the help of a wedding planner, it's all about organization and delegation.

A couple of things dictate how you're going to handle planning all the details of your wedding: how much money you have to spend and how much time you have to invest over the course of the next few months. If you have at least 12 to 15 hours per week to devote to wedding planning and are a fairly organized person, you can do all the planning yourself with a friend or two to help carry out some of the footwork. If your professional demands are great and you have discretionary funds to invest in the planning of your wedding, then we suggest you go with a professional planner. In either case, you will find information and advice in this chapter that will help you keep it all in perspective, which is what you need at this point.

Throughout life, young girls dream of this day.

Budget Meets Dream

NOW IS THE TIME TO REMEMBER all those old childhood dreams. What sort of dress did you envision wearing? Did you see yourself swooping gracefully around the dance floor with your handsome groom looking deep into your eyes with every step? Did you see yourself floating down a grand staircase to strains of *Lohengrin* as all the wedding guests raised their eyes to greet you? Or standing in a garden surrounded by your closest friends and family under a rose arbor?

Work together to plan to realize your dreams.

The composer of "The Bridal Chorus" from *Lohengrin* (known informally as "Here Comes the Bride") was Richard Wagner, a favorite composer of Hitler's and an anti-semite himself. Reputedly, the Nazis used to broadcast his music through speakers in the concentration camps. Thus, you will rarely hear this song played at a Jewish wedding. Ironically, *Lohengrin* is a romantic opera about a doomed marriage, which makes it an odd choice for the procession of so many generations of Western brides.

The first thing you need to do is write down every scene you envision of your perfect wedding day, every thought that comes to mind that would make it glorious and just what you have always dreamed of. Ask your fiancé to do the same. Chances are, the bride's list will be a lot longer and more detailed than the groom's. When your lists are complete, you should sit down together in a relaxed atmosphere and go over your ideas for the wedding, immediately eliminating any aspects you both feel strongly that you don't want to include, inking in the ones you both are sure you want, and leaving some others to be discussed. Some compromising might be in order; the things you agree on are easy; unreasonable expectations that don't take into account your budget or your lifestyle will need to be examined a bit more closely. Is there a way to have that designer dress with the 20-foot train without spending the entire wedding budget on the dress? You may need to devise come creative solutions if you want to fulfill some of your more elaborate dreams. But anything is possible as long as you start planning early.

Cathleen & Chris

Cathleen says, "I wanted to elope, but my husband wanted a big wedding with all his family. So we struck a deal: If I agreed to a large wedding (100 people), I got to plan the entire honeymoon. This was fine with him, and so it was! Once I actually started planning the wedding, I had a blast! Chris gave me *carte blanche* to pretty much do as I pleased, as long as his family and friends were all included. Obviously I consulted with him on all the major things, and it ended up being a fun, non-traditional wedding ceremony."

After you've agreed on a list of must haves, some maybes, and a few no ways, it's time to think about how much you will actually have to spend on this major event in your life. It is, after all, a major event, and therefore it should be an occasion for spending as much as you want or can afford. It is also one day in your life, and you should plan for all you want it to be—and then plan for how you can accomplish what you want in a somewhat reasonable manner.

Plan

Your first budgeting task is to determine how much money you have to invest in the wedding of your dreams. How much will your parents contribute? How much will your fiancé's parents pitch in? Once you have a total amount that you think you can depend on as "your total wedding budget," you might want to try one of the many wedding budget calculators available online. A good one is at elegala.com. You don't have to register or provide any information; just go to www.elegala.com, type in the amount of your budget, and hit the Submit button. You'll see a list of all the items you'll need to purchase, rent, or pay for, and a suggested amount that you should budget for each item determined by the total amount you have available.

The web site, elegala.com, has free budget software plus a wealth of other helpful wedding planning advice.

Put some thought into where you want to put the bulk of your money. What is of critical importance, and what is optional or less noticeable if you don't spend buckets of money on it? Several years from now, you will still have at least one wedding photograph on your dressing table or night stand or maybe even hanging in the hallway. The cake will be long ago eaten and forgotten. The dress will be packed away. The flowers that mattered so much on your wedding day will be reduced to a few pressed petals or perhaps a preserved bouquet in a box in the attic. Do not stint on the cost of your photographer and videographer. You'll want the best pictures you can get. If you must stick to a budget as you plan, a successful bargain hunt for a great dress is quite possible, but don't gamble on a cheap but unproven photographer. This is one item where you don't want to take any chances.

Of course, some costs are fixed and some are discretionary. You can't choose how much you will pay for the license, but practically everything else is either negotiable or can be done by you or a creative friend. If you have a close friend who is a dressmaker, you can probably save some money on the dress that can be put toward the cost of food at the reception. If you want to make the invitations yourself, that's a few hundred dollars that can be spent on flowers to create a beautiful backdrop for your vows or on a better photographer.

Theresa & Randy

Theresa's wedding to Randy was a New Year's Eve fantasy. The chosen theme was Somewhere Over the Rainbow, and she looked beautiful with her long blond hair in her white dress with a spray of red roses. The ring bearer and flower girl were both too cute, and everyone spent an hour gathering for family photos after the wedding. There were photo sessions at the church and at the reception.

But disaster struck. The photographer was a friend of a friend who offered to take the wedding pictures as a gift, and something went wrong. Today, 30 years later, there are only a few fuzzy pictures taken with the Kodak cameras of guests, only one or two of them actual posed shots of the bride, groom, and wedding party.

After calculating how much you have available and how much the experts say you should spend on each item in your budget, you should begin to personalize those expenses. If someone is doing the flowers as a gift, you can take the suggested amount for that expense and apply it somewhere else in your wedding budget.

Getting Organized

WHETHER YOU DECIDE TO HIRE a professional wedding planner or not, you'll need to be very organized over the course of the next few months. You might consider keeping a file or files of all the people you'll deal with, the estimates you'll get for various items, the contacts you'll make, whether the religious officiant you want is available on the same date as the reception venue you have your heart set on, and much more. We suggest you purchase a large three-ring binder and a three hole punch along with some tabbed dividers, a business card holder, and some see-through sheet protectors (also with three holes to fit in the binder). Your first purchase should be from an office supply store, and it will be your constant companion over the coming months. Everything that pertains to your wedding and every person you talk to, along with their phone number, cell phone number, e-mail address, and mailing address, should go in that binder in an organized way.

As a modern bride, you'll want to search the Internet for many things. When you run across an item of interest, one you want to go back to later or use for comparison shopping, add the web page to your Favorites folder. Set up a subfolder called Wedding Planning and fill it with the sites of interest you find as you "shop" on the web. Just do a quick Google search for "wedding planning," and you'll see how very much is available on the web to help you with your planning. You'll find places to purchase everything from the dress to the cake, but even more importantly, you'll find limitless information about everything you want to know.

A few sites we suggest you visit before you begin to seriously plan your wedding:

Whether you are Canadian or not, frugalbride.com has tons of advice and tips that you'll find useful as you begin planning.

Theknot.com is among the best sites for wedding planning.

Weddingchannel.com is another good place to go for wedding planning help.

There are hundreds more, but these are three of the best. Don't depend on just one source though. Find information at these sites and others; then keep records in your three-ring binder.

In fact, as you search through various sites, you will probably want to set up more specific folders in your Favorites folder for such items as dress, flowers, invitations, and so forth.

Start Early and Stay Organized

You'll stay well organized with your three-ring binder in which you will put everything that you accumulate as you start to plan; use it faithfully and no piece of information that you need will be lost. But where to start? That's where some lists and forms come in handy. Following is a list of decisions you need to make and things you need to do early in your planning. Make these decisions right away, and then get down to more detailed planning.

Why We Do That

In 15th and 16th Century agrarian Europe, *betrothal* was the name for the time between an agreement to marry and the actual wedding. Betrothals could last a long time, literally for years, because often the agreement to marry had been made long ago when the bride and groom were children. The agreement, of course, was between their families, but the bride and groom were bound by it. Goods were exchanged, dowries settled, land changed hands; a marriage was of much more economic import than it is today. The families agreed to join together in the person of the bride and groom, and it was settled, often with a handshake. Today, the bride and groom meet, fall in love, and bring their families along in their decision to wed. In older times, the bride and groom were brought together by a family decision; now families are brought together by the decision of the couple. Then and now, the period of betrothal is a time to become acquainted—then for the bride and groom, now for their families.

Here are some things you'll want to plan for as early as possible before your wedding:

- ☘ Talk to your fiancé and both sets of parents to determine the source of funds for your wedding.
- ☘ Determine a budget for how those funds will be spent.
- ☘ Choose a maid of honor, best man, bridesmaids, groomsmen, and ushers.
- ☘ Develop a record-keeping method.
- ☘ Start to plan the guest list.
- ☘ Decide whether you'll include children in the wedding.
- ☘ Find a site for the ceremony and reserve your date.
- ☘ Ask your preferred officiant to reserve the date.
- ☘ Select your reception site and reserve the date.
- ☘ Select and reserve the band or DJ of your choice for the date of your reception.

> **The last four items may require some coordination and compromise, depending on your preferences. If you want a particular date, no matter what, you may need to be flexible on other choices. If you are determined to have a particular venue for the reception or a particular band to play at your reception, you may have to be flexible on your planned date.**

The following are also things you'll want to think about early on:

- ☘ Take into account any upcoming events among your family and friends as you choose a date. Is your best friend/maid of honor due to have a baby close to your planned wedding date? Will your younger brother be graduating from high school the week before your chosen date? You want each event in your lives to have its own special time, so you should take these "unmovable" dates into consideration.
- ☘ Remember to take into consideration any huge events that take place in your city. Check with event planners at the reception site or hotel to make sure you aren't choosing a date that falls in the midst of a rowdy convention or playoff tournament that would interfere with the solemnity of your wedding.
- ☘ If you are planning an outdoor wedding, consider the time of year and the place you live. Northern Michigan in the summer might mean mosquitoes and midges and black flies ruining your ceremony. (Those things can ruin a camping trip; I can't imagine the harm they might cause when you're trying to exchange solemn vows.) The same is true in many parts of the country. Be aware of such hazards wherever you live.
- ☘ Speaking of insects, check the locust reports for your area. In June 2004, more than one bride at an outdoor ceremony found herself serenaded by the 17-year type—to the point where it was impossible to hear the vows being exchanged. You don't have to be overly squeamish to scream when one of those red-eyed, green-winged, alien-looking monsters lands on you either; they can wreak havoc on any genteel gathering.

Maria & George

Maria and George got married in a garden in a park on July 4 at 2 p.m. In addition to the sweltering heat, bees-plagued guests and interrupted the ceremony. Summer outdoor weddings have the potential to cause all the participants to sweat fiercely, ruining make-up jobs and sweat-staining gowns and tuxes—not the best photo ops.

ᦹ If you've checked the insect report and found it to be promising and you still want to plan your wedding for your parents' backyard, check well ahead of the planned date for any flower or shrubbery planting that needs to be done or dead limbs that need to be removed from trees. Is the exterior of the house in need of paint or mainte-nance? Start to rectify this early on.

ᦹ Climate in some parts of the country can really have an effect, not just on your wedding day plans, but on honey-moon travel as well. Consider snow-storms in Vermont and hurricane season along the Gulf Coast as you make your plans.

ᦹ If you or your fiancé need any dental work or elective surgery, get that taken care of early on too. Recovery times vary with procedures. You will want to look your best and you don't want pain to interfere with any of the festivities leading up to the wedding day.

Keeping Records

In whatever way is most convenient and natural for you, you should keep records of all orders placed, invoices paid, amounts still outstanding, and gen-eral accounting records of the whole affair. Now is the time to set up that system, well before you start spending money and placing orders. Keep these records in some kind of accounting software if that comes naturally to you (not if it extra studying to learn a new software program though). If you are already proficient in Excel or Quicken or Microsoft Money, all are good ways to keep records. If not, a few pages of your three-ring binder should be dedicated to keeping your budget in order.

One of the most critical tasks of wedding planning is keeping track of each expense.

Make sure you keep copies of all the contracts you sign in your three-ring binder too. You'll certainly have a detailed contract with your reception site and possibly a separate one with a caterer. There will also be contracts with musicians, photogra-phers, videographers, tux rental shops, and bridal boutiques, and you'll want to keep them where you can refer to them quickly should there be any miscommunication about who should be doing what on the big day.

Choosing the Date and Time

AFTER YOU'VE TAKEN INTO account any upcoming graduations, childbirth, insect invasions, holidays, and NCAA playoffs, you'll start to narrow your choice of a wedding date to a particular time of year or month. Perhaps you want to have your wedding on the anniversary of your first date, on Valentine's Day, or another date that holds special meaning for you. Start checking these dates with the reception site; the church, temple, or synagogue; the band or DJ you want; and your family and chosen attendants.

Start by doing some phone work. Find out available dates for key venues and vendors, and begin coordinating your plans.

Season

Do you picture an autumn wedding with attendants wearing shades of gold, yellow, and rust and you carrying a bouquet of chrysanthemums? It's a lovely time of year with leaves falling and hillsides bursting with color. Or does a spring wedding with flowers abloom everywhere and the weather starting to warm up but not yet sweltering sound like your ideal? Maybe you have always wanted a winter wedding with masses of red roses shipped in for the occasion and the church all warm with candlelight.

The style of wedding you have can be affected by the season. If you plan an outdoor wedding in August, you want to steer clear of black tie and a high-necked, long-sleeved gown or any stiff and uncomfortable fabric such as velvet or taffeta.

Flowers that are available in the spring aren't so abundant at other times of the year.

Courtesy Shutterstock © Olga Lyubkina

Summer lends itself to some interesting menu choices for the reception that might not be so easy to manage during other seasons.

Courtesy Shutterstock © 6051186858

And this beautiful table is perfect for a winter wedding.

Courtesy Shutterstock © Nolte Lourens

This casual wedding cake is perfect for a fall wedding.

The most popular months for weddings currently are June, August, September, and December. You might want to consider other months and seasons when there will be less competition for reception and ceremony sites and caterers; other vendors, such as florists and bakeries, are likely to be able to give you more personal service during these "off" months as well. Consider an October or April wedding.

Day of Week

It seems that practically everyone gets married on Saturday afternoon or evening, and Saturday is certainly a convenient day of the week for the most people to drop everything and attend a wedding. But consider a Friday evening or Sunday morning wedding instead. It might be much easier to have the reception site or DJ of your choice if you are a bit flexible on the day and time you get married. You should consider the work schedules of the majority of your guests, but Saturday is by no means the only available day for a wedding. In fact, according to the following traditional English rhyme, the current practice among most Americans of marrying almost exclusively on Saturday may be to blame for many a loss in Las Vegas and possibly a couple of stock market crashes.

Time of Day

Not all weddings must take place in the afternoon or early evening. It is perfectly acceptable to plan a morning wedding followed by breakfast, brunch, or lunch. If you are more flexible regarding the time of day for your ceremony, you may find that more venues are available to you. It is common for banquet halls and caterers to set up a room for a midday reception the night before, serve lunch or brunch to a party that ends by 3:00, then "turn the room over" for an evening affair that begins at 7:00. In just a couple of hours, an experienced crew can clean up, rearrange, and set up a room for a completely different type of party.

Why We Do That

What's in a month? June is the traditional month for weddings, but why is that? Again, our agricultural background is still affecting how we conduct our lives today. Springtime was a time of freedom for the hardworking medieval farmer. By May the crop was in the ground, and so every young man's mind could "lightly turn to thoughts of love." And by June...well, by June it was time to end the courting nonsense and get back to work. So June became a popular month for weddings among the working-class farmers and tradespeople.

In Ancient Greece, January was a preferred month for weddings because it was the month dedicated to Hera, wife of Zeus and Goddess of Marriage and Monogamy. (She spent a lot of time driving off Zeus' many mistresses, by the way.)

Christianity introduced the idea that marriage could not take place during the solemn period of Lent, and today many churches and pastors still refuse to perform weddings between Ash Wednesday and Easter (roughly from mid-February through mid-April; it varies from year to year). So if you are planning a spring wedding in a church, you should double check to make sure you won't run into a scheduling conflict with Lent. Queen Victoria, who was married in February, declared that marriage was a solemn ritual and therefore it was most appropriate to marry during Lent. Royalty has a way of circumventing the religious rules laid down for the rest of us.

Sandy & Dave

Sandy and Dave were married on a Thursday evening because they wanted to schedule their wedding on the anniversary of their first date. They wanted a simple ceremony with a great party afterward, and they knew most of their guests would welcome the chance to schedule a long weekend. This was also the perfect way to add an extra couple of days to their honeymoon. Instead of leaving town Saturday evening or Sunday morning, they were leaving the hotel bound for their honeymoon cabin in the north woods on Friday morning.

The time of day and the time of year you choose for your ceremony will affect the quality of the light. Consult with your photographer and see if she has any suggestions for this. There's a big difference in light quality between an overcast late afternoon in February and a bright mid-afternoon summer day. This can be managed as long as you consider it ahead of time and discuss lighting and flash bulb needs with your photographer.

Religious Restrictions

If you have your heart set on a church or temple wedding but aren't a member or a practitioner of any particular faith, there are a few things you should be prepared for. Many Christian churches (Catholic and Protestant) will not allow weddings to take place during Lent (approximately mid-February through late March or mid-April). There are churches that will refuse to allow you to be married in their sanctuary if you have been married before. Others will not allow you to plan a formal church wedding if you already are living together. And, of course, Sunday may not be a good day to get married in church because it's already booked.

Jewish weddings may not be conducted on the Sabbath; other holidays (Rosh Hashanah, Yom Kippur, Passover Shavuot, and Sukkoth); the three weeks between the seventeenth of Tamuz and the ninth of Av, which generally fall in July and/or August and commemorate the destruction of the Temple; or the Omer period (between Passover and Shavuot), seven weeks that usually fall in April and May. Sunday is a popular wedding day for those of the Jewish faith, but Saturday evening an hour and a half after sundown is acceptable (after the Sabbath has ended).

Whatever the house of worship you choose as the place for your wedding, you should consult with the priest, pastor, minister, or rabbi who will conduct the service. He or she will be able to give you restrictions that apply in that particular congregation for the dates and times for weddings.

A Vision of Your Big Day

EVERY MAJOR PROJECT YOU undertake requires a plan and a budget, and your wedding may well be the most major project you've ever undertaken. Don't just dive in and start ordering things and spending money. After you've consulted with everyone and decided on all the aspects that are most important to you and your family and talked in general terms about financing your dream of the perfect wedding, after you've chosen a date, found a site for the service and a site for the reception, it's time to get down to making choices. You need to choose a dress, flowers, photographer, invitations, and more...much more... in great detail. You'll be choosing menus, tasting wedding cake, and deciding which flowers to use in your bouquet. No detail is too small to cause an anxiety attack in a stressed out bride. The more in charge you are now, the less likely you will be to "lose it" on your wedding day. This should be a whirlwind time of joy and happiness, but it can be marred by overspending and incurring unwanted debt unless you plan carefully. Chapter 5, "Strictly Business," will help you plan a budget, decide how you'll pay for everything, and help you plan the most elegant wedding and reception you can afford in the time you have allotted for the preparations. After Chapter 5, we will get down to the fun part of the planning—choosing all those details and attending all those parties in a state of supreme confidence and control.

Courtesy Shawn and Eli Kammerman

This happy couple put their plans in motion to realize a lifelong dream of the perfect wedding.

Part II

Serious Planning

ANY MAJOR UNDERTAKING IN LIFE *begins with the excitement of the idea, proceeds through various levels of planning (from general to very fine details), and culminates in the fulfillment of a dream. You'll do a lot of things in your life, professional and personal, from graduation through retirement and from childhood through parenthood and senior citizenship. They all follow the same pattern. Dream, plan, and work to realize the dream.*

Your wedding is no different from all those other major and minor life achievements: the hard work is in the planning. If you have a good plan, the execution is easier. In Part II, we explore the plans. From figuring out a budget and organizing contracts and paperwork through the shine on the flower girl's shoe, the more organized you are early in the plan, the better your overall result will be.

Strictly Business

"I think that everyone should get married at least once, so you can see what a silly, outdated institution it is."

—Madonna

(presumably before her sumptuous wedding to Guy Ritchie in December 2000)

W E TEND THESE DAYS TO GET married at a later age than in previous decades. The average age of a bride in the 1950s was somewhere in her early 20s. In 2006 it was 27, with many first time brides waiting until their early to mid 30s or even later to walk down the aisle. What seemed relevant in terms of etiquette and financial responsibility during much of the 20th century now seems passé. Still, when it comes to weddings, we like to adhere to tradition, although we would argue that the opulence and conspicuous consumerism practiced by many brides today is hardly traditional; couples marrying in previous decades would never have dreamed of incurring debt for their wedding festivities, while today we take it for granted that no expense is too great on this one day.

We'll outline for you in this chapter what's considered proper along with how things are actually happening in the 21st century (and point out some historical facts to help explain how our current "traditions" came to be). These days, the father of the bride, who traditionally footed the bill for the entire wedding, may have long since sunk his life savings into a motor home and hit the road in search of adventure. The bride's mother, who in the past had the responsibility for planning the ceremony and reception, issuing invitations, and hiring a photographer, is traveling with him, likely accompanied by a small dog dressed in a sweater. Meanwhile, the bride is earning a six-figure income of her own. The result is that the traditions of who pays for what have, in reality, been greatly modified.

Courtesy of Michael and Marni Migliaccio

Today's bride and groom are much more financially independent, and take responsibility for the cost of their own wedding. Because they don't have to feel that they are raiding their parents' retirement accounts, they can spend as freely as they wish.

The Budget, or Who Should Pay for What

THE FOLLOWING INFORMATION is taken from an etiquette guide printed in 1992.*

The bride and her family were responsible for:

The bridal consultant if one is used

Invitations, announcements, and enclosures

The wedding gown and accessories

Flowers and decorations for the ceremony and reception, bridal bouquet, bridesmaid's bouquets

The photographer and a videotape if one is made

Music at ceremony and reception

Transportation to ceremony and from ceremony to reception

All expenses of the reception

Bride's presents to her attendants

Bride's present to groom (optional)

The groom's wedding ring

Awning for entrance to ceremony and runner for aisle

Police escorts or traffic officers if needed

Transportation and lodging for the clergyman if from another location and chosen by the bride's family

Accommodations for bride's attendants

Bridesmaid's luncheon

The groom and his family in 1992, according to Post, were responsible for:

The bride's engagement and wedding rings

Groom's present to the bride (optional)

Gifts for the groom's attendants

Accommodations for the groom's attendants

Boutonnieres for male members of the wedding party

Ties and gloves, although those are most likely provided with the tux

The bride's going away corsage (a somewhat antiquated notion now)

Corsages for immediate family members (although this was probably included in the bride's florist order)

The minister's or rabbi's fee

Transportation and lodging for the clergyman if from another location and chosen by the groom's family

The marriage license

Transportation of groom and best man to ceremony

Expenses of the honeymoon

All costs of the rehearsal dinner

Bachelor dinner (optional)

Transportation and lodging expenses for groom's parents if necessary

*Information from *Emily Post's Etiquette*, 15th Edition, by Elizabeth L. Post, 1992, New York, Harper Collins Publishers.

The bride's attendants were responsible for the following:

- The purchase of their dresses and accessories
- Their own transportation to and from the ceremony
- A shared gift from the attendants to the bride
- An individual gift to the couple
- Organizing a shower or luncheon for the bride

The groom's attendants were responsible for the following:

- Rental of their attire
- Transportation to and from the wedding
- A shared gift from the groomsmen to the groom
- An individual gift to the couple
- A bachelor's dinner or stag party for the groom

And, finally, guests, of course, were responsible for their own transportation and accommodations, although it was (and still is) the custom for the family (either the groom's or the bride's) that lives in the host city to reserve a block of rooms in a hotel near the ceremony and reception sites.

Today's Fiscal Responsibility

To be fair, Ms. Post in 1992 does give a nod to the growing tendency for the groom's family to share in the planning and expense for the wedding, but she still places most of the responsibility for the wedding on the parents of the bride. Today, the bride and groom themselves are more apt to share a greater load of the expense for their own nuptials, and this is probably a direct result of their being older and already living independently.

> **In 1922, Emily Post's advice was less detailed, as was the general atmosphere surrounding a wedding. The mother of the bride first made sure the minister was available to perform the ceremony on the date she had chosen and that the church was available. She then visited a stationer's shop with her daughter to choose invitations. After that, she decided how many guests she could afford to feed and then consulted with the groom's mother on the guest list. The wedding was financed by the bride's family, and the groom paid for the wedding trip and the engagement ring. A simple arrangement, one that over the ensuing century has grown much more complicated, albeit more realistic and, thankfully, shared among more people.**

A great majority (79%) of brides and grooms contribute toward the cost of their own wedding. Today only 53% of the bride's parents and 31% of the groom's parents contribute to the cost of the wedding. In most cases, it is a joint venture, but more brides and grooms than ever are helping to pay for their own nuptial festivities.

In the past, the wedding ceremony marked not just a joining of two people in a new enterprise called marriage, but it also marked a rite of passage that proclaimed to the world, "We are adults now," in a way that was understood by the community.

As recently as 25 years ago, young people tended to live at home until they either married or went to college; indeed, if they went to college, it was to live in a dorm or a sorority or fraternity, which served as an extension of their parent's home. Notwithstanding the current trend for single adults to move back home after college until they have established themselves in a career, the end of the college years usually marks our society's agreed upon coming of age these days, not marriage. Nowadays, having a career and a home of your own often precedes the wedding, and many people live together before they marry. The result is that more people now design their own ceremony, pay for it themselves, and spare no expense in the process. Weddings have grown more and more elaborate and lavish as a result, not only of conspicuous consumption and consumerism, but also of the increased means of the marrying couple themselves—not to mention the precedent being set by celebrities and royalty that is the main fare of our evening TV news. Weddings have become more expensive, and the bride and groom are footing the bill themselves.

Why We Do That

Not only did weddings in the past proclaim to the world that two people had become adults, they actually said something else— that the two of them would be having sex and, as a result, children. Advances in birth control have made it possible for people to have the one without the other today, so a wedding is no longer simply considered a license to have sex. But it is still considered a step toward the stability necessary before a couple begins to have children. Thus, many couples live together while planning their wedding.

Your Station in Life

The type of neighborhood you live in and your socio-economic standing tend to determine how much you spend on your wedding, where it will take place, and who will pay for it. You are more likely to get married in a church if you live in Tennessee than in New York City, far more likely to get married in a church if you live in New York City than if you live in Beverly Hills, and no matter which city you live in, if you live in an affluent professional neighborhood, you are likely to spend twice as much money on your wedding than other brides and grooms who live in middle class neighborhoods in the same city. The area of the country you live in even affects the age at which you are married. Brides in New York and in Lexington, Kentucky are, on average, 27; in Indiana and Iowa, their average age is 25.

Information provided by The Wedding Report at weddingreport.com.

Worksheets and Calculators

THE FIRST THING YOU NEED to know, of course, is how much money you will have available to spend. You don't have to actually have this amount in an account somewhere when you start the planning. You will probably spend somewhere between eight months and two years planning your wedding, depending on the availability of sites for the reception and ceremony and a particular date you have your heart set on. (Many couples waited years to be married on the particularly auspicious date of 7/7/2007, and there's a waiting list of four years' duration to have your ceremony performed in Times Square.) The longer you take to plan the wedding, the more you can spread the cost out over that time period. Of course, you can also use credit cards, but then you run the risk of starting off your marriage in debt, and you don't really want to do that.

So figure out an amount that you will have to spend. Some of it may come from your parents (both bride's and groom's), and some will come from the two of you. You might even find other more creative sources of wedding cost revenue. It might be important enough to you to cash in some CDs or bonds, and other relatives, grandparents, for instance, might make a contribution. Get commitments from parents and other resources. Decide how much you will have in discretionary funds over the next several months. Discuss other sources of income, add it all up, and determine your total budget. Then you can start breaking that amount into reasonable sums for each item.

A typical budget might look something like this:

Bride's dress and accessories	7%
Hair and makeup	1%
Groom's attire and accessories	3%
Reception and ceremony site rental	10%
Officiant's fees, gratuities, and license	1%
Flowers	3%
Food	30%
Beverages	8%
Cake	3%
Decorations	3%
Music	10%
Photography	5%
Videography	3%
Invitations and postage	2%
Programs	1%
Transportation	1%
Attendants' gifts	3%
Miscellaneous	6%

Suggested wedding budgets vary by a few percentage points, and this one does not include the cost of the rings or the honeymoon; and, of course, you should tailor yours to fit your circumstances. Take advantage of talents and business and social connections among your family and friends to save big on some items too. If Uncle George says, "I can get that for you wholesale," listen and consider. If Cousin Betty is a pastry chef who is donating the cake, that will be 3% of your budget that you can use to upgrade some other item on the list. If a video of the whole proceeding isn't something you will treasure, but you'd like the very best photographer available in your area, you should be able to budget more for photography alone.

Use this budget, or one you find online at any number of sites (do a Google search for "wedding budget"), and begin tailoring the one that makes most sense for you to fit your needs. If you have $30,000 available to spend and you know the cost of your attendants' gifts won't be anywhere near the $900 suggested by this budget worksheet, you can adjust and plan to spend more on the cake or the food.

Approximately 50% of your total budget is going to be spent on things that are consumed at the reception—dinner, beverages, cake, champagne to toast with, cake cutting fees, and rental of the site. The rest will go for wedding attire (particularly the bride's dress), photography, music, and flowers, along with a few relatively minor expenses such as invitations and transportation.

You can find wedding calculators online at several web sites. Try a few out and see which one makes the most sense to you. Following are a few results I found by plugging in various amounts.

◌ **Blissweddings.com**

Follow the links to the budget planner here. I plugged in an amount of $30,000 here and the calculator suggested $15,000 for the reception, but only $600 for the ring. Of course, these amounts are adjustable according to your needs. You should place your priorities as you wish; I think I might be inclined to spend a bit more on the ring and a bit less on something else.

◌ **Eventageous.com**

Click on Articles and Resources at the top of the page and scroll down to Wedding Budget Worksheet. This site asks for a total budget amount and the number of guests. The calculations here are broken down into a bit more detail, and it's very nice because you can pick and choose which items to include in your calculations. For instance, if the rings have already been bought and paid for, you don't need to consider them so just uncheck that item in the list.

There is also a great Master Checklist here that you should print and use to keep track of every detail from babysitter's phone number to restrictions on what can be thrown. You might want to print multiple copies of parts of this form before you decide on ceremony and reception venues and use them to compare the facilities.

cg Outoftheordinary.com/
   weddingbudgetcalc.php

Or go to Outoftheordinary.com and click on Budget Calculator on the left of the screen. This site also asks for a budget amount and the number of guests and then calculates how much you should budget for each category.

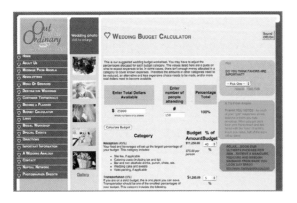

Geography Matters

A typical Midwest bride will spend somewhere between $10,000 and $30,000 on the entire wedding (rings, clothing, ceremony, reception, and gifts). In Beverly Hills, that total amount is nearly $60,000, while in some other areas of the country, the average is less than $10,000. No matter how much you spend though, the proportion will be approximately 50% on the reception, 10% on attire, and 15% on photography and music. The remaining 25% will be divided among wedding rings, flowers, and miscellaneous expenses, such as the license, transportation, and those commemorative wedding napkins and matches or favors and hotel room gift bags for out of town guests.

Head Count

Your budget is directly tied to the number of guests you invite. The more guests at the wedding, the greater the amount you'll need to entertain them all. If you have a limited budget or want to do something really extraordinary for your close friends and family members, the best way to manage the cost is to cut the number of guests. It is more costly to feed 300 people a buffet supper of cold cuts and salads than it is to feed 20 people fresh shrimp and mahi mahi in an exotic locale.

Prenuptial Agreements

A S LONG AS WE'RE TALKING about money, we should discuss the option of a prenuptial agreement. Is this sort of unromantic contract really necessary for you? After all, you have met the man of your dreams, you never argue, and nothing will ever go wrong in your life. You have planned where you'll live, how many children you'll have, and even talked about how you'll retire to Arizona one day. He isn't Donald Trump, and you aren't Christina Aguilera. So why do you need to be so businesslike?

Wedding Checklist

❑ Reserve Banquet Hall
❑ Reserve Church
❑ Make Honeymoon Reservations
❑ Select Invitations
❑ Select Caterer
❑ Interview Bands
❑ Select Bridesmaid Gowns
❑ Interview Photograph⌐
❑ Select Florist
❑ Compile ⌐
❑ Res

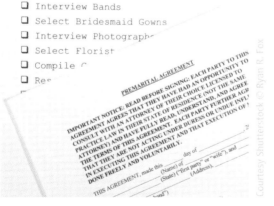

If you are comfortable with each other, you should be able to talk about whether a prenuptial agreement is appropriate for you.

While you are planning your wedding, take some time to plan your marriage. If you haven't talked about how you will manage money and what your attitudes toward child care are, you have much more important topics to discuss than the color scheme for the ceremony. Will you each hold separate checking accounts? How much do you think you should be able to spend without consulting your spouse? Will one of you be responsible for paying the bills or will you take turns; just how will you divvy up that responsibility in your new business arrangement? What is your attitude toward credit, toward savings, toward retirement planning? When you have children, will one of you stay at home to care for them?

Somehow a prenuptial agreement seems to say "I love you, and I plan to spend the rest of my life with you; we're both about to vow to stay together 'til death us do part' and 'for better or worse,' but I don't completely trust you, and I think you may leave me some day." Well, yes, as unromantic as that may sound, it's pretty much what you are saying. Do you really need to do it?

That depends, but think about this: 50% of the marriages in this country end in divorce. That's right, 50%; that's the divorce rate in the United States. If you live in a community property state, that means that everything you own, including all the income either of you earned during the course of your marriage, is considered to be held jointly. If he makes half a million a year and she earns nothing, in a community property state they each earned a quarter of a million. Perhaps even more importantly, keep in mind that married couples share their debt equally. This means that if one partner has spending issues and runs up thousands in credit card debt, both partners are liable for repayment of the debt. It is absolutely critical that a couple discuss and agree to certain spending guidelines early on to avoid financial stress in the marriage.

Thinking about these things tends to pull the plug on romance, sure, but now, early in the planning phase, is when you need to get this discussion out of the way, decide whether a prenup is right for you, sign whatever legal papers are necessary, and then forget about it and get back to the fun of being in love and planning a wedding. Just take a day off from feeling giddy with happiness and look into the legality of the agreement you are about to enter into. People have been left alone, bereft, bankrupt, and brokenhearted, and a bit of legal business now might just save you some day from being all of those at once. You can protect yourself from bankruptcy, and if you both enter into an equal arrangement, what's the harm? You're making sure if you ever do get left alone, bereft, and brokenhearted, at least you won't have to move in with your parents until you recover from a bad business agreement as well as a bad marriage. If the matter of a prenup strikes such a nerve in either partner that the engagement is ended, it is better to have that scene play out now rather than several years later when additional assets—not to mention possible children—are involved.

The jury is still out on the reason fully half the marriages in the United States end in divorce. The real culprit is probably a lack of commitment to the very institution of marriage, but as a couple you need to work on communicating, not just on the things you love about each other or the things you like talking about together, but also about the areas where you have real differences. And you need to consider the vows you are about to take as a serious promise, not just "as long as you remain young and beautiful and healthy," but also "when you get old and deaf and hair grows out of your nose." You are promising to remain together as a couple even on those occasions when you don't like each other very much.

Community Property vs. Common Law States

If you live in a *community property state*, any income or property acquired by either of you during the marriage is considered to be jointly held. It is as if that asset is an asset of the marriage, not of either individual. This rule of marital law has not been spelled out so clearly in the *common law states*, where the decision is made based on precedent and how the court rules, rather than stating clearly that the property of the marriage is held jointly by the two people in the marriage. So in the event of a divorce, or the dissolution of your marriage, if you live in a community property state, any property that you acquired during the course of the marriage must be split 50-50 between the two of you (or, in some jurisdictions, as the court rules).

Why We Do That

When marriages were arranged by families and the bride and groom often didn't even meet until their wedding day, more work went into the prenuptial agreement and less into wondering whether the two people involved had found their soul mate. The two families could barter and bargain unhindered by love or dewy-eyed admiration for each other. Marriage was a business deal, and romance was not a factor; indeed, the couple often "learned to love one another" after having spent a few years working together, sleeping together, and having children together—financially protected by the bargaining done by their parents long before their wedding day.

Divorce rates were pretty much zero in those days. Then again, the death rate was a lot higher, so if you weren't happy with your spouse, you could just wait for him or her to die (or go ahead and die yourself, because death was the only escape possible from "till death us do part"). A prenuptial agreement serves the same purpose that the arranged marriages of the past served—it protects both members from financial ruin if one of them ends up abandoning the other. It just makes good sense if you are entering into the marriage with any kind of property or income of your own or if you have no income or career and plan to devote yourself to being a true helpmeet for your partner, especially if you live in a community property state.

In common law states, this may still be true, but it will be decided by the court and by agreement between the two parties rather than on the basis of an already existing law.

The following nine states are jurisdictions where community property laws are in effect:

Arizona	Louisiana	Texas
California	Nevada	Washington
Idaho	New Mexico	Wisconsin

Notice that most of these states are in the western half of the United States. That's because the idea of community property has its roots in the laws of Mexico, whose laws have their roots in the laws of Spain. Common law is a distinctly English type of law, and it's what most of the law in the United States is based on. It's the influence in California, Texas, Nevada, and most of those other states from Mexican law that makes them a bit different.

Laws vary from state to state, whether they are community property or common law states, and you need to investigate the precedents set in your own state of residence. You should also read Publication 555 from the Internal Revenue Service for more information about what these laws and court proceedings might mean to you. Your individual circumstances are unique to you. There may be children from previous relationships involved, or one of you may have assets in the form of investments such as stocks, annuities, and retirement pensions. You need to sit down and talk about the assets (not to mention the debts and prior commitments) that each of you is bringing to the marriage. Look into whether a prenuptial agreement makes sense in your case. You certainly do want to protect any assets that should rightfully belong to your children one day.

Other Business Concerns

AFTER YOU DECIDE WHETHER you'll be opening a joint checking and savings account, after you decide who's going to be responsible for keeping records and writing checks each month, after you decide how you will share financial responsibilities and what is an acceptable amount of money for each of you to spend frivolously without consulting the other, and finally, after you decide whether a prenuptial agreement is appropriate for you, you will also want to update any insurance policies or pension funds that you now hold singly. Your responsibilities are growing, and you might need more life insurance. You will want to make sure that each of you is covered by the other's automobile insurance and that you both have health insurance. You should also investigate whether it would be financially beneficial for one of you to carry the other as a dependent on your company's health insurance policy. As your legal and social status changes, you might look into how being married will affect your income tax. Perhaps you should change the number of dependents you report on your W-4 forms at work.

If you are changing your name, you'll need to inform the Social Security Administration and request a new card. This applies to women who change to their husband's name and to both if you decide to hyphenate. If you have children and want to make clear your wishes regarding them, now is a good time to write a will too. You need to state who you want to be their guardian in the case of your death (this may or may not be your new spouse), and you need to make sure any property you own that is to become theirs is specified as such. In many states, the surviving spouse automatically inherits all.

If one of you is switching to the other's health care coverage, you need to inquire about windows of opportunity for doing that too. You may have a short period of time after the wedding (as you do after the birth of a child), or you may have to wait for your company's open enrollment period.

Even though some of these legal considerations can't be carried out until after your marriage becomes official, it isn't too soon to start a list of them and make sure you do all the paperwork as soon after the wedding as possible. It isn't even too early to begin thinking about writing a will. For some of this, you might find it beneficial to consult an attorney. Just as you have a family doctor, a family lawyer is not a far fetched idea. It's not just something rich people have. Everyone on occasion needs the advice or services of an attorney.

Wrapping Up the Business Aspects

WHEW! THAT WASN'T MUCH FUN, was it? But now that it's all out of the way, or at least has been given a thought and added to one of your growing number of checklists, we can get back to the fun part of planning your wedding. In Chapter 6, "Choosing the Sites, the Theme, the Tone of Your Wedding," we'll dive right into the romantic whirlwind of your wedding day.

The site you choose for your wedding sets the tone: an estate wedding with lawn tents or a casual beach wedding with umbrellas just in case.

Courtesy Lisa Boyadjian and Chris Duval © Abbie DeLeers

Choosing the Sites, the Theme, the Tone of Your Wedding

For the happiest life, days should be rigorously planned, nights left open to chance.
—Mignon McLaughlin

A T LAST, IT'S ACTUALLY TIME TO begin planning your wedding. You have the ring, you've told all your close friends and family, announced the upcoming nuptials in the local newspaper, and basked in all those happy congratulations and well wishes. You may even have been pestered with questions about where you'll live, when you'll start having children, and other personal information that people seem to feel free to ask at this time in your life (and you have handled it all with grace and aplomb). You've even planned the budget for your wedding and resolved some of the potentially thorny issues of your new legal and financial status. Now you are overwhelmed with pressure to choose invitations, the dress, the flowers, the cake, and music for both the ceremony and the reception.

Start with the big picture. Before you begin to focus on those highly important details, it is time to choose where your wedding and reception will take place and to consider what general atmosphere, even attitude, you want your wedding to have. Then you'll be able to move on to the next phase—choosing who will be participating in the ceremony with you, the color scheme for your wedding, and what sort of food you will serve. In short, it's time to determine the style your wedding will have. A wedding is an event, rather like a Broadway play: Will yours be lavish and over the top, somber and formal, joyous and filled with meaning, or casual and laid back? Will you choose to honor your love, your families, your ethnicity, or your culture? What means the most to you and what feeling do you want to express on this day? What do you want to emphasize as you exchange vows? How do you want your guests to go away feeling? Your decision regarding sites, formality, number of attendants, and color schemes will help to narrow your choices and get you started on all those other decisions. Now is the time to start booking the sites and reserving the key vendors you'll need to hire.

Courtesy Sarah O'Donnell Panella and Jason Panella
© Elizabeth Furbish

The scenery sets the tone for your wedding.

The Ceremony

THE DETERMINING FACTORS in the theme, the overall *feel*, of your wedding are the site of the ceremony (religious or not), the relative formality of the service (barefoot in the park or white tie and tails in a cathedral), the time of day, and how many people you want to invite. All of these things need to fit together.

If you and your fiancé are of the same faith and having a religious ceremony is important to you, choosing a site for the ceremony should be easy. It will be in the church or synagogue of your choice, and the officiant will be a clergyman of your faith. You may have to decide in whose home church you want to hold the service or whether you want to have it in a particularly picturesque church that neither of you attends, but other choices and details of the service should be easily agreed upon.

You really do not want to have eight attendants in white tie attire if you picture your wedding taking place on the beach or in your parents' backyard. And it might seem out of place to wear a wreath of ivy and a simple peasant gown with bare feet if your ceremony will be in St. Brad the Divine Cathedral. Setting has everything to do with atmosphere and theme.

Make sure the lavishness of your setting is coordinated with the formality of your attire and even the relative formality or casualness of the type of food served. You don't want to be trying to eat fried chicken outside wearing a taffeta and lace dress with a long train. Set the tone with your site selection and keep it in mind as you choose food, flowers, and music.

Courtesy Scott and Reneé Boshears © Adlam Herod

A joyful church wedding is what we most often picture when we say "traditional."

Housbondes at chirche dore I have had five...

> —From *The Wife of Bath's Prologue*,
> Geoffrey Chaucer, ~1400

Before the 13th century, weddings were civil affairs. In 1215, marriage was one of the holy sacraments listed by the Fourth Lateran Council of the Catholic Church; this was reaffirmed at the Council of Trent in 1563. Before the 13th century, marriage was considered a serious commitment, and only those who had reached the age of consent (12 for girls; 14 for boys) were allowed to exchange vows, but it was not a religious undertaking. As a learned member of the community, the local priest was often invited to weddings, but he had no official role in the vows until after 1215, and even then priests and friars had to make it a point to encourage their charges to come to the church to exchange their vows. Even after marriage became a sacrament, weddings took place outside the doors of the church. After the vows were exchanged, everyone entered for a proper Mass, during which the couple knelt at the altar while attendants held a canopy over their heads (reminiscent of the Jewish chuppah). Often, couples married themselves and later asked for a priest's blessing on their union.

Why We Do That

Marriage enjoys a curious state that straddles civil law and religious edict. Today you may be married in a church and have the blessings of an entire religious organization, but without a license from the state, you are not legally married, and in most states the person who performs the ceremony must himself be licensed to do so. In most states, weddings may be performed by clergy and by some of the following offices: a ship's captain, a judge, a clerk of the court, a justice of the peace, or a sheriff. An interesting trend today is for someone (anyone who is willing to complete the paperwork) to be ordained online to perform wedding ceremonies for his or her friends; however, that person must still be licensed and recognized by the state where he performs his duties.

If neither of you has a particular religious affiliation, you may simply agree upon a venue for your ceremony and then follow the rules set forth by the site you choose for your wedding. That's simple too. Complications may arise, however, when you want to combine elements of two different faiths or if you wish to marry in a church you have no affiliation with. You may find that more conservative priests, rabbis, and ministers refuse to participate in mixed ceremonies, and you may run into other religious impediments you did not expect.

Why We Do That

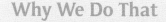

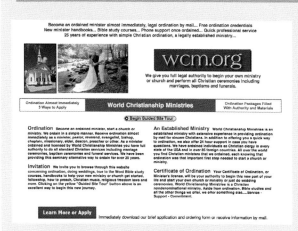

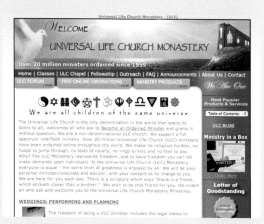

You don't have to attend seminary for years to be able to officiate at your friends' weddings.

For a list of the laws regarding who may perform marriage ceremonies and to see how the laws regarding marriage vary from state to state, go to http://usmarriagelaws.com. New York City, for instance, does not recognize online ordinations by the Universal Life Church; in fact, the marriage laws in New York City differ greatly from the rest of the state. Be aware of the laws in your state as well as the requirements of your religious denomination.

Check the laws in your state to find out if your unique and unusual wedding plans are legal.

You can, of course, choose to have your ceremony performed by one or the other of your religious affiliations and find some other way to incorporate the beliefs of the other person. Or you may opt to have your ceremony at a neutral site and choose a member of the clergy who is willing to perform a ceremony that is not specific to any particular church.

Reneé & Scott

Reneé, who is a teacher, and Scott planned to be married during spring break, which happens to come the week before Easter in her school district. They had no particular faith affiliation but did want a church wedding. They first inquired at a Christian church that was close to where they lived together and where Scott had attended kindergarten and participated in sporting events throughout his school years, although neither of them was a member of that church. The minister told them he was unwilling to officiate at the type of ceremony they planned; he felt it was unseemly for them to have a church wedding while they were living together unmarried. He was willing to perform a quickie ceremony now and then do the big church ceremony later, but he wasn't willing to help them plan a church wedding while they were not married but living together. They rejected that option.

Their next choice was the Lutheran church where Reneé's mother was a longtime member. There they learned that no weddings took place in that church during Lent, and of course, spring break happened during Lent. They opted for this church, though, because they really liked the pastor, so they changed the date of their wedding to a day in August.

You might need to make some compromises and change your plans a bit when you start to investigate churches or other sites for your ceremony. Availability is not the only issue you might run into, but if you are willing to be a bit flexible regarding the date or some other aspect, you will eventually find the perfect place for your ceremony.

In any case, now (as early as possible in the planning stages) is the time to choose the site for your ceremony and someone to officiate your exchange of vows, and that means you'll be choosing the tone for your wedding. Following are some possible venues to consider:

A church one or both of you belongs to

In a church neither of you has any affiliation with (including cathedrals, chapels, temples, and synagogues)

At the courthouse by a justice of the peace

A public park, conservatory, or garden

In a historic mansion or house that is rented for such occasions

On the beach

At a resort

In a separate room of the hotel or country club where the reception is to be held

In your home or your parents' home, inside or out

In someone else's private home

In a museum

On a golf course

At a winery or orchard (a beautiful choice—all those vines and flowers and trees and ponds)

The mood captured on a lawn overlooking the Pacific in Hawaii might be difficult to duplicate anywhere else.

Get Specific and Ask the Right Questions

Once you've narrowed down your choice of site and know what you're looking for, visit the site and talk about any restrictions involved that would make this a poor choice for your wedding ceremony. Make sure the site is available on the date you need it. If you've chosen a church or synagogue or a public place, such as a museum, make sure photographs are allowed on the premises and find out if there are any other strictures you should know about. Is there a fee for using the facility?

Is there a possibility other weddings might be scheduled in that location on the same day as yours? Are there policies you need to be aware of concerning decorating? Does the church you've chosen also act as the host of the local Little League? Does it share parking facilities with any other nearby organizations? Try to find out what else might be taking place on your big day in or near the place you decide on for your ceremony. Is there a limit to the number of people who are allowed in the building at one time. Fire codes often limit the number of occupants. In the Appendix to this book, you'll find a list of questions to ask about the sites you are considering.

Make sure the site you choose for the ceremony will actually hold the number of guests you want to invite. If you plan to have the wedding in a small picturesque chapel or your parents' 12×14 living room, you will have to tailor the guest list to fit in that space. Also make sure there is ample parking for the number of guests you will have.

Cathleen & Chris

Cathleen and Chris were married in a small rose garden at a senior citizen community's golf course. It may not be the first place that comes to mind, but don't discount senior citizen communities as a possible wedding venue. Many have banquet facilities that are quite nice, and Cathleen found one that was reasonably priced simply because they gain enough money from association fees and golf course events that they are able to keep their wedding costs fairly low. Cathleen's and Chris's wedding was about half the price of a normal golf course wedding—a wonderful bargain!

If there is a particular clergyman you'd like to have officiate at your wedding ceremony, make sure he or she is available on the date you've chosen as well. If it is important to you to do so, you will want to ask if the pastor or rabbi you've chosen will allow you to write your own vows. What is allowed and what is not allowed in the site you have chosen for your ceremony?

Why We Do That

Sacred spaces: an altar, a chuppah, a rose arbor...if we recognize and celebrate no other rite of passage, we like to create a special space for our nuptials. The wedding is universal, and it is a rite we like to reserve for a sacred space, even if we don't particularly involve ourselves with sacred spaces for any other reason. We have a real need to create or visit such a place when we exchange wedding vows, be it in a church or a rose garden.

You can create your own sacred space in the midst of beautiful scenery.

Changing Religions to Get Married

Some mixed faith couples choose for one of them to convert to the other's religion so that their marriage can be sanctified by the faith of their choice. If you feel strongly about doing this, you should begin early in the preparation phases for your wedding day to plan for the classes and training that often go into "signing up" with a new faith. Especially if you have been married previously, even though you are now legally divorced, that marriage must often be annulled by the church. Often, there are tenets of faith to learn, baptisms and communions to plan and participate in, and other requirements to fulfill. It can take longer than a year to carry out all the necessary rites that go into joining a new religion, so if you know you'll be doing this, it's best to get started right away. Some couples do this because they want the full Catholic or Eastern Orthodox Mass at their ceremony or because they want to make a commitment to raise their children in a particular faith.

Just be sure you allow plenty of time for all the paperwork, class work, and vows that go into switching religions. Consult your officiating minister, priest, or rabbi if this is something you are contemplating.

Reserve Musicians for the Ceremony

When you are interviewing the pastor or his assistant, inquire about music. Is an organist or pianist available through the church? Or maybe you'd rather have your cousin Jim play guitar as a backdrop for your wedding. Make sure outside musicians are permitted as some churches have restrictions on not only the kind of music (religious or secular) that can be played, but also who can perform. Some limit musicians to their own organist, pianist, or music director. In the case of an Eastern Orthodox ceremony, you will require a cantor to assist the presiding priest. Some churches provide the cantor, while others require you to provide one. Music is a crucial element in setting the tone for the day. You might find it to be an excellent way to honor your heritage too. You can do that with bagpipe music before the ceremony if one or both of you have Scottish forbears, or you might choose to honor your Spanish ancestors with Spanish guitar music. There are many possibilities. If one of you hails from the mountains of North Carolina or Virginia, a zither might be an appropriate instrument to have someone play at your wedding.

If you are asking a family member or friend who is an amateur to play music or sing at your wedding, be sure to ask early and give them plenty of time to rehearse. Don't ask anyone to sing or perform at your wedding, though, unless you are sure of their abilities. Nothing is more embarrassing than having your aunt sing "O Promise Me" in a high falsetto and then find herself unable to reach the high notes. If a friend will be playing organ or piano, make sure one is available at the ceremony site. Check with your contact at the site to make sure the music you want is allowed and there's room for the musicians to perform.

Coordination

YOU'LL NEED TO COORDINATE your planned wedding date with your choice of ceremony site, reception site, musicians for both, caterer, and the clergy who will officiate. Now is the time to keep your three-ring binder and calendar handy as you make calls, check availability, call someone else, and narrow down your choices to a date, a wedding site, a reception site, the clergyman who will perform the ceremony, an organist or other musician to play at the ceremony, a DJ or band to play at the reception, and the availability of all your attendants. Just dive in and make the calls; it will all come together.

Keep that three-ring binder handy to store the names, numbers, and contact information of all the people you talk with during this "setting up the framework of your wedding" phase. You'll also want to keep copies of all the contracts you'll be signing in it. As the big day approaches, you'll want to be able to quickly put your hands on all records of all your agreements.

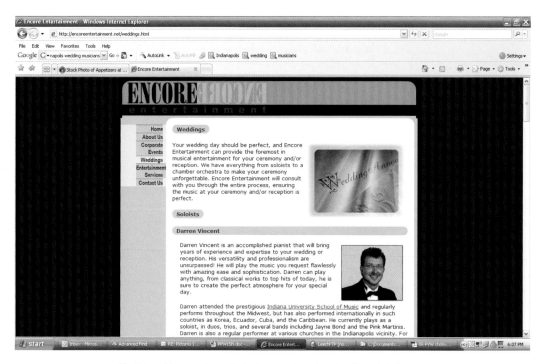

The Internet is a great way to start comparison shopping for entertainment.
Get recommendations from friends and inquire at local music schools too.

The Reception

I'll kiss all the ladies, the young and old, and then

I'll have myself another drink, and kiss them all again.

I'll dance at your wedding, I won't miss that wedding,

I'll dance at your wedding, am I gonna shine

At your wedding and mine.

—From "I'll Dance at Your Wedding" by Herbert Magidson/Ben Oakland, performed by various artists, including Bing Crosby and Frank Sinatra, 1948

Next you need to reserve your reception site and a caterer if food service isn't provided by the site. Most hotels and country clubs sell you the food, recommend their preferred DJs and pastry chefs for the cake, and don't charge extra for the room. Finding this "all in one" sort of deal reduces some of the stress of searching out all these vendors on your own, but you might feel that you are giving up making these individual choices on your own. Many of these all-inclusive sites make their money from food sales, so they don't charge extra for the ballroom or the place where the reception takes place. In the case of hotels, they also make their money from your out-of-town guests; if you block a set of rooms for your out-of-town guests, they get a group rate, too. If a hotel wants to sell you food for your reception and rooms for your guests and then wants to charge you for the use of their ball-room for your reception, they really need to have a good explanation for why they're doing that. As is the case with any contracted job, get several bids for your wedding reception. You are paying for all the service you get with such a reception site. The markup on the food is more than you would likely pay if you booked a hall and hired a caterer. This is the time to comparison shop and ask for bids.

Insist on sampling the food that will be served at your reception. Every venue you consider should be anxious for you to sample the food that you will be buying in great quantities from them. Schedule a time when you and your fiancé, preferably along with one or both of your mothers or any other helpers you designate, can go visit the reception site and be served samples of the dishes you want to serve.

As you drive the route from the wedding, make notes of the directions and any hazards you notice along the way, as well as landmarks that would be helpful in giving driving directions. You can print a map from Mapquest or one of the other online mapping services to enclose with your invitations, but you should double check those carefully against the actual experience of driving from one location to another. The mapping services are great, but there still are some streets and addresses that they don't cover exactly enough to provide good directions to. Check with town hall for planned construction projects along your route as detours can easily cause confused out of town guests to miss the entire wedding or reception.

From a strip mall banquet facility to a paddlewheel steamboat, a hotel ballroom to your own backyard, from a local mansion dedicated to catering to a mountaintop retreat, the site of your reception can be as simple, as elegant, or as unique as you want. You can have it all done professionally, sit back and enjoy, and do nothing more strenuous than write checks and toss your bouquet. Or you can plan to have volunteer helpers and save a bundle on a less staid and formal affair. The site of your reception and who you choose to do the work determine many things, such as what sort of food is available and how much room your guests will have to maneuver around in.

From the collection of Judy Doell

Young ladies of the 1950s look stylish and proper serving cake and punch at a friend's wedding.

From the collection of Judy Doell

Thirty years later, the style is a bit less formal, but the job is the same.

When you consider a site for the reception, take some time to drive the route between the ceremony and the celebration. Do it on the day of the week your wedding is planned for and at approximately the time your guests will be making the trip. Now is the time to plan at what point you'll be taking pictures and what your guests will be doing while that takes place. Will you have a formal receiving line immediately following the wedding and then go back inside to pose for formal photos while your guests wend their way to the reception site. How much time will that actually take? What will your guests be doing while you're involved in the photo session? Timing these things is something you'll want to discuss with the photographer and the catering director. The bar should be open when your guests arrive, and some hors d' oeuvres being served at this time would be thoughtful.

Basically, there are two kinds of sites—the complete "all in one package" kind of place where you buy their food, use their staff, and follow their rules, and they handle pretty much everything once you arrive for the reception. Or the other kind where you rent the room and then hire your own caterer and staff or enlist friends and family to handle much of the decorating and food preparation. Either type is likely to have its own rules concerning liquor though. The serving of liquor is regulated by state laws, so unless you opt to have the reception in your own home, you will likely be required to buy any liquor you serve from the site or through an approved vendor, regardless of how you handle the food. In fact, even serving liquor to guests in your home is subject to liability laws, under which you can be held responsible for your guests' actions afterward. It's a good idea to check with your caterer or with local law enforcement to find out just what your liability is in either case.

Space Concerns

No matter how elegant your attire, no matter how wonderful the food or beautiful the cake, if people can't maneuver around the space provided for the reception, they are going to be miserable and will probably leave early. (Lack of air conditioning on a hot day can make them miserable too, by the way.) How many tables of eight will the space available to you hold? Will there be plenty of room for your guests to walk around, get to the dance floor, the bar, the buffet table, and the cake? Is there "milling around" room? Is the room you are buying exactly the room you will get? Some ballrooms can be divided, and overzealous salespeople can and will cut your space a bit and crowd the tables up a bit so they can sell a portion of your room to another party. Be sure when you sign the contract with the reception site that you are guaranteed to get the space you bargained for.

How much space will you need? Does the venue use round tables (preferred) or eight-foot long tables that make you feel as if you are dining in a refectory with monks or maybe onboard a submarine—not conducive to relaxation and good times. If you are using round tables, no more than eight people should be seated at each table, and there should be at least three feet of floor space between the backs of chairs at adjoining tables—room to scoot the chair out, get up, walk away, and get back without having to step over people. You do not want your guests crowded into too small a space.

It is recommended that you allow 12 square feet per person for dining plus 8 square feet per person for dancing. This means that, after the buffet table and bar are set up, after the cake table and gift table have been placed, you should have 2,000 square feet of sitting, maneuvering, and dancing space for every 100 people. Ask to see the room that is offered to you set up. If necessary, visit the site before you sign the contract, on a Saturday when it is set for a wedding reception that is similar in size to your planned-for reception.

> **If you are getting married in the summer, make sure you request that the air conditioning be turned on and set well below 70 early on the day of your reception. Hotels and country clubs often have a computer-controlled HVAC system that is scheduled to come on an hour or two before your event. If the room is hot, that system will never cool it down enough in just a couple of hours. Furthermore, unless the temperature starts out well below 70, once 100 or 200 people start milling about, drinking and dancing, and waiters start hauling out buffet pans and sterno food warmers, it will soon be an uncomfortable 80, and the system will never catch up. Better to have the first few guests arrive thinking "It's kind of chilly in here" than to have them all leave right after dinner thinking "It's too hot; sorry, but we need to get out of here." Of course, they'd never say that to you, but it's what they'd be thinking.**

Arrange to speak to not just the salesperson who sells you the space and food, but also the banquet manager who is charged with delivering what the salesperson sells you. Talk to her or him about every item in the contract and make sure he understands how you visualize the room on the day of your reception. Talk to the banquet manager about where the bar will be, how the tables will be arranged, where the cake table will be, and how much space will be allotted for a band or DJ and for a dance floor and where these will be placed. Walk the space and have a picture in your mind of how things will look on your day.

Concern for All Your Guests

Good manners are defined as not just propriety, but also graciousness and kindness toward others; treating your guests well never goes out of style. Remembering small details about your guests, who is diabetic, who drinks only fruit juice, who might need extra space for a wheelchair shows your thoughtfulness. This is, after all, a party, and you are the hosts. The comfort of your guests should be your top priority.

Check to make sure the chairs are comfortable, sturdy, and upholstered. Your guests will not be as happy on folding wooden chairs as they will be in the kinds of chairs that have upholstered seats and backs and are stackable. You may have to pay extra for more comfortable chairs, but they are well worth the expense. The tables, as mentioned, should be round, and guests should not be crowded around them.

Why We Do That

The wedding feast is a tradition that is as old as the ceremony. And when we speak of "going to a wedding," it is sometimes as if the ceremony is something to be gotten through just so we can go to the reception. In a sense, the wedding is the reception, the meal and dancing that follow the ceremony. The first recorded miracle performed by Jesus was to turn water into wine for the guests at a wedding feast.

During the Middle Ages, a feast was part of a wedding, whether the hosts were royalty, middle class, or peasants. In 1376, wealthy Italian merchant Francesco di Marco Datini ordered his servants to purchase 406 loaves of bread, 250 eggs, 100 pounds of cheese, half an oxen, eight sheep, 37 capons, 11 chickens, 2 boar's heads, and assorted pigeons and ducks, along with gallons of wine, in order to feed the guests at his wedding to his 16-year-old bride Margheritis Bandini. (Pretty much defines "robbing the cradle," doesn't it?)

Devoting a whole weekend to a wedding is not something we've recently discovered either. The usual wedding feast during the Middle Ages lasted three days and included gift giving, entertainment, eating, and drinking. It sometimes ended with the guests escorting the newlywed couple to their bedchamber.

Courtesy, Shutterstock © Eric Limon

Start with comfortable chairs and sturdy round tables; then move on to create your simple and elegant table setting.

Check also to make sure that there is space available nearby for your guests who smoke. Of course, you must be considerate of the nonsmokers, especially small children, pregnant women, the ill and infirm, but it is the smokers who tend to be left out in the cold these days, quite literally. They are all your guests, and you should display hospitality and concern for the comfort of all. Try to make sure everyone is accommodated, even if it simply means making sure an overflow patio or a porch with comfortable seating will be available so anyone who wants to get away from the main celebration for a few minutes has a convenient place to retire to.

There should be adequate lighting in interior and exterior spaces, including parking lots and walkways. Laws now require wheelchair ramps in most public places, but there are still some historic mansions with less than adequate access for all. If your reception is held on an upper floor, make sure everyone has a way to get up there. There is probably an elevator, but it may be in an out of the way spot.

Make sure there is access to the room for your handicapped and elderly guests. Check the bathrooms to be sure there are commodious stalls for wheelchairs. Of course, again, make sure there is plenty of parking space available nearby and guests don't have to park down the street. In some urban areas, the only parking may be in paid lots or garages. Is that going to be acceptable for your guests? Also ask about air conditioning and heat, entrances and exits from the reception space, kitchen facilities and water availability, bathrooms, and cloakrooms if the weather is cool. Where are they? How close are they? And are they being shared with other events taking place at the same time? If your wedding is during the winter, will nearby lots and streets be plowed? You can't fend off a blizzard, but you can ask about normal maintenance after a snowstorm.

Consider the Work That Must Be Done

For how long a time will the room be yours? If you are planning an afternoon reception, will your guests be hurried out so the banquet crew can set up another wedding in the evening? That's okay as long as you know when you have to vacate the room. Allow plenty of time for the band or DJ to break down and carry out their equipment. Find out how soon before the reception your band or DJ will be able to set up. Inquire about security...can they set up their instruments early in the day and feel secure leaving them while they go out for a bite or even attend the wedding? Allow time for your groomsmen to carry gifts to cars after the reception ends. And it takes time to divvy up all that leftover wedding cake. In fact, you'll also want to ask if the hotel or country club staff will help with packing up the cake.

Make sure there's room for waiters to maneuver among your beautifully decorated tables.

Will you simply opt for some background music, maybe a three-piece string quartet or jazz group, while your guests balance martini glasses and hors d'oeuvres plates and take part in educated and upscale conversation? Music during the reception sets the tone for the type of party you want your wedding celebration to be. Most wedding receptions include a dance floor, but yours doesn't have to be the main focus of the event if you don't want to go that route. Still, some music is nice.

A DJ, of course, is generally less expensive than paying several musicians to perform. The DJ is also more flexible. He can play any type of music from hip hop to '40s big band swing to reggae and everything in between, just by opening a different crate of CDs. And DJs can be very personable, very "let's get this party started."

If you want live music, however, you or your friends may have a favorite band whose music you often dance to for hours. Just don't hire any band you've never seen and heard perform yourself, and remember that bands aren't always as flexible as DJs can be. Often, if your older guests hear the right type of music ('40s swing Louis Armstrong type music, '50s rockabilly, or '70s disco), you might find yourself amazed at terpsichorean talents you've never seen them display before. That won't happen if you lock yourself in to the style of one band that you and your friends love. Again, what is the mood you want to set at your reception? Do you want to emphasize and honor family, or do you want the "family" type guests to leave after dinner and let you get down to partying the night away with your college pals? Neither is wrong, but you may have to make a choice, and the type of music you choose is one of the biggest factors in the tone and temperament of the evening.

How many servers per guest will be available for dinner service? You'll need approximately one server per 25 guests for appetizers and for buffet-type meals and one server per 16 guests for table service. How many will remain to clear away glasses during dancing? About one per 50 will suffice to just stroll around the room and keep things tidy after dinner. The greater number of them should clear as much as possible of dinnerware, glasses, silverware, and napkins, and then a minimal staff should be left to discreetly hug the walls or slip in and out as needed.

Reserve Musicians or DJ for Reception

Will you have a DJ or a band for dancing? Do you envision a major blowout party lasting until well into the night or a quiet, more staid affair?

Again, as with everyone you hire, choose the band or DJ you want, sign a contract, and then keep that contract in your three-ring binder. Some things that contract should spell out:

The time they will arrive and set up

How long they will perform

What time they will stop playing

Financial terms of the contract (rate per hour)

Overtime rates

How many breaks the band will take and how long they will last and whether there will be recorded music during the break?

Whether the band leader or DJ will act as master of ceremonies throughout the reception

The contract should also cover liability insurance, terms of payment, and bonding information

It happens often that just as the party gets warmed up and everyone is having a great time, it is time for the band to quit playing. Make sure you find out if they are available to continue, how much it will cost you, and if the country club or hotel will allow them to continue playing beyond the scheduled end of your reception. This often happens at about the same time the second keg runs out and someone tries to convince you that a third one is a really good idea. Trust me—it is not. A better idea is to ask the band to play some "slow it down" music for the last set they are scheduled to play and to schedule some coffee service late in the evening.

You should also be absolutely certain that the band members know where your reception is to take place and have a map to the facility. Have them communicate directly with the sales manager to make sure the people who'll be providing them with electricity and risers understand their needs. Keep in your three-ring binder contact information for the band, and make sure they have a number to reach the person you've delegated to handle logistics on your wedding day—your assistant, maid of honor, best man, or one of your parents.

And don't forget: It is considered good manners to provide a meal for your performers, one or two alcoholic beverages, and unlimited nonalcoholic beverages throughout the night. Music is thirsty work! Don't forget them when the cake is served either. The better you treat your musicians, the more fun they'll have, and therefore, the more fun everyone else will have. (Do not, however, make the mistake of serving them unlimited alcohol throughout the evening. One drink is hospitable; more than two is doing yourself a disservice.)

Smart Moves

Finally, insist on getting pricing information from everyone you deal with in the form of bids. You want to be able to make some choices regarding where you have the reception, what kind of food is served (and how it is served), and you want to know what the going rate in your region is for these things. The best way to do that is to get bids from at least three or four different venues. Along the way, you'll pick up some creative ideas that you might want to use whether you hire that particular vendor or not. When you settle on a reception site, a caterer, and musicians, pay the least amount down that you can negotiate, and do it with a credit card. In the case of a no show or other wedding day disappointment, your credit card company will make it a lot easier for you to be reimbursed by a nonperforming or nondelivering vendor. It's just a smart way to handle your investment.

Kindly respond on or before
March 20, 2010

M _____

will _____ attend

Getting Down to Some Details

*A happy bridesmaid
makes a happy bride.*
                    —Alfred Lord Tennyson

THE DATE, THE TIME, AND THE PLACE are determined, and with them, the tone and level of formality have been decided, too. The guest list is being honed, and you have a good idea how many people you'll be inviting. You have enough information now to go ahead and choose your invitations. If you haven't done so already, you will want to consider the color scheme for your wedding now because, if possible, you want to incorporate the color scheme, or even a motif that's important to you, into the invitations. You may have already begun involving others in your plans. Certainly your mother, your fiancé, his mother, and sisters, if you have them, have been consulted already as you decided on the guest list, a date, a season, a time of day, and places for your ceremony and reception. It's time now also to consider who your attendants will be and how many you want. Having the principal players in mind before you go shopping for dress styles and colors will be a big help.

Being a winter bride gives you different choices for floral motifs and color schemes.

Your color scheme should reflect your own personal taste and preferences as well as the season during which your wedding will take place. Springtime weddings should take advantage of the flowers available at that time: hyacinths, daffodils, tulips, and more. Summertime is the time for roses, from deep red to nearly white. Fall is the time we associate with the changing colors of leaves, with chrysanthemums spilling out of pots in their deep yellow, orange, rust, and burgundy colors. Wintertime colors might correspond to poinsettias and evergreen boughs with pine cones and holly berries, or ice blue with white might be another winter color choice.

The season you choose for your ceremony can be a real determining factor in the all important color scheme of your wedding, as well as the style and fabric for dresses. A summertime wedding might lend itself to a simple off-the-shoulder eyelet cotton or silk gown, while during the winter, you might indulge in velvet with an ermine muff. The attendants' dresses, the flowers you and they carry, centerpieces, the color in the groom's and groomsmen's cummerbunds and suspenders, as well as the color you choose for your wedding stationery (not just invitations but menu cards, programs, and thank you cards), accent colors on the cake, trim on your dress...all these and more will be determined by the color scheme you choose now. Unless you have one color that has always been the one you dream of when you dream of your wedding, you have a big decision to make; luckily, making it is a lot of fun.

Courtesy Heather Kaufman Urschel

Don't forget also to take into consideration the décor of your wedding and reception sites. If the carpet, walls, and lighting of the hall where you've chosen to have your reception are all various shades of green, you might want to opt for bridesmaids' dresses and floral decorations in a contrasting color. Stay away from green, blue, and lavender in this case.

Honoring your heritage might affect your choice of color scheme or décor too. You might want to pick up a color from the Scottish plaid that might be featured in kilts and shawls. Or you might want to use red to honor your Asian heritage.

This wedding included the Robertson clan's Scottish plaid and motto ("Glory is the reward of valor") in the groom's and his brother/best man's attire.

The use of red on the invitations and programs makes a beautiful statement of this couple's Asian heritage.

Color Scheme

THE THREE PRIMARY COLORS are red, blue, and yellow. Everything else is a combination of these. The secondary colors, orange, green, and purple, are what you get when you mix equal portions of red and yellow, blue and yellow, and red and blue, respectively. Shades depend on the saturation of color, so pink is just a much lighter saturation of red, and peach is a lighter saturation of orange. Mix in a little gray or white and you get all the many hues that are available. There are thousands of ways to combine these three primary colors to make new colors and then to use them together to create a color scheme.

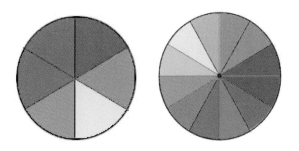

The three primary colors are red, yellow, and blue. Secondary colors are orange, green, and purple.

Emotions Associated with Color

Ask 10 people what their favorite color is and four of them will respond "blue." If they're all men, six will say blue is their favorite. Blue is comforting, restful, peaceful. Then again, consider electric blue, navy blue, neon blue; those don't sound so restful. Conversely, blue is also thought of as depressing; we get "the blues" or we feel "blue" when we are sad or down. Blue evokes feelings of happiness, creativity, and patience.

Green is the second favorite for both men and women. We associate green with Mother Nature, with grass and leaves, with life. From grass to flower stems to the deep green of an evergreen forest to the bright green of a lime, green seems to come in more hues than any other color. And it seems that way for a reason: It is the color with the most hues available to perception by the human eye. We simply "see" more green than we do any other color. Green, like blue, is considered a "cool" color; it generally has a relaxing and calming influence. Green evokes feelings of peace and harmony and symbolizes fertility.

Yellow is a "hot" color. It is stimulating; it wakes us up. Yellow also "pops" in a flower arrangement. Of course, yellow comes in many shades, from pastel to brilliant and shining, like the sun. Yellow evokes feelings of friendship and cooperation.

Orange, somewhere between yellow and red, is also stimulating, a hot color. It particularly is said to stimulate appetite and conversation. Maybe the more of it your guests see, the more they'll enjoy eating and talking. Orange evokes feelings of energy and symbolizes knowledge.

Red is the hottest of all. If orange encourages your guests to eat and talk, red will get them up dancing. Red is the color of blood, the color of war, the color of excitement and joie de vivre. Red is the color of celebration and passion; it's the color of luck.

Purple, a combination of hot red and cool blue, can be a bit unnerving. It's also said to be mentally and spiritually calming, perhaps because it speaks to our needs for both relaxation and excitement. Purple evokes feelings of mystery, royalty, and spirituality.

Pink is the color of innocence, of love and friendship. It's a feminine color.

Brown is the color of stability, of dependableness, of your dad's old sweater. It's also the color of the earth.

Black is for drama. You need some black in every situation. Usually at a wedding the groom's and groomsmen's tuxedos provide all the black you need, but if you opt for them to wear a different color, consider using a bit of black somewhere else—just for drama and contrast.

Gray evokes the fog rolling in, a sense of mystery. It also infers feelings of depression. Still, used as an accent, it can be effective.

White, of course, is the bride's color. But it can be used elsewhere to great effect. As an accent color on the bridesmaid's clothes, the white of the men's shirts, linens, stationery. White is the color of purity, of cleanliness, of a fresh beginning, of spirituality. White on white is particularly classic.

Some Facts about Color

Green is the color we associate with Ireland; red with China; blue is associated, not only with depression, but also with protection against evil spirits. Lavender, pink, and pastel colors are associated with spring; white and blue, as well as deep red, with winter, bright yellow and orange are summertime colors (think Gerbera daisies), and, of course, the fall colors are rust, orange, brown, and burgundy.

Every year there's a hot new color combo: red and teal, chocolate and pink, tangerine and teal, navy and pink, black and pink, navy and lime green, to name just a few that have cropped up in recent years. Then there are the old favorite combos like the various shades of pink, rose, red, and burgundy. Your color choice is going to be uniquely yours. Shop around, consider the season and what's in bloom (and therefore less expensive), and then make your choice based on your own favorite color. It will be a reflection of you.

One of the better ideas right now is to choose one color and then pick dresses for all your bridesmaids in various styles that best complement their figures, all in that same color. The unifying motif is the color. Here are some places to go to find more advice on color. Check it all out, then pick what you know you like.

www.weddingbasics.com

www.yourweddingcompany.com

www.brides.com   This one has a color wheel you can spin to see various color combinations (midnight, blue, and lilac, for instance, or pink, peach, and blush).

Consult a Florist

As you begin to pin down the plans for your wedding, it's a good idea to contact a florist early on. Even if you aren't yet ready to decide which florist you want to hire for your wedding, you can ask for ideas about what flowers will be most available on the date you've chosen and ask some general questions about pricing. Don't forget; the season you choose for your wedding often determines what flowers will be available. Any holidays around the date of your wedding can also affect availability. If your wedding date falls near to a holiday whose major association is with flowers (Valentine's Day or Mother's Day, for instance), expect to order early and possibly pay more...or find a shortage.

Why We Do That

Just as we commoners now want to emulate the weddings of royalty and celebrities, the middle class of the Middle Ages wanted to lift themselves up a bit in society by adopting what they observed in the nobility of their time. Princes, princesses, queens, dukes, earls...anyone with a title...set the tone for the rest of society, just as movie stars and celebrities do today.

Royal families had flags, banners, and family colors, which were always featured in their rituals. So when the merchant class began to get some money and wanted to flaunt their newfound wealth at weddings, christenings, and the like, one of the first things they felt the need for was a color scheme. Since no traditional color was usually associated with her family, a bride of the merchant class during the Middle Ages simply chose her own color scheme for her wedding. And the tradition continues through the present. A bride must still chose "her colors" for her wedding day.

Some interesting observances about color: The Houses of Lancaster and York, symbolized by red and white, respectively, and more specifically later as red and white roses, were made famous in the Wars of the Roses. Purple, of course, has long been considered the color that denotes royalty. In fact, in some past eras, only royalty was allowed to wear purple.

Invitations

WHEN YOU INVITE YOUR GUESTS to your wedding, you're telling them that a very special day is coming and you'd like them to be there. The invitation can also serve as their first clue as to the level of formality of your wedding. If you send invitations that are home-made from recycled paper and tied with raffia, in which you invite your guests to your wedding in the park, that's a clue—this is not going to be a formal, black tie affair with a seven-course sit-down dinner following. If that's the kind of wedding you're planning, you need to choose an invitation that is much more formal.

There are thousands of Internet sites where you can choose from tens of thousands of invitations.

This one has a shop-by-color page:

www.Weddingpaperdivas.com

This one offers a free wedding planning guide, and a free guest book with orders over $200:

www.Beautifulweddinginvitations.com

And this one has a large selection, including the invitations featured in this chapter:

www.1st-class-wedding-invitations.com

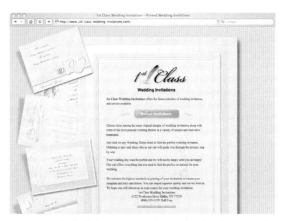

You can find all the invitations featured in this chapter and many more at www.1st-class-wedding-invitations.com.

© Williamhouse

© JRC

Why We Do That

In 12th Century England, everyone in the neighborhood was invited to every wedding. Word of mouth and perhaps even town criers helped spread the word, and everyone was always up for a celebration—because they didn't have a tee time already scheduled on Saturday morning anyway, and there wasn't much to watch on TV. Later, as more people were able to read and a land owning class emerged, monks were pressed into service to apply their calligraphic skills to the art of the wedding invitation for the new upper class. And, then, of course, the invitations were hand delivered to the gentry in the surrounding countryside. The peasant rabble was still invited, but maybe just to the grounds of the estate, certainly not inside the castle.

Each landed family had its own crest, or coat of arms, and this was incorporated into all communications. It was a highly recognizable "signature" in the days when not everyone was able to read.

© Williamhouse

© Williamhouse

© JRC

© Williamhouse

Save the Date Cards

Now that you actually have the date set, you might want to send *save the date* cards right away. These less formal pre-invitation cards are a popular way to ensure that your guests know about your wedding well ahead of time. You can be sure that while you are busy making plans and choosing a dress and flowers, some of your favorite people are blissfully going about their business planning a trip to Europe or a cruise and might already be making reservations. Letting them know well ahead of time the date you've chosen for your wedding is a nice thing to do for you both. Think of it as giving them the option of making their plans around your date; just don't feel insulted if they opt to carry on with their long planned for vacation. The save the date card provides an opportunity to have fun with your design or hint at the story of your engagement.

Design by David Traier.

Other Stationery Items

Remember when every wedding reception came with hundreds of napkins imprinted with the bride and groom's names and the date of their wedding, and there were similarly imprinted matchbooks in ashtrays on every table? Times have changed, and the matchbooks are less prevalent, but they've been replaced with some more useful items for your guests to take away as a souvenir of the day. The same vendors who sell invitations also provide many other items, so it's a good idea to coordinate and order some of these items at the same time you order your invitations and save the date cards. You should consider including some of the following items when you order your invitations:

- **Peel and stick bows for the invitations**: Little pre-made satin or chiffon already tied bows that come in a variety of colors to stick on your invitations and give them just a little extra touch of elegance.

- **Menu or place cards**: These are handy items that lend a touch of elegance and thoughtfulness to your place settings. Menu and place cards are an excellent place to add personalization to your wedding in the form of your paper, color, and design choices. As a matter of proper etiquette, you should only use your new monogram after the wedding ceremony —at your reception rather than an engagement party or rehearsal dinner.

- **Pew cards**: Include these with the invitations of close family members if you are having a really large wedding and want to make sure family members get rock star seating. You don't have to specify a pew; just put "Inside the Ribbon" on the card. The recipients then present this card to the usher who seats them, and he will have been told what to do.

- **Note pads engraved with your names and the date:** You can put these, along with ink pens engraved with your names and the date, at each place setting. Guests can use them to write requests to the band, give a bridesmaid their phone number, or just doodle. These are also thoughtful items to include in welcome bags in your out of town guests' hotel rooms.

- **Napkins**: This familiar item continues to be the most useful. Use the cocktail size to decorate the cake table and place on the bar. If you are having an informal wedding without linen napkins, place these preprinted paper ones on the buffet table or at place settings. If you find traditional preprinted name or monogrammed napkins a bit tired, you can liven them up by choosing a personal cartoon or caricatures of the bride and groom, poignant quotes, romantic poetry, lines from your first dance song, or whatever else your imagination can dream up.

- **Matchbooks**: These haven't been completely forgotten either. They still come in handy for lighting candles and even the occasional cigar or cigarette. Still a thoughtful item to place on tables in a smoking lounge or cigar bar area at the reception. Of course, if yours is a non-smoking facility, it is best to forgo the matchbooks completely.

- **Thank you notes:** You'll need informal ones for shower gifts and more formal, blank ones, for wedding gifts. The ones for the wedding gifts can coordinate with your invitations; might as well order them at the same time.

Speaking of Favors

Favors for guests have long been a sticky spot for couples. The expectation is there, so couples feel obligated to provide a favor, but at the same time everyone is tired of the same old, same old. You may be tempted to give all your guests shot glasses, champagne glasses, personalized photo frames, and other such items with no long-term value whatsoever. If you do feel compelled to gift your guests with a remembrance of your wedding (which is not a bad thing at all), do try to make sure you give them something they will find useful at some point in the future. A CD of the music played at your wedding might conceivably be of some use when someone runs across it in the glove box while on a road trip a year later. A shot glass? Not so much. Sweet treats, flower seeds, and other useful options are thankfully coming into vogue. Favors are a perfect opportunity to show some creativity by choosing something that will get your guests talking. Here are some sites we found where you can find unique and useful wedding favors. And some shot glasses, too.

www.favorfavor.com

www.favorideas.com

www.americanbridal.com

www.wrapwithus.com

Check them out. Do a Google search for wedding favors and find hundreds of others.

Presentation should not be overlooked when considering your guest favors.

Kristin & Scott

At their October wedding, Kristin and Scott provided delicious caramel apples covered with nuts for their reception guests.

Mitzi & John

In honor of their engagement in Paris, a thoughtful and talented bridesmaid hand made chocolate Eiffel Tower treats to create unique favors.

Courtesy Mitzi and John Koontz

Courtesy Shutterstock © Danilo Ascione

Attendants

FTER YOU'VE CHOSEN THE VENUE and the date for your wedding, the next thing you need is a helping hand or two. You need to choose your bridal attendants next because they're going to help you through the rest of the pre-wedding planning and preparation, and they'll really come in handy on your wedding day.

You are supposed to have an equal number of bridesmaids and groomsmen, but nowadays brides and grooms are beginning to value their friends as people, not as male or female friends, so if the bride wants her male best friend to stand up with her or the groom's best friend happens to be a woman, it's okay to cross those gender lines. Follow your heart here—not tradition. And be prepared to rearrange the recessional after the ceremony so that no one has to walk back up the aisle alone.

The faces of the bridal party in this 1940s wedding demonstrate that weddings are always a time for happiness.

From the collection of Judy Doell

How Many?

You can have any number of attendants at your wedding, as many as you can afford to buy flowers for and as many as you want to cart around in limousines all day. The best plan might be to keep it simple. Have as many as you need. You need about one usher per 50 wedding guests. You need a maid or matron of honor to help you get dressed, to give you a bridal shower or two, to hold your bouquet while you exchange ring; you need a best man to hold the rings and generally make sure the groom gets to the ceremony. Choose wisely. Your honor attendants will likely be the ones who help you with much of your planning, act as the voice of reason when you are stressing over the difference between French blue and periwinkle ribbons in the bouquets, and be there to support you during the inevitable meltdowns with your beloved. Beyond those needs, you probably have in mind a few close friends, brothers, or sisters who you'd like to invite to be more than just another guest at the wedding.

More than six of each, however, can become a burden to keep up with, especially while wrangling everyone for photographs, and four is usually quite sufficient for even a large wedding. During Victorian times, a dozen or more bridesmaids was common, and the greater the rank of the bride, the more bridesmaids she had. Of course, the more formal your wedding, the greater the number of attendants you'll need because a formal wedding involves more details that someone will need to take care of for you.

How to Choose Them

Choose your attendants from among your closest friends and relatives: college classmates and roommates, high school friends, your sister, the groom's sister, close cousins, and other relatives. Choose people who will take their duties seriously, who are dependable, and willing to support you in all your pre-wedding parties, teas, and showers.

Choose the ones you love and hold dear. Choose people who you know have your best interests at heart. Need we add do not choose your attendants according to their body image or whether they make you look good. This is no time to be petty or childish; it will come back to haunt you in the future if you are. A trend of late is to choose attendants' dresses in styles that are flattering to each one's particular body type but are all of the same color. All of your bridesmaids do not need to be tall, willowy, and model slim. Love is more photogenic than physical beauty.

Flower girls should be between the ages of three and eight, as should ring bearers. After eight, girls can be considered junior bridesmaids and boys can be junior ushers. You can also make pre-teen and teenage boys responsible for decorating the car or other such fun pursuits. They will be taking part in the wedding in a way that is most appropriate to their talents and preferences. No matter how much you adore your two year old niece, do not have unrealistic expectations of her. She is simply not ready to march down the aisle unaccompanied while hoards of strangers stare at her no matter how adoringly. If you wish to include especially young children, you may opt to dress them to coordinate with the wedding party and participate in photos, but be prepared that they most likely will not make it through the ceremony without incident. Some couples have included younger children in their ceremonies in creative ways such as having a parent or grandparent wheel them down the aisle during the processional in a lovely flower or garland covered wagon. If young children will play an important part in your ceremony, find creative ways to include them without sparking sensory overload and subsequent meltdowns.

This beautiful flower girl nearly steals the show.

A ringbearer in a top hat—too cute!

Responsibilities of the Attendants

When you do ask your friends to be your brides-maids, junior bridesmaids, or groomsmen, make sure they know what their responsibilities are. Consider their current lifestyles and capabilities before you ask, and don't be offended if they can't afford it or are reluctant to take on the responsibility. Be gracious when you ask and be prepared to help with any financial concerns or other reluctance.

Here are some lists for you to work from:

Bridesmaids and Maid or Matron of Honor

- Pay for their own dresses and accessories
- Do not pay for their own flowers
- Pay for their own travel expenses
- Maid or matron of honor should give the bridal shower
- Attend rehearsal and rehearsal dinner
- Choose and present a joint gift for the bride from all her attendants

This matron of honor knows the bride likes to keep her lipstick fresh.

- Stick close to bride throughout the day of the wedding, helping with her veil, train, flowers, keeping her lipstick fresh and ready with a handkerchief or any other small item needed
- Maid or matron of honor holds bride's bouquet during exchange of rings at altar. She also holds the groom's ring until the bride is ready to put it on his finger.
- Maid or matron of honor signs the marriage license as a witness
- Be helpful with guests, offering directions to all and assistance to any older guests
- Maid or matron of honor may offer toast to the couple at the reception, but this is optional
- Maid or matron of honor takes responsibility for the bride's gown after she changes to leave for the honeymoon (although the mother of the bride often takes the gown home or to the cleaners while the couple is honeymooning)

Groomsmen, Ushers, and Best Man

- Pay for renting and pick up their own tuxedos and accessories and make sure they attend fittings
- Pay their own travel expenses
- Best man organizes and groomsmen attend a bachelor party in honor of the groom
- Attend rehearsal and rehearsal dinner
- Best man is responsible for getting groom to the ceremony on the day of the wedding and remains by his side to provide any aid needed in dressing

- ℂℬ Join together to choose and present a joint gift to the groom

- ℂℬ Ushers seat the guests before the ceremony and release them, one pew at a time, after the ceremony

- ℂℬ After guests are seated and before processional begins, ushers are responsible for placing the runner in the aisle for the bride and her party to walk on

- ℂℬ Best man signs the marriage license as a witness

- ℂℬ Best man is in charge of the bride's ring until the ring exchange takes place

- ℂℬ Best man is responsible for handing gratuity from the groom to the clergy

- ℂℬ Best man is responsible for toasting the couple at the reception

- ℂℬ Best man assumes responsibility for the groom's tuxedo after he leaves for the honeymoon. If necessary, he returns the groom's tuxedo along with his own to the rental company.

Believe it or not, most of the hard work and decision making is now done. Next comes shopping and parties. You can do that, can't you? You have the theme, the color scheme, and the general plan in place for your wedding. You know when and where it will be, and you have delegated a lot of responsibilities to your most trusted friends and relatives. Now it's just finding a gown for you, dresses for the attendants, registering for flatware and china, hiring a photographer, a videographer, and a florist, and getting dressed up for a lot of parties in your honor. There are still food items to decide on for the reception, including the cake, but first, let's get the look right. Let's go dress shopping! The most important item you'll purchase for the wedding, your wedding gown, is the one we'll talk about next in Chapter 8, "Shopping for *The Dress...* and More."

Why We Do That

In ancient Greece, very young brides often needed the assistance and advice of older women as they made the transition from young girl to wife. Older female relatives literally surrounded the early teen-aged bride as she made her way to the wedding. In Rome, marriages had to be witnessed by 10 people, so many of those naturally were relatives of the bride who, again, escorted her to the ceremony.

Bridesmaids and groomsmen came about as a way of thwarting the attempts of any jealous ex-lovers (or, in some cultures, evil spirits) bent on stopping the wedding, stealing the dowry, or otherwise ruining a perfect day. They dressed in clothes similar to the bride and groom to serve as decoys and so the bride and groom could be literally hidden in a mass of like-dressed people.

Later, the bride became a more powerful planner in her own wedding, and brides began to choose their friends as escorts to the ceremony. The bridesmaid's role as defender against evil spirits took on a more symbolic meaning, but still, the more helpers a bride had, the more moral support she had. Of course, one of her friends might have been a more talented make-up artist while another was better at organizing, so each managed to find a job to do.

Shopping for The Dress... and More

Custom has decided, from the earliest ages, that white is the most fitting hue, whatever may be the material. It is an emblem of the purity and innocence of girlhood, and the unsullied heart she now yields to the chosen one.

—Godey's Lady's Book, 1849 ed.

IT'S BEEN OVER 150 YEARS since *Godey's Lady's Book* declared white to be "an emblem of the purity and innocence of girlhood," and brides today, who almost universally no longer consider themselves pure, innocent, or unsullied, still almost unanimously prefer white wedding gowns, although today we do include some other colors—there are even several shades of white available in gowns. And certainly, there are many fabric and fabric combinations to choose from. Finding the perfect dress can be as frustrating as it is exhilarating, but many brides say the same thing: "When I found *my* dress, I knew it immediately." It's as if you ran into a long lost friend in the airport. There are people all over the airport, just as there are dresses hanging from every wall rack and display case in the bridal shop. But the one that is yours will be recognizable immediately.

Caroline Flagler, Senior Vice President of Merchandising at David's Bridal, says prospective brides usually start shopping with one of two mindsets. Some don't know where to start and seem bewildered by the array of choices and styles available. Others have an idea what they want. The secret, in either case, to a successful shopping trip is to be open to suggestion and willing to try on several different styles.

Sandy & Dave

Sandy actually bought one dress, a simple knee length white dress that showed off her summer tan, thinking it would be perfect for her casual afternoon wedding to Dave. Then, a few days later, while shopping for accessories, she found it—the dress she knew she was meant to wear, a simple white eyelet cotton with a peasant neckline. This was 20 years ago, and these were off the rack dresses neither of which cost more than $100. She hadn't planned to make any alterations, so it was a simple matter to return the first dress and wear the second one.

It isn't usually that simple in today's world, where you are often asked to sign a contract when you order a wedding gown, so wait for that epiphany—that moment when you just absolutely know you've found your dress. And then restrain yourself. Come back the next day, shop a bit more, ask your mother and your maid of honor, and if you still are sure, buy the dress.

You should keep an open mind regarding style and material, length, and all the other variables that go into creating a wedding gown. Don't decide ahead of time that only cap sleeves are right for you and thereby overlook the strapless dress that would be perfect if only you would just try it. Try on dresses that don't seem so appealing on the hanger, too. Your dress may just be hanging there waiting for you to put it on and bring it to life.

Wedding Gown Vocabulary

IT HELPS TO LEARN THE TERMS used to describe wedding gowns. You'll be choosing between general dress types, necklines, sleeves, lengths, and color.

General types of dresses are:

- **Ball gown:** A fitted bodice with a full skirt, often accompanied by many petticoats to make it look all the more full. Think Cinderella.

- **Empire:** A fitted bodice with a slim, slightly flared skirt that begins just below the bustline.

- **Sheath:** Fitted bodice and straight skirt.

- **Mermaid:** A sheath with an extra bit of flare at the bottom.

- **A-Line:** Fitted bodice with a less pronounced waistline than the others. Skirt flares gently, not so full as the ball gown.

Neckline choices include:

- **Sweetheart:** The classic, gently curved.

- **V-neck:** Comes to a point, cut deeply between the breasts.

- **Strapless:** Straight across top of breasts, form fitting.

- **Scoop:** Rounded, somewhat revealing.

- **Sabrina:** Straight across, shows off collarbone.

- **Portrait:** Gentle folds of fabric frame the face.

- **Jewel:** Very plain, very simple, shows off a string of pearls perfectly.

- **Halter:** Cut low between breasts and straps fasten at back of neck.

- **Bateau** (or boat neck)**:** Cut straight across like a sailor's jersey, reveals small amount of collarbone at neckline.

- **High, no collar:** Usually has a band that fits closely around the neck, often topping off a lace bodice.

- **High with collar:** Like a man's shirt with a collar.

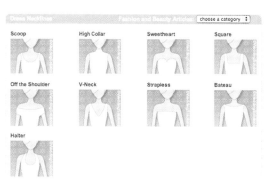

There are many variations and all these styles can be varied by using different fabrics. The most popular currently seem to be the sweetheart and strapless styles.

The cathedral train makes a dramatic statement, and the sweetheart neckline highlights the bride's beautiful smile.

Sleeves are another consideration:

- **Cap**: Barely there, "capped" over the shoulder.
- **Three-quarters**: Loosely falls to a point midway between the elbow and wrist.
- **Long, fitted**: Fits snugly from shoulder to wrist, often made of lace or gauzy material.
- **Off-the-shoulder**: A neckline type; arms are covered, but the shoulders are bare.
- **Dolman**: Very dramatic, large opening with lots of flowing fabric between body and arm.
- **T-shirt**: Just a sleeve, like a T-shirt sleeve, simple, classic.

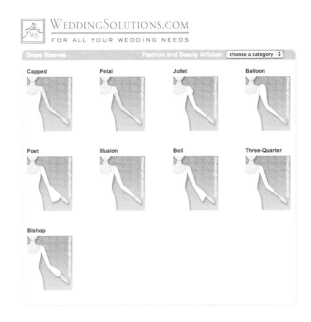

110

You may choose a gown in any of the following lengths. In past days, the time of day of your wedding determined the length of your dress. Brides never wore floor length dresses in the afternoon. Tea length and ballerina were appropriate afternoon lengths, and above the knee was never considered correct. Now, you are limited only by your own preference and good taste.

Lengths include:

- **Mini:** Short short. Think Pamela Anderson's choice in wedding attire.

- **Knee length**: For a less formal but conservative wedding. You might choose to wear a knee length white suit.

- **Tea length**: Mid-calf.

- **Ballerina**: Long but not to the floor, almost ankle length.

- **Floor length**: Skims the floor. A floor length ball gown is the dress associated with the most formal of weddings.

© Waldek Photography

Back of gown with a splash of color.

And, of course, there are many fabrics to choose from. The fabric you choose, along with the style of dress, creates the overall effect. A loose flowing fabric used to make a sheath dress creates an almost slip-like look, and a suit made of brocade is very conservative looking. Fabric choices for wedding gowns include:

Full length skirt, high neck, pouf sleeves.

- **Cotton, linen:** Used in casual wedding dresses, these are cool, crisp, and clean looking.

- **Chiffon:** Sheer and lightweight, made of silk, rayon, or synthetics.

- **Crepe:** Looks slightly crinkled.

- **Georgette:** Like chiffon, only with a duller looking finish.

- **Jersey:** A knit of wool, silk, or rayon.

- **Satin:** Beautiful lustrous fabric used often for formal wedding gowns.

- **Shantung:** A woven blend with a nubby finish.

- **Silk:** There's nothing like it. A product of the silk worm.

- **Taffeta:** A shiny, lustrous, smooth fabric.

- **Tulle:** Sheer, mesh-like, somewhat stiff. Often used in petticoats and crinolines.

- **Laces—Alencon, Chantilly, and Irish, and Belgian:** These are used for trim or as a layer over the top of more solid backing materials. Lace can be hand made or machine made.

- **Brocade:** Heavy decorative embroidery.

There are shades of white! We all know about white, ivory, off-white, cream, and even winter white, but did you know there is also stark white, diamond white, eggshell, and champagne white, which is sort of pinkish? Try a few different shades next to your skin to see which is most flattering.

Making the Choice

YOU HAVE LITERALLY HUNDREDS of thousands of wedding gowns and dresses to choose from, and you are limited only by your own taste and budget. All the styles are available in various price ranges. If it's important to you to have a one-of-a-kind designer gown and you can afford it (prices range from $2,000 to $25,000 and more), go ahead and splurge on this once-in-a-lifetime purchase. A few of them are listed here:

ଔ **Custom designers:** Vera Wang, Demetrios, Badgley Mischka, Amsale, Reem Acra, Alfred Angelo, Alfred Sung, and more. If you can afford a trip to New York or Paris, Los Angeles, or even Austin to visit these custom providers of dream wedding gowns, you should do it. If you can't, at least visit their web sites to learn where the latest trends in fashion originate.

Some other places where you might want to look for your dress include:

ଔ **Chain store bridal boutiques:** Stores that cater to brides and carry all things wedding: bridal gowns, gloves, tiaras, veils, bridesmaids' dresses, flower girl dresses, shoes, fans.... You will need an appointment. The sales staff will be very helpful, but make sure you get some other opinions before you make any decisions.

Caroline Flagler, Senior Vice President of Merchandising at David's Bridal, shared these insights into shopping for your perfect dress:

White is still by far the color of choice for brides, but the latest trend seems to be toward adding a color accent of some sort, either in the form of a panel insert in the skirt or a sash. Tone on tone brocades and textures are "hot."

The architectural look, incorporating both black and white with an additional "pop" of an added accept color is a look that is coming into its own now.

In response to the question "How do you know when you've found the dress that was meant to be yours?" Caroline says the consultants at David's Bridal notice two common responses. One is tears. The bride, her mother, and anyone shopping with her will shed a tear or two. The second is touching. As soon as a bride sees herself for the first time in the dress that she'll wear in her wedding, she begins to touch it. It's an expression of ownership.

 📖 **Local bridal salons**: Personal service at a local level, usually friendly, accommodating, and they'll recognize you every time you visit.

❧ **Bridal departments in major department stores**: Pick your dress. Order your size. Have it delivered. Some department stores still have their own in-house alterations people. If not, go to a seamstress or tailor and get the job done. Others carry designer labels such as Vera Wang and hold semi-annual trunk sales.

❧ **Online and catalog shopping:** You can go here and look, then go shopping and try dresses on. It might take a little work, and there will still be alterations to arrange, but if you start early enough in the process, you can find a great dress at a good price by shopping online. Even J. Crew has a wedding shop.

If you buy a dress "off the rack" and are torn between the size 8, which almost fits but is a little tight in the bust, or the size 10, which almost fits but is a little loose at the waist, opt for the larger size. It is much easier to cut a dress down to size than it is to add material to make it bigger.

Do not, under any circumstances, convince yourself that you will buy the size 8 and then diet to fit into it! Eating healthy and being as fit as possible is something you need to do in preparation for your wedding, but don't count on attaining any particular results, namely, a dress size.

- *Consignment shops*: These little shops are in strip malls and trendy shopping areas all over large cities and small towns. You never know what sort of bargain you might find. It might be worth an afternoon expedition.

- *Thrift stores*: Again, it's bargain shopping, but if you get into it, check here for some real deals, especially if you think you might be interested in vintage gowns.

- *Designer trunk shows*: Look for these at large department stores and bridal salons in your town. Famous designers bring their goods right to your hometown so you don't have to go hang out in Paris with the Hilton girls and Oprah. These are usually held in spring and fall at the beginning of the "fashion season," and you may still need an appointment.

- *Bargain basements*: The famous Filenes Bargain Basement in Boston sells designer dresses at very low prices twice a year in a melee that has been dubbed "the running of the brides." Twice a year hundreds of women gather to compete, perhaps even wrestle each other to the ground, for possession of the perfect dress. You can get a designer gown that would normally sell for upwards of $10,000 for less than $1,000, but you may have to fight for it. In 2007 sales were also held in Chicago and Washington D.C, and bargain basement wedding gown sales are popping up in other areas where Filene's stores are located.

116

C3 **Bridal shows and expos:** First there were home shows, then boat and sport shows; the bridal industry, made up of hundreds of various vendors and changing fashions from year to year, is a natural for the expo business. Check events calendars near you for these twice-yearly events. You can meet designers, dress shop personnel, emissaries from the chain bridal salons, as well as every other type of wedding vendor imaginable, including jewelers, caterers, wedding planners, florists, photographers, and more—all under one roof. In one day you can get leads and ideas to help you in your planning. Often the exhibitors offer special pricing, incentive packages, or discounts to show attendees as well.

Don't forget to browse the bridal magazines, too. There are dozens of these available in every bookstore and newsstand, and they really do have all the latest trends and fashions—assuming you want to be trendy and fashionable. You can also find advice in these magazines for updating your mother's or grandmother's gown to make it your own if that's something you'd like to do.

When you set out on your dress shopping expedition, you might want to take along shoes of the approximate color and height that you'll be wearing on your wedding day. Take a variety of undergarments with you as well. The stores will have some of these items available for you to use as you try dresses on, but they are rather generic, may not be available in exactly your size, and the shoes have been worn by many people before you. Take your own.

Accessories

IN ADDITION TO THE DRESS itself, you'll need a few other items. Your bridal salon will help you sort out which ones are required for your gown and the look you want to achieve. Just remember, it's a total picture. Accessories and jewelry help complete the picture that is you on your wedding day.

> Caroline Flagler, of David's Bridal, says: Choose your jewelry to complement some detail of your dress. For instance, a dress that has seed pearls might best be accessorized by a simple string of pearls. Conversely, if you want to wear your mother's diamond necklace, keep that in mind as you shop for the dress. Also choose the neckline of your dress and any jewelry you want to wear with your face shape and hairstyle in mind. They are all elements in the final picture.

Trains

Trains, like the gowns they accessorize, come in different lengths. These include:

- **Sweep:** Sweeps the floor.
- **Court:** Just a bit longer, but doesn't trail behind you.
- **Chapel:** Trails behind you about three to four feet.
- **Monarch:** Very long, very formal, trails six to eight feet behind you.

You'll also want to bear in mind what you'll do with the train after the trip down the aisle is finished. Bridesmaids will need to be available to arrange it after you arrive at the altar and to help arrange it before you start back up the aisle as a married woman. Some trains are detachable, but for others, later on at the reception, certainly before a lot of dancing starts, you'll need help with a process called *bustling* if you choose a very long train.

Veils

This article of wedding attire can be affixed by a tiara, a wreath of flowers, or simply affixed directly to the hair with ribbons or a head band. Veils come in a variety of lengths and can be worn as a simple headpiece that covers the hair and shoulders or used as a veil for the face until the groom performs the traditional act of lifting the veil to kiss his bride. The veil is optional. If you feel uncomfortable wearing one, feel free to go without it, or opt for a beautiful accessory—flowers in your hair, a simple barrette, even a satin headband..

Make sure your hairstyle is coordinated with your veil and headpiece. A simple comb can be used to hold the veil in place.

Veils, too, come in varying lengths and styles. A few of the more common terms you'll hear used to describe veils are

- ✆ **Fingertip**: Falls to your fingertips.
- ✆ **Blusher**: Short, just covers the face.
- ✆ **Mantilla**: Lace secured with a comb in the style of Flamenco dancers.
- ✆ **Elbow**: Extends to your elbows.

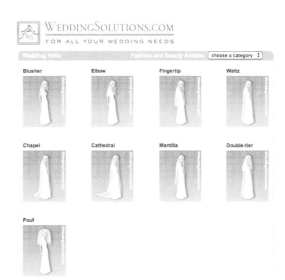

Why We Do That

In some Middle Eastern traditions, the veil was, and still is, worn to cover the bride completely from view. Indeed, many women in some Islamic cultures still wear the burqa whenever they go out in public. The veil worn at the wedding was used to cover the bride's face and hide her from the groom until the ceremony was over. Grooms did not see their brides' faces until they were married to them.

In ancient Rome, the veil worn by a bride covered her from head to toe and was saved to be used as her burial shroud.

Choose your veil at the same time you choose your hairstyle. Take the veil to the stylist who will be doing your hair on your wedding day and discuss how your hair should be arranged with the veil and tiara or headpiece so that it all works together both before and after the veil is lifted off your face.

Why We Do That

Queen Victoria, unlike royal brides before her, chose to wear her veil off her face for her wedding to Prince Albert in 1840. Her subjects expressed a desire to see her face on her wedding day, and she, the popular young queen, granted them their request.

Never known for her beauty, she was, by all reports, a beautiful bride. As one columnist of the day put it, "She had her day of beauty."

Tiaras

Tiaras are the headpiece of choice, but there are other means of securing the veil. You might want to do it with a barrette, a comb, an elegant bun ring, or a hat. Some of us just look really good in hats, and if that's true of you, run with it.

Gloves

Gloves are experiencing a comeback. A strapless gown worn with long gloves is a classic look that can't be matched. Gloves come in various lengths too, but the long, elegant, formal ones that end above the elbow are perfect with a strapless dress.

A perfect classic look is a strapless gown with elbow length gloves.

Courtesy John and Mitzi Koontz © Waldek Photography

Undergarments

Look at your dress. Of course, if it is strapless, you
will need a strapless bra or built-in wiring to keep
it snug and in place. For all dress styles, keep in
mind all the different foundation garments and
lingerie you may need to create the smoothest
lines and hide any slight imperfections in your
figure. Your seamstress will guide you in determining the best options for your gown and your body
type. To avoid pulling and tugging on your strapless bra, your seamstress will sew it or tack it in
place or may even sew in supports or padding to
fill out the bodice. Above all, though, as you put
your wedding ensemble together, keep comfort in
mind. The dress, the shoes, the undergarments—all
should work together so that you feel at ease as
you walk, dance, hug, and reach out to your guests.
A happy bride is a comfortable bride. Before making your selections walk around, dance (fast and
slow), sit down (you will eventually have to eat or
rest!), and hug someone. You will be doing all of
these things on your wedding day and you will
want to do them comfortably. Put some time into
choosing bras, slips, and hosiery that make you
feel feminine but lithe, smooth but unbound.
You'll be glad you did.

Other Accessories

Fans, handkerchiefs, handbags—these and other
items you'll need are all available at bridal salons,
department stores, and online or can be custom
made to your order. The more you can accessorize,
the more finished your wedding day ensemble will
be. Just make sure you get several opinions and
don't go overboard. Sometimes "less is more."

Fans can help provide a vintage Victorian mood for your day.

*Pearls, handkerchiefs, and handbags are just a few of the
accessories you'll want to try with your wedding gown.*

Shoes

Your choice of footwear should be determined by one thing only: comfort. Have you ever seen a picture of a bride sitting in a chair in her beautiful satin, silk, and lace dress surrounded by yards of Chantilly lace and tulle? Your wedding day is a day you will spend on your feet, and you want your shoes to be the most comfortable possible. If you can find dressy shoes that feel really good on your feet and that you won't mind standing, dancing, walking, and smiling in for about eight hours, that's wonderful. If not, we suggest you take the practical route and opt for ballet slippers or another kind of flat, comfortable shoe.

If you do decide to wear "real" heels on your wedding day, make sure you take the shoes for a practice walk or two, and not just for half an hour walking in your carpeted living room. Wear them to walk on a sidewalk, a tile floor, getting in and out of the car, and keep them on for a few hours a couple of times before the wedding day. You need to scuff up the soles a bit anyway so that they aren't slick as you start down the aisle. If you simply cannot bring yourself to sully your perfect shoes before your big day, visit your shoe store to purchase stick on sole grips so you don't slide down the aisle. You may want to try gel or support inserts for added comfort as well.

Comfortable footwear is a requirement.

Shoes are always important to women, but for the bride and the bridesmaids, it's a quest to find just the right ones. This bride and her attendants have perfect shoes for the occasion—stylish and comfortable.

Courtesy Mitzi and John Koontz © Waldek Photography

Why We Do That

A pillbox hat and a stylish suit were considered highly appropriate for afternoon, informal weddings in the 1960s, but this era also saw the advent of the "hippie" bride, barefoot with flowers in her hair.

In the '70s, brides often opted for shorter, above the knee dresses, sometimes in color. Or short short wedding gowns such as those modeled by Twiggy.

Mod bridal dress patterns are still available at www.etsy.com.

Still More Shopping to Do

YOU HAVE YOUR DRESS, your accessories, your shoes, and your underwear. Next you want to choose what everyone else will be wearing. The maid or matron of honor, the bridesmaids, flower girls, junior bridesmaids—whoever else you've chosen to be in your wedding party. The groom and his groomsmen also will need to be dressed in a style and level of formality that complements your dress. And let's not forget the parents of the bride and groom. You still have a lot of shopping and planning to do, but the big decision has been made. You have the perfect dress!

Bridesmaids' Dresses

The latest trend is to choose your color or color palette and then let each bridesmaid select a dress in that color, using fabrics that you all choose together, that best suits her body style. Your maid of honor might wear a scoop necked sheath dress with cap sleeves while one bridesmaid wears a sweetheart neckline with three quarter length sleeves and a second one wears an A-line sleeveless dress with a high neck, all made of the same fabric in the same or similar colors.

Fashion seems to be moving away from solid color dresses too. Prints and tartans are showing up in weddings, as are mixing and matching colors. It's always a good idea to choose dresses that the bridesmaids can wear on other occasions, too. Having everyone dressed the same, in long dresses with big bows in the back or floor length ball gowns of taffeta and brocade, pretty much ensures they're buying an expensive item they'll never get to use again. Try to be considerate and choose attire for them that can be worn again. Take them shopping with you and let them be involved in the choice. You get to be the final arbiter, of course; it's your wedding. But do be considerate of these people who are giving you their time and devotion and who are, by definition, close friends.

Cathleen & Chris

Cathleen says, "Bridesmaid dresses! They're usually not reusable and can be expensive; it seemed presumptuous of me to ask my friends to buy their own. So my Mom and I searched the Internet and found a clearance sale on a full-length "special occasion" dress that was formal but not actually intended for weddings. It was just pretty much a crepe empire-waist sheath dress—very simple, and something that my maids of honor wouldn't mind wearing. They cost $30 each. I really wanted to pay for the girls' dresses, and that was very affordable. (I just didn't want to ask someone to be in my wedding and then expect them to shell out large sums of money to do so. I didn't want to do that to them.)"

Do a lot of talking and planning with your bridesmaids before you go shopping so that you all start with a common goal or idea in mind. Share pictures in catalogs and from online shopping forays to get the ball rolling. Be a consensus builder, not a despot. You should have already chosen a color scheme and style for your wedding, so within those parameters, start the discussion of dress styles for your bridesmaids. Junior bridesmaids, if you have any, may wear an age appropriate dress in the same color or fabric as the other bridesmaids.

The options for flower girls are endless. You may choose dresses in the same color as your bridesmaids, a coordinating or contrasting color, or a white dress with color accents. As with junior bridesmaids, the only firm rule is to choose something that is age appropriate. It also is considerate to invite the parent of the girl to help you select the dress. Keep in mind that money may be an issue for parents with young children, so be mindful of the price or find a dress that may be worn again—perhaps for a holiday.

Beyond the choosing, there is the practical matter of fit and measurement. Everyone needs to go shopping in the same place and be measured—at the beginning of the process and just before the final fitting. It's important that your bridesmaids' dresses fit well and that they are comfortable wearing them. They all have jobs to do on the wedding day, so they need to be comfortable in their clothes, just as you do.

Shop for bridesmaid dresses in the same places you shop for your dress. Chain bridal retailers, department store bridal departments, and bridal salons are all good places to find these dresses that add so much to the feel of the day. If you are the princess for one day, the bridesmaids are your court. They are like beautiful red or yellow (or green or mauve or orange) roses surrounding you, the one white rose.

Why We Do That

Bridesmaids' duties have changed throughout history. Celtic bridesmaids often planted sprigs of myrtle on each side of the newlyweds' house. If a sprig took root, it foretold a wedding in the near future for the bridesmaid who planted it.

Mothers of the Bride and Groom

Customarily, the mother of the bride chooses her dress and then lets the mother of the groom know its style and color. The mothers' dresses should complement the wedding colors, but they should not match the bridesmaids' dresses. If the bridesmaids are wearing burgundy, for instance, the mothers might choose dresses in pink or a pale beige. They should not clash with, but rather, complement the bridesmaids.

This mother of the groom's dress coordinates perfectly with color scheme and degree of formality of the wedding party.

Groom's and Groomsmen's Attire

In most cases, the bride should most certainly have a hand in choosing the groom's and his attendants' clothing on the day of the wedding. Sometimes men have a difficult time understanding the difference between white tie and black tie or even between a suit and a sport coat and slacks. Tuxes are far beyond their daily concerns, and if you, the bride, want your men looking good in their tuxedos, oversee the whole process yourself.

If your wedding is more informal, you'll just want your groomsmen to be dressed in their best suits. It won't matter so much if they aren't exactly matched, but you may wish to specify dark or light suits. Of course, if you are to be married barefoot on a beach, you may want to request linen pants and white shirts. If you are going the formal route, however, you'll need to consider a few choices. The following sections give some insight into dealing with the tux shop.

If some or all of the men in your wedding are not accustomed to formal dressing, consider suspenders with a vest rather than a cummerbund. Cummerbunds tend to feel loose to men, like a belt that's about to come undone, and they can't seem to refrain from fidgeting with it. There are many stylish options available in vests, and the groom can select a different style or one with more elaborate detail to set him apart from the groomsmen. Fathers can also select vests to coordinate with the mothers' dresses for a polished look.

The Tuxedo, the Suit Itself

Tuxedos come in various styles from morning coats to white tie and tails for very formal wear to crisp white linen trousers with a navy jacket for summertime afternoon weddings, either indoors or out. Morning coats were at one time reserved for very formal morning weddings. Morning weddings are increasingly common, and the morning coat with striped trousers, top hat, and ascot is a really great formal look. White tie and tails is still reserved for after 6:00, and it can certainly lend an air of elegance to your evening wedding. If your groom is a military man, his dress blues are a particularly striking choice. It adds an incomparable degree of personalization and meaning to your attire choice. And no one can resist a man in uniform!

For more casual afternoon weddings, consider a dinner jacket and dark trousers. The standard tuxedo with cummerbund or suspenders and vest (waistcoat) is appropriate at any time of day.

If you will have a ring bearer in your wedding party, you may have limited choices for formal attire in his size. Ask your tuxedo shop personnel to show you the options. Also, keep in mind how quickly children grow, and make sure he is measured again closer to the wedding so any necessary adjustments can be made to the order.

The staff at tuxedo shops are skilled at suggesting the proper attire for your wedding and can help you choose shoes, accessories, hats, canes, spats, ties, ascots, and more. Look through magazines to get some ideas for the look you want the men in your wedding to achieve and show your favorites to the tailors at the tux shop. Handsome cuff links make good gifts for your groomsmen and add style to your wedding party. Cuff links also offer another opportunity for personalization, so find something that really speaks to in a unique way.

© www.aaronlockwoodphotography.com

Courtesy Tiffany Webster Larsen and Chad Larsen

This groom and his groomsmen lend their own air of elegance to a formal wedding.

Fit

You can choose any style tuxedo or suit for the men in your wedding to wear. They can all match to a "T," or they can be in calculatedly mismatched suits. But if the suits don't fit well, they will look sloppy and slovenly. And mostly, the men themselves will just appear to be uncomfortable, like they can't wait to change into their jeans. No matter what they wear, once the picture taking is over, expect all the jackets to be left on chair backs and the shirt tails to come out during the first fast dance.

You can head off some of the discomfort, though, by insisting that everyone show up to be measured for their tuxes well ahead of time. And then show up again a week or so prior to the wedding for a final fitting—just like the bride and bridesmaids will be doing. It is a good idea to schedule this for everyone at once and turn it into a fun time.

A little nervous, but in that suit, does it matter?

Courtesy Tiffany Webster Larsen and Chad Larsen

If you ask each man to go on his own to the tux shop to be measured, it is a chore that most of them will dutifully accomplish. To get more enthusiastic participation in this process though, we suggest that you organize a group affair. Gather everyone at the tux shop to be measured, and then head over to the local pub for nachos, beer, and a game on the big screen TV. You can relax knowing everyone has been properly fitted, and the guys will be even more impressed with the great catch their buddy has found.

Be sure the tux shop has instructions to make everyone try on every piece, including shoes, when they pick up their tuxes for the wedding. Inevitably something will be the wrong size and it is better to find out at the shop rather than while dressing at the church. Many wedding day disasters have occurred when a groomsman discovered the wrong color shirt or too small shoes too late .It couldn't hurt.

Assign this small task to a trusted person, one of your bridesmaids, a responsible usher, or the groom's father (who probably doesn't have much to do anyway): Request a handful of collar extenders from the tux shop. These little elastic loops with a button on one end are perfect for easing neck strain on the wedding day. No matter how many fittings they have, it seems that collars always end up being too tight for breathing on the wedding day. Anyone with a few of these in his pocket becomes an instant hero.

Fathers of the Bride and Groom

Don't forget to include the fathers of the bride and groom. Most tuxedo shops offer free rental to the father of the bride or the groom with a minimum wedding party order. They don't have to be dressed like the groom and the ushers, but they do need to look polished. Their attire needs to complement the style of the wedding. Luckily, you don't have to ask them to coordinate the color of their suits, but again, if you're having a beach wedding, for instance, you might want to suggest linen trousers. Ask them all (stepfathers, too) if they own the proper attire. Unless you know them to be very fastidious, don't take their word for it either; ask to see them in the suits they plan to wear. The father of the bride especially has a pivotal role to play in the processional—assuming he's walking you down the aisle—so how these men are dressed is also important. Plan ahead, make sure all these details are worked out, and you won't be disappointed on your wedding day.

Courtesy Chris Small and Tom Small
© 2006 Holly Istas Photography

Courtesy Shutterstock © Lisa F. Young

Courtesy Shutterstock © PeterG

129

Florists, Cakes, Photographers, and More

*I perhaps owe having become
a painter to flowers.*

—Claude Monet

YOUR WEDDING IS STARTING to take shape now, and you should be able to visualize what you want everything to look like. You're still hiring people and signing contracts, so keep your three-ring binder handy. You'll need it in the coming weeks.

As with the caterer and the dresses and tuxedos, you may already have in mind some ideas for the flowers, the photography, and the cake at your wedding. No doubt you've been to friends' weddings and seen spectacular cakes and beautiful flower arrangements. You may even have noticed at other weddings you've attended the really impressive Hummer limo that was used to carry the entire wedding party from ceremony to reception or the antique Bentley the bride and groom were driven away in as they left the reception. Great! You have some leads. Contact your friends and relatives and start making notes in your three-ring binder about vendors you want to interview.

While the Internet is great for comparison shopping, the importance of a personal meeting cannot be overemphasized. One bride interviewed a florist who plopped several standard FTD arrangement books in front of her and left her to look at them alone, while the florist she selected took her through several photo albums of her own work, asking what she liked and didn't like, what colors she had chosen, what types of flowers she preferred, and on and on. The first florist was just a merchant. The second was an artist and found creative ways to stretch the couple's budget to get the look they wanted for their wedding and reception.

Check the Internet again—this time for two types of information. First, there's the possibility of purchasing some things online; but, second, many local vendors will have web sites where you can find out the types of services they provide and possibly even get estimates. You can also just get an overall idea, by looking at photos on the web, of the kind of results they achieve. Photographers, especially, have portfolios on the web. Florists love to show pictures of their work, and even cake decorators have web sites where you can see some samples of their work. It's a place to start, but don't make a decision until you've interviewed at least three of each type of vendor—even more if you are not satisfied by the first three you talk to.

This is the time when your shopping skills are going to come in handy. Go and talk to these people and see their handiwork in person. They are artists, and we all have our own taste in art; you may prefer classic flower arrangements and highly decorated cakes with bridges, moats, and waterfalls. On the other hand, you may prefer the minimalist movement with a single rose bud and a simple white cake with a few rose petals sprinkled over it. Whatever your preference, now you need to begin looking for florists, bakers, and photographers who are able and willing to make these aspects of your dream a reality.

Getting married in the rose garden at Timber Creek Lodge, Sun City Roseville, California—flowers came with the site.

Flowers

FLOWERS SET THE STAGE FOR YOUR wedding. They, along with the colorful bridesmaid dresses, provide much of the color of the day. Flowers can be used as background arrangements, carried by the women in the wedding, worn in the lapels of the men, worn as corsages by the mothers of the bride and groom, presented as a tribute to other important people in your life, and used as centerpieces on tables at the reception. You can choose them for their color, their beauty, their meaning, and for their various aromas.

The Bride's and Bridesmaids' Bouquets

The trend these days in bridal bouquets is small and tailored in bright colors that match the general theme of the wedding, but if you want to carry a long trailing mass of lilies and carnations, you should do exactly as you please. One of the most beautiful old photographs we found while doing the research for this book is on the first page of Chapter 1, and one reason it's such a great photo is that big beautiful bouquet. Lily of the valley and orange blossoms, roses and orchids in long cascading bouquets were the style set by royalty for many years. Recent trends toward simpler, more compact bouquets are certainly more cost effective and still beautiful, but that long trailing bouquet is just awesome. Bridesmaids' bouquets are often just smaller versions of the bride's flowers, with colors coordinated with their gowns. Often the bride's bouquet has her "colors" in it while the bridesmaids, often already dressed in those colors, carry white flowers. You can do this as you see fit. If white on white for yourself reflects your style, then the bridesmaids can carry something more colorful.

Why We Do That

Flowers have long played a part in weddings of many cultures, and men have not always been limited to wearing a small boutonniere in their lapels. Roman grooms were crowned with wreaths of ivy, and during the Elizabethan age in England, men wore nosegays as part of their elaborate attire.

On her wedding day, Queen Victoria wore in her hair orange blossoms sprinkled with diamonds from her royal jewels.

Early European brides carried piquant bouquets of garlic and spices, which were thought to help drive away evil spirits.

In ancient Greece and Rome, shafts of wheat and grain were thought to invoke fertility.

Some of the meanings associated with certain flowers:

Baby's breath is believed to ensure a fruitful marriage.

Stephanotis are thought to bring good luck, especially for the bride.

White flowers symbolize innocence, as do pink.

Forget-me-nots are a symbol of true love.

Rosemary for remembrance.

The bride, believe it or not, created this bouquet herself.
If you're talented enough, you might want to try
making some of your own floral creations.

As you walk down the aisle carrying your bouquet, consider how it will look to your guests. You don't want to show them a bunch of stems. Point the bouquet forward, and wrap the stems in ribbon or some tulle to hide the blunt ends.

If you wish to carry a Bible or prayer book, keep the arrangement simple by carrying a single white or red rose with it.

The flower girl is an integral part of many weddings. You don't see her strewing petals as she walks down the aisle so much these days, but that was her original purpose: to spread the bride's path with flower petals. It's a tradition you might want to try resurrecting for your wedding. At a recent wedding, the pair of flower girls were so enthusiastic in performing their petal sprinkling duties that the priest congratulated them on a job well done, creating a memorable moment of laughter among the guests. Let the petals fall!

Tall brides can carry large blossoms like sunflowers; shorter brides might want to stick with rosebuds and baby's breath. Consider the style of your dress when choosing your bouquet. A ball gown looks good with a round bouquet. A-line dresses are complemented by more irregular, trailing bouquets. Sheath dresses look pretty when accompanied by large single flowers or loose arrangements.

This bride chose a vintage look with a long cascading bouquet.

Centerpieces, Altar Flowers, Pew Pieces

In addition to the flowers you carry on your wedding day, you'll want to decorate the ceremony site and the tables at the reception with flowers. An inexpensive method is to tie big bows for the ends of the pews and thread them with baby's breath or greenery. Save the big flower arrangements for the altar, and be sure to assign someone to carry them to the reception so they can double as background beauty there as well. Set an arrangement on the buffet table, the cake table, and the head table where the wedding party sits.

> Let the bride's and bridesmaids' bouquets double as centerpieces for the main table or decorate the cake table at the reception.

Corsages and Boutonnières

All mothers and stepmothers should receive a corsage. It is a nice touch to also provide them for grandmothers, special aunts, godmothers, or any woman who is special in either of your lives. Or you might just present these special women with a single long stemmed rose. If you have musicians, singers, or readers who take part in the ceremony in any way, a floral tribute of some kind might also be in order: corsages or long stemmed roses for the women and boutonnieres for the men. You may want your floral tributes to do double duty. For instance, a floral arrangement placed on the piano or beside the harp during the ceremony can easily be reused as a gift table decoration at the reception.

The groom, groomsmen, and ushers should all wear boutonnieres. The groom's boutonniere should be slightly different than the groomsmen's. Fathers of the bride and groom and stepfathers should be presented with boutonnieres. Flowers should not be worn with any military uniform.

The groom should wear a boutonniere with just an extra bit of colorful ribbon or a flower from the bride's bouquet.

Other Decorative Items

Of course, decorations don't have to be flowers. Ribbons, balloons, greenery, evergreen boughs, candles, anything can contribute to the festive nature of the hall where your reception is held.

If you want rose petals in the aisle, freeze-dried are a great alternative to fresh. They're less expensive, they last longer, they aren't as slippery, and you can order them on the Internet and have them shipped right to your house. They look as good as regular petals.

Order freeze dried rose petals online and have them delivered.

Shutterstock © Netea Mircea Valentin

Priscilla & Josh

When Priscilla's and Josh's guests walked in through the beautiful garden where their wedding took place, they walked beneath a large banner embossed with their names and the date (using their wedding colors). Approximately 25 decorated trees lined the walkway that was the entrance to the wedding site. These trees were decorated in their red, eggplant, and gold colors. White twinkling Christmas lights were everywhere. As the guests arrived, they were met by the aroma of a delicious hot apple cider punch for their enjoyment as they entered the hall. The theme was Christmas, so Christmas music played in the gardens. All the senses of sight, smell, taste, sound, and touch (with "real" snow on the ground) were satisfied.

Courtesy Priscilla Webster Mellette and Josh Mellette © Cameron H Photography

A winter wonderland was created for this Christmas wedding in Florida.

Heather & Mark

Heather loves hemlock trees, and the house she and Mark were living in when they got married had a beautiful hemlock tree in the front yard. As they were having a winter wedding, with a winter color palette, evergreens in general were a big part of their flower arrangements. They took many clippings from that beautiful hemlock in the front yard, and their florist used them in the bouquets and other flower arrangements.

Courtesy Shutterstock © Ronen

Shutterstock © Gordon Swanson

Mitzi & John

Mitzi's mother and grandmother are allergic to fragrant flowers, so instead of rose corsages to match the bouquets, the florist thoughtfully selected less fragrant flowers from the overall floral scheme and pinned them to the ladies' purses. The mother of the groom was pleased with this alternative as well because it prevented nasty pin holes from ruining the delicate fabric of her dress.

Shutterstock © Norman Chan

The Cake

A MODERN WEDDING CAKE is a thing of beauty, covered in fondant or buttercream icing with doves, cherubs, lace, and flowers galore. It should be placed as the centerpiece of the room where the reception is held, although it should be in a place well out of the way of boisterous dancers. It will serve as part of the decoration and as dessert. It's also the central piece in one of the traditions associated with the wedding: the cutting of the cake, when the bride and groom join hands and cut their first piece of dessert to be enjoyed as husband and wife.

You may want to take as much care in choosing your cake as you did in choosing your dress. Top bakers are booked up months in advance, so if you want the very best, start your cake quest early. Talk with the chef who will be baking your cake about flavors and styles to choose from. The wedding cake, often a tiered affair, is a miracle of modern architecture, or perhaps sculpture, requiring columns, supports, and icing to hold it together. You certainly want to make sure yours is created by a professional who knows what she's doing. Insist on seeing pictures of cakes this person has created before.

Linda Shonk, renowned pastry chef and wedding cake artist, has this piece of advice: "You can have it all. You may see an elaborately decorated cake in the bakery window or in the bakery's portfolio and think it's a thing of beauty and exactly what you want for your wedding. But if that bakery makes their cakes from mixes or otherwise cuts corners, you and your guests will be disappointed in the taste. Insist on a taste test. If you are considering different flavors or varieties, taste each one. Beauty and flavor—that's what it takes to make a superlative wedding cake.

"Make it a point to observe actual cakes they are delivering that week too, not pictures of cakes they baked last year. Excellent chefs who take pride in their work know they are only as good as the cake they just baked."

A toast before cutting the cake.

Courtesy Shutterstock

Courtesy Shutterstock © Eric Limon

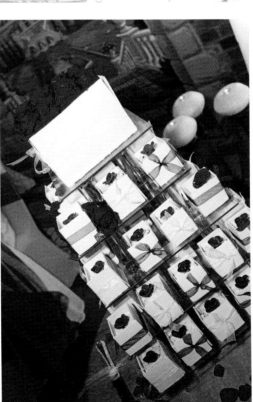

Courtesy Shutterstock © Nolte Lourens

Your cake can be as complicated, as elegant, or as whimsical as you wish.
You are only limited by your imagination and the talent of your pastry chef.

Insist on tasting the goods ahead of time, too—hey, why not? Tasting cakes can be an afternoon's entertainment for you, your mother, and your maid of honor. And there is a great difference in how bakeries prepare the cake itself. Ask how they do it. Ask what the ingredients in the icing will be. You can have any flavor cake you want too: current favorites are white, chocolate, cheesecake, red velvet, raspberry, strawberry, or chiffon. If you have a favorite, request a taste test and order it. Any flavor cake can be made into a wedding cake by a creative baker.

If you want a really big cake to use as a centerpiece but you're only expecting 75 guests at your wedding, discuss this with the pastry chef. It's possible to bake a small cake and then place it on a piece of cake-shaped Styrofoam that has been iced to match your cake. Voila! You've got your huge cake for impressive photographs with no leftover cake to be disposed of.

Conversely, if you expect hundreds of people but don't want to pay for the gigantic seven-tiered creation it would take to feed them all, have a three-tiered cake for cutting and photo sessions, and get a couple of sheet cakes to go along with it to serve all your guests. If you want the sheet cake to come stacked and filled like a tiered wedding cake, that's usually just as expensive as getting the real thing. Talk to your pastry chef; many options are available, including cupcakes.

You probably will have leftover cake, though, and therefore you should make sure that, along with the cake, the bakery also delivers a few of those white bakery boxes for sending cake home with your guests. You'll also need one for that top layer if you wish to save it.

This beautiful cake takes center stage.

Put a trustworthy friend or family member in charge of storing that cake top for you. Some couples save this top in the freezer to enjoy on their first anniversary. Some report that it tasted just as good a year later as it tasted on their wedding day. Some say not so much. Decide whether you want to risk it. Home freezing guides suggest not freezing baked goods for longer than a couple of months, but this is a special case. It's pretty certain, though, that you won't eat all of it if you keep it for a year, but you might enjoy just having a token bite for the sake of tradition.

The cake deserves a spotlighted table with skirting and greenery. Make sure you speak with your caterer about the way the cake will be displayed and make sure the chef who bakes it delivers the cake in plenty of time to put it in place and then embellish the table with some trim, such as skirting on the table, greenery, and carefully arranged napkins, forks, and plates. Candelabra and spotlights help to display the cake in all its glory as well. You should also coordinate with your florist to get any special floral accents on the cake table. Another popular idea is to decorate a very simple cake with a cascade of fresh flowers or flower petals. You will want the florist or the cake artist to place those and not leave it for the waitstaff to do.

Why We Do That

The tradition of serving guests a slice of confection known as a wedding cake began in ancient Greece, as did so many other wedding traditions. But the Grecian bride and groom didn't so much serve a cake as they did simply eat a bite of bread. The bread was broken over their heads to ensure fertility and prosperity. Then the guests scrambled for crumbs that fell to floor so as to share in the good luck being wished on the happy couple.

Europeans took this idea a bit further when bridesmaids tried to pile the small cakes high on the day of their friend's wedding. The higher the pile of cakes, the more friends the bride had. Eventually, the idea of holding the cakes together with a glaze of honey and sugar came about. This is still done by French chefs; the creation is called a croquembouche, and it is a tower of pastries held together with a sweet glaze; it is the traditional French wedding cake.

Until a couple hundred years ago, most wedding cakes were more like today's fruitcake or plum pudding—heavy and filled with fruit and nuts. When millers began milling flour into the fine white powder we use now, and when baking soda and baking powder became useful as leavening agents, it became possible to create the towering creations we indulge in today.

Interestingly, the latest trend is to serve smaller, individual cakes or cupcakes; it seems the fashion in wedding cakes may be heading back to the small cakes broken over the heads of the early Greek and Roman brides and grooms.

Courtesy Ryan and Jennifer O'Donnell © Stewart Pinsky Photography (Mini-cakes by Pacific Cakes of Maui)

Individual cakes are an elegant alternative to the huge iced confections that dominate many receptions.

Okay, you probably won't actually die if you freeze the top of your cake and eat it a year later. But one bride says that 12 years later, her top tier is still in the freezer awaiting the brave person who will thaw and eat it. They even moved and took that cake with them! Consider enjoying your cake top on your one month anniversary as a more appetizing alternative.

On your first anniversary you can order a replica of your cake top from your bakery. You can even notify your bakery ahead of time that you're planning to do this so they can advise you on the necessary lead time to fulfill your order. Be sure to bring in pictures of your cake top—get good close ups to show the details! You don't have to limit yourself to this trick on your first anniversary only either. You can make an anniversary tradition out of serving your top cake tier over and over.

Why We Do That

In the 1970s modern brides and grooms felt that it was their responsibility to entertain their guests. It was already a custom for couples to cut the cake and then feed each other a piece of it, but someone thought "wouldn't it be funny if we smeared cake all over each other's faces." And so a new and horrifying tradition came about. Make a pact to not do this at your wedding. It might have been acceptable in the casual '70s, but today's bride often spends hours having her make-up applied professionally for her wedding day. Smearing cake in her face is not a good thing to do. Brides, be sure to address this with your groom prior to the reception. If you are the fun-loving, laid back type who thinks it is funny to have a food fight, it's your day. But, if you consider it rude and disrespectful to smash a handful of cake into the face of your beloved instead of gently feeding it to one another, make your feelings clear. No groom wants a disappointed or upset bride on his wedding day.

Courtesy Cathleen Small © 2006 Holly istas Photography (Cupcakes by Dainty Pastry of Roseville, California)

This couple included a small cake for the cutting ceremony and served cupcakes to their guests—easy, convenient, and economical—not to mention quite trendy.

Choosing a Photographer

IF YOU HAD YOUR ENGAGEMENT photo taken by a professional photographer and it turned out to your liking, you're well on your way to choosing a wedding photographer. The engagement photo served as a test for your photographer's skills. As with other vendors, word of mouth is your best bet for recommendations. Friends will be more than happy to show you their wedding photographs. Get recommendations, check out web sites of photographers, and then visit them for an interview.

Your wedding is developing its own style, one that reflects your personalities. You want the photos taken on the day of your wedding to reflect that style. Interview photographers as you did florists and bakers. Many have online portfolios to make it easier for you to shop around a bit before you start the interviewing process. As you look at those portfolios or the ones the photographer shows you in his studio, make sure she is able to capture the emotion of a moment, to tell a story with pictures. Pictures and memories will be all you have to share of your wedding day with your grandchildren someday. Make sure both are well preserved.

Be sure when you are interviewing a photographer that he or she is the one who will actually be assigned to your wedding. Many photography studios employ several photographers, and of course, some are better than others. You will begin to establish a relationship during the interview with the person you're talking to. You will want the photographer who shows up at your wedding to be someone you are already comfortable with.

Mitzi & John

This couple was fortunate to have several friends who had chosen Waldek Photography with stunning results. They were particularly pleased having witnessed firsthand Waldek's unobtrusive, quiet style of capturing unscripted moments of the day. His photojournalistic style and artistic use of color, black and white, and sepia tones made him a "must have" for their wedding. They verified his availability when selecting their wedding date—he was that critical to their plans.

Some of the formal, posed photos you'll want to make sure you get include:

Bride and groom at altar

Bride alone with her dress and train on full display

Bride with parents

Groom with parents

Bride and groom with each set of parents and with all

Other family groupings

Bride with her attendants

Groom with his attendants

Bride and groom with wedding party

If you aren't thrilled by the idea of taking up to four hours for photography, ask to see some samples of your photographer's candid shots. Some are better at this than others. You may want candid shots of the following:

The bride leaving home in curlers and jeans

Various photos of the bride and bridesmaids and her mother getting dressed

Putting the garter on the bride's leg

Groom and best man before the ceremony

Groom getting dressed with help from best man

Groom with father before the ceremony

Bride with flower girl and ring bearer

The bride standing with her father waiting for the processional to begin

This photographer was ready to capture a memorable moment.

From the collection of Judy Doetl

Courtesy Mitzi and John Koontz © Waldek Photography

In the 1930s an official wedding photo was a stiff-looking affair. These days it's gotten much more informal.

You should try to take advantage of any special architectural or sculptural opportunities your city offers. Small towns also offer scenic or historic buildings, and the countryside is teeming with views that could serve as a great backdrop for you and your bridal party to pose in front of. Brides often pose for photos at the Alamo, for instance. Even if you don't live in San Antonio, there are unique buildings and artwork featured in most U.S. cities. Give some thought to places where you might want to have your picture made on your special day.

Courtesy Mitzi and John Koontz © Waldek Photography

A wedding party poses in front of this famous sculpture by Robert Indiana.

During the ceremony and reception photographers should be unobtrusive. They need to get their candid shots so that no one even notices they are there. Be sure to check with the officiant at your wedding about taking photos during the ceremony. Some churches and synagogues do not allow photographs during services. Make sure your photographer understands what is allowable.

Some photography packages include a beautiful album with your professional prints. Don't forget to buy an album and picture frames to put your informal photos in. Of course, you can find albums in such places as card shops and scrapbook stores, but for something unique and custom made, do some shopping at these web sites:

Artzproducts.com

Leathercraftsmen.com

Zookbinders.com

You don't want to overdo it, but having a couple of other amateur photographers in addition to the professional you hire for the ceremony is often a good idea. These people should not intrude on the formal photos being posed for the professional shots or otherwise get in the way of the main photographer, but they may get some candid shots the main photographer won't get while she's occupied elsewhere. Discuss this first with your "official" photographer though; some object to other photographers being present. This is a good way to get coverage of your entire reception, because many photographers leave after the main reception photo ops have finished—the cake cutting, first dance, and such. If your photography package is for a set number of hours, having another person in charge of capturing the classic moments with your family and friends is essential.

During the artistic revolution of the 1960s, photographers tried many new perspectives for wedding photos.

What about disposable cameras on the tables so that all your guests can take pictures? Reviews are mixed on these. Some couples swear they got some of their best shots from them and others say the effort and expense were wasted for one or two decent photos and lot of junk. Now that disposable digitals are available, I'd give it a shot. You can review them before you have them printed, so there's less chance for waste. Of course, everyone today is carrying a cell phone that's capable of taking photos, so you'll get lots of candid shots taken by friends. The more ways you have to remember you wedding, the better, and one or two of these informal, unasked for shots may end up being your favorites. But don't think they can take the place of a professional photographer. You cannot do without this necessity.

Heather & Mark

Heather says she loved having table cameras. "The evening is such a blur for the bride and groom, being ushered from one thing to another, trying to briefly get around to everyone and fulfilling all those cake cutting, garter throwing, and other photographic moments. Those cameras were great for really finding out what was going on, and what everyone thought of our night. I was so relieved to see that everyone looked like they were having such a great time."

Videographer

With today's lightweight, handheld video cameras and digital cameras that double as moving picture cameras, you'll likely have lots of videos taken of your wedding by amateur photographer friends. But that doesn't mean you won't want to invest in a real life videographer. Ask your photographer about this service. Since they'll be there anyway with their lights and cameras, having someone shooting videos as well as photos might work out just fine. And you should get a better deal on videography services if you use the same company for both.

Again, make sure video cameras are allowed inside the church or synagogue during the service.

Videos can be priceless, too. There's no other way to get such great footage of Uncle Charlie doing the limbo or your cousin Tammy dancing with your best man. Film can capture a moment, but moving pictures capture every moment. Make sure your videography package includes your entire reception, if that is what you want. Some brides have been disappointed to find that their videographers have packed up and left after the traditional reception photo ops were completed. Another nice touch is for your videographer to approach guests during the reception or set up a message station in a quiet alcove or hallway so your guests can leave you video messages. These messages will be treasured for years to come, especially those from grandparents and parents.

Transportation

Y OU'LL WANT TO GIVE SOME thought to how the whole entourage is going to be transported from their homes to the site of the ceremony along with all the curling irons, make-up mirrors, and safety pins that go into the perfect wedding day (not to mention coolers of iced down drinks and a snack in case someone gets hungry while the dressing is going on). Everyone in the wedding party, including parents and grand-parents, needs a ride from his or her home to the ceremony and from the ceremony to the reception; in addition, the bride and groom will need to be carried away in style after the reception.

The easiest and most convenient way to handle transportation needs for the bride and groom is to hire a limousine for the day. There is usually a minimum amount of time you'll have to pay for anyway (three or four hours), so this rented vehicle can serve as the bride's ride to the church, the couple's ride from the church to the reception site, and perhaps a few other errands that need to be run.

Make sure the company you hire has reliable vehi-cles, a good service record with recommendations, insurance, and bonded drivers. Ask how the driver will be dressed for your wedding and find out whether a tip is expected—it usually is.

There are some really unique choices for trans-portation on the day of your wedding. Search online for local companies that provide this serv-ice, and know that you have many choices. Vintage vehicles, stretch limousines, and buses that can carry your whole wedding party from the wedding to the reception are just a few of the choices you'll want to consider.

In addition to your own transportation needs, there are certain people you will want to accom-modate on your wedding day. Your parents, of course, will probably have their own transporta-tion, but they might be too distracted to remember their parents. Don't just leave the arrival of your 90-year-old grandmother to chance. Assign a rela-tive, an uncle or cousin or someone not so central to the rest of the wedding day activities, to make sure she gets to the ceremony on time and to the reception and then is delivered home afterward. This might mean that someone will have to leave and take her home and then return for any cele-bration that goes on late into the night since most older people prefer to go home after the cake is cut. Of course, if your Granny likes to party, she should stay as late as she wants!

And, if you have children, they should have top priority. If at all possible, they should ride with you to the ceremony and the reception. If you would rather just the two of you ride in the limo, make sure your children are happy with the arrange-ments you make for them. You don't want them to start off their new life feeling left out of anything, especially a ride in a cool car.

Consider coordinating rides for family or friends flying in for your wedding. If hiring limos or taxis are out of your budget, ask outgoing, reliable friends to shuttle a specific couple or family to and from the airport and to and from the wedding festivities. This is a nice way for your friends to meet each other and feel welcome since you cannot possibly be everywhere at once.

Getting around on the day of the ceremony can be half the fun.

Part III

All the Revelry That Comes Before

AS HAPPENED WITH THE VICTORIAN *bride of yesteryear, your wedding sends you off on a social whirl of shopping and parties. You'll be the center of attention at many gatherings in the coming months, and you have many details still to work out. Showers and bachelor parties are common, but you'll also be invited to (and hosting) brunches, golf outings, dinners, and maybe even ski trips—all designed to introduce you to each other's family and friends. You aren't just creating a new family by getting married; you're each becoming part of an already existing one as well.*

You also have some legal issues to handle. Marriage license and a name change are just two of the legal considerations you'll need to address.

Finally, this is the time to start planning your honeymoon. Where will you go on your first trip as a married couple? We're gearing up now for the walk down the aisle and all that comes immediately after it. Just a few more items to think about now.

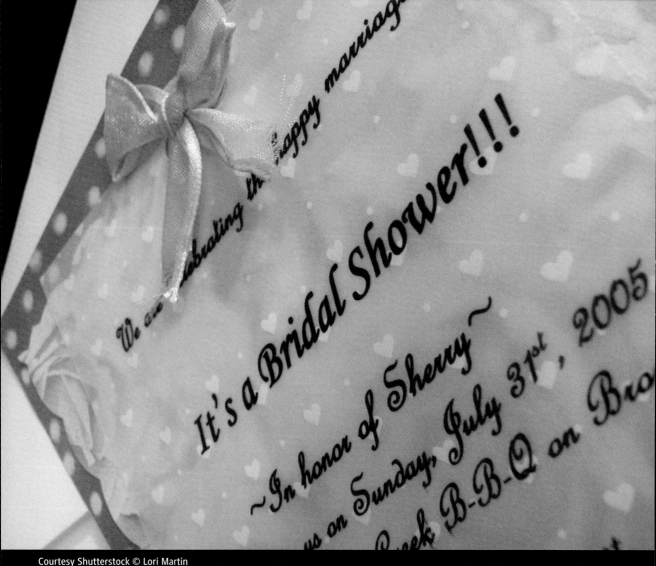

We are celebrating the happy marriage

It's a Bridal Shower!!!

~In honor of Sherry~

...s on Sunday, July 31st, 2005

...reek B-B-Q on Bro...

Pre-Wedding Parties

*What counts in making a happy
marriage is not so much how
compatible you are, but how you
deal with incompatibility.*

—Leo Tolstoy

Y OU'LL NEED TO INSERT A calendar of the coming months in your three-ring binder. Use it to keep a record of all the parties and appointments that will be on your schedule. There will be bridal showers, bachelor and bachelorette parties, a bridesmaids' lunch or brunch, a groomsmen golf outing, perhaps a few football games, and other fun activities scheduled. Your calendar is going to be very full.

*Summer entertaining: roses, champagne, fruit, a garden—
perfect setting for a bridal shower!*

Showers

A FEW MODERN BRIDES OBJECT to the idea of showers because they are grown up, professional women who already own all the toasters and fajita makers they need, and they paid for it all themselves, thank you very much. In preparation for writing this book, we interviewed several brides, and even the ones who were most adamant about not wanting gifts discovered that old habits die hard and if you're getting married and inviting people to a wedding, they are just going to give you a gift. So most brides say they gave up in the end and decided to register to make it easy for people. And to make sure that the gifts they received would be something they'd actually like to own. And isn't that the point anyway? People want to share in your happiness. They want to help you get off to a good start in your new life, and this is the way it's done.

Here, then, are a few rules and guidelines for showers because if it's going to happen, you might as well do it the right way.

First, the idea of a women-only shower is only one way of conducting this ritual. Men help with the gift registry, and they often attend the shower. After all, they'll be using the dishes too, not to mention washing them often. They have a right. In fact, couples showers are increasingly popular as they bring the bride's and groom's friends together to form connections before the big day. Couples showers often carry a theme such as an entertainment, boating, home improvement, camping, or any other interest you share as a couple. On the other hand, if you want to keep it all female, there certainly is historic precedent for that.

In decades not so far in the past, a bride often had several showers. These were specialty showers, ones where the gift was supposed to fit into a certain category, such as kitchen, linen, and personal; there were even Tupperware showers. A girl often had several sets of friends—classmates and sorority sisters, family, and friends from work, and each group found a time to shower the bride-to-be with gifts. Family and friends were invited to the kitchen and the linen shower, but only close girlfriends, perhaps sorority sisters, attended the personal shower. It wasn't considered proper to open such personal items in the company of the mothers of the bride and groom.

Courtesy Shutterstock © Natalia V. Guseva

Lingerie in pretty feminine boxes is a perfect shower gift, especially at a shower that includes just close girlfriends of the bride.

One of the oft mentioned responsibilities of the maid of honor is to give the bride a shower. Some etiquette guides say that a close relative should not be the one to host your bridal shower, and that may be so...unless your maid of honor is your sister, in which case, she'd be perfectly justified. We think it's all right for the mother of the groom to give the bride-to-be a shower too, especially as it might serve to introduce her to other female family members and friends of the groom. The mother of the bride...unless there is absolutely no one else willing to do it, that's still frowned upon in most societies.

It is not considered proper etiquette to include with the wedding invitation any notation about where the bride is registered, no matter how practical an idea that may seem. A shower invitation, however, presumably because it comes from the shower hostess and not from the bride herself, should include this vital information. For those wedding guests who are not invited to any bridal showers, word of mouth (or some good detective work) must suffice for them to know where to go searching for your names in a bridal registry in order to purchase a gift they can be sure you'll like.

Why We Do That

The personal shower in recent decades has been replaced by a night on the town called the bachelorette party. Although the idea of going out with your girlfriends, riding in a limo, drinking too much, making fools of yourselves, and tucking bucks into some stud dancer's G-string sounds appealing and you might even consider it to be fair play since the groom is probably having a similar evening with his friends, we beg you to reconsider. What if, instead of a night on the town, your girlfriends took you shopping at Victoria's Secret and maybe even Bath and Body Works and each one bought you some small item of apparel or personal indulgence? What if, instead of ending the night with a hangover and a plastic straw in the shape of a penis, you ended up with some real goods: lingerie, peignoirs, nightgowns, lace panties, bubble bath, lotions and other such sexy stuff that might come in handy on your honeymoon? Think about it. It might be a suggestion you want to whisper to your maid of honor.

Showers can have a theme in keeping with the wedding, a theme of their own, or even none at all. They are, by definition, kitschy. You can carry the traditional bridal shower to the extreme, playing shower games and serving cake and punch—this was standard procedure throughout the last century. Or you can eschew the games, serve wine and cheese, kick back, and have a more modern gathering. How many you have and the way each is hosted is entirely up to you and your friends.

Bachelor and Bachelorette Parties

BACHELOR PARTIES HAVE LONG been with us. It was thought that the groom should have one last chance to kick up his heels as a single man, to totally indulge himself in the freedom of a men-only night on the town. This often involved a visit to a strip club where much was made of his impending loss of freedom. Or worse. If you need a reminder of what a bachelor party should be, rent *Bachelor Party*, the 1984 movie starring Tom Hanks. Let's just say it involves three things no bachelor party should be without: hookers, drugs, and a donkey.

Seriously, the bachelor party should be a time for some male bonding. It's the responsibility of the best man to see that the groom is entertained in this way. It can be as elaborate as a trip to Vegas or as simple as a day of golf with some buddies or a concert of a favorite band.

What happens in Vegas stays in Vegas.

Bachelorette parties are a recent addition to the pre-wedding hoopla. They started being a popular pursuit when women decided they wanted in on the "final fling" action, too. It's fun to get out and kick up your heels with your girlfriends as the stress of making decisions about so many things is nearing its culmination—when you go on display as the center of attention at a day long affair with hundreds of eyes focused on you—yes, a little stress relief is definitely called for.

Bachelorette parties may be simple nights out on the town, or they might involve such tame pursuits as massages and facials and yoga classes. Let yours be personal and designed as a stress reliever.

Why We Do That

According to Clarissa Pinkola Estes, in *Women Who Run with the Wolves*, women of all cultures have traditionally gotten together for some "sacred obscene" times with a bride before her wedding. This ritual served the purpose of introducing a very young teenage girl (in past cultures, the age of wedlock was about 13) to her new duties as a grown up married woman, including the very grown up activity of sexual intercourse. A lot of joking and fun happened, but in the process, the young girl was educated by older women in the art of seduction.

We don't seem to need this ritual so much any more; after all, now it is common to put off marriage until we are in our 30s, so we've had plenty of time to learn much more than the teenage brides of less developed cultures. Still, those personal showers of the '50s and '60s with the comments of friends as each new filmy piece of lingerie was unwrapped, and now the bachelorette party where brides presumably have their last chance to flirt and dance with strangers, serve the purpose of letting women bond in a ribald and open way.

Special Gatherings

A WEEK OR SO BEFORE the wedding, after the dresses have been fitted for the last time, after everyone has decided on hairdos and make-up hues and shoes, a bridesmaids' tea is in order. It doesn't have to be a tea; it can be lunch, breakfast, or even brunch; it is a gathering, hosted by the bride, in which she brings together the important women in her life. It isn't necessary, but it's a gracious thing to do. Invite the groom's mother and sisters (if he has them) along with your own mother, sisters, and the bridal attendants—and any other special people you want to thank for seeing you this far through life.

The bridesmaids' tea is the time for you to present your attendants with their gifts from you and to publicly thank them for their participation in your major lifetime event.

The groom, too, will want to host a similar affair for his attendants and close male relatives. The fare here and the entertainment can be more casual and laid back. A golf outing or fishing trip may provide the perfect quiet getaway for the guys.

Even an afternoon of chicken wings and football on TV can be a great break for your busy fiancé to unwind. This is the time for the groom to present his attendants with their gifts. If neither of you find the time or resources to host such an event, the rehearsal dinner is your next opportunity to present thank you gifts to your attendants.

Why We Do That

A quaint custom is the trousseau tea, the practice of inviting close friends and family to your home to view the wedding gifts you've accumulated. Writing in 1992, Elizabeth Post advises the bride-to-be that this can be done prior to the wedding or, if the reception is at home, gifts may simply be displayed on tables in a room near the main party, where people can simply wander in and out, examining the goods. Ms. Post says this should never be done at a country club, hotel, or hall—only at home.

It wasn't considered showing off the accumulated booty, but a thoughtful way to express your appreciation to the gift givers. Checks were to be displayed with only the signature showing, the top one covered in opaque paper and a piece of glass placed over all to discourage the curious from checking amounts.

This may still be practiced in some regions, but it is a custom that seems to have fallen by the wayside. Now the gifts are piled on a table at the wedding reception, stored somewhere until the bride and groom return from their honeymoon, and then opened privately.

A pretty cake in the wedding's color scheme is an appropriate dessert for the bridesmaids' tea.

Courtesy Sweet Art Galleries and Linda Shonk

Rehearsal and Rehearsal Dinner

BECAUSE WEDDINGS HAVE BECOME so very personalized in recent years, with couples writing their own vows, musicians performing, readers reading, and singers singing, and because new rituals have been added to the ceremony in the form of unity candles, sand blending, and handfasting, a rehearsal for all the players has been deemed necessary the night before the ceremony. That added event has given us another opportunity to get together and share a meal with loved ones. In fact, the rehearsal dinner is smaller and more personal than the reception on the day of the wedding. This is your chance to spend a little time with people who are dearest to you and to thank them for their contribution to your lives.

The rehearsal dinner follows the rehearsal at the ceremony site and is usually hosted by the parents of the groom, although many couples pay for this themselves, too. The guest list should include the bridal party, parents of the bride and groom, and other close family members.

This gathering can be as formal or informal as you want it to be, anything from a pizza party to a sit down meal with waiters pouring wine. The traditional seating for a rehearsal dinner includes a U-shaped table with the bride and groom sitting at the head of the table, their parents arranged next to them in a way that emphasizes the blending of the families (mother of bride next to groom, father of groom next to bride). With so many families including stepparents and other significant people who don't necessarily fit into that formal seating arrangement, it has become common to dispense with formal seating arrangements. If out of town guests arrive in time for this gathering, they should also be invited.

The rehearsal dinner is an ideal time to distribute your attendant gifts or wedding day accessories.

Your rehearsal dinner can be held in an elegant private room at your favorite romantic restaurant...

Or a casual poolside party at your future in-laws' home. Choose the best expression of your entertaining style as a couple.

Cathleen & Chris

Chris's parents hosted the rehearsal BBQ. According to Cathleen, "There were a ton of people coming in from out of town and we wouldn't get to see them much, we wanted to spend time with them. And because they'd all be staying in the hotels we had reserved, we didn't want them to be bored. So instead of a traditional rehearsal dinner, Chris's parents rented a conference room and patio at the hotel and had a local supermarket provide all the food—prepared salads and meat for Chris's dad to BBQ. We invited all the out-of-town guests and very close family members, a total of 60 people, and had a wonderful time. It was very laid back, very casual. Just everyone gathering to eat and chat and have fun."

Post Wedding Brunches

ESPECIALLY IF YOU HAVE MANY out of town guests who will be leaving the morning after the wedding, you or your parents might want to host a post-wedding breakfast or brunch. If you've secured a block of rooms in a hotel and several of your guests are staying there, you can often simply ask that a gathering room or hospitality suite be set aside for your guests to participate in one final meal before everyone goes their separate ways. Most upscale hotels serve quite sumptuous breakfasts to their guests anyway, with every imaginable breakfast food and chefs taking orders for eggs and waffles. If most of your wedding guests are staying at the same hotel, this is certainly an option.

You might also opt to have your parents host a small breakfast at their house for out of town guests who are headed back home the following day. The bride and groom, depending on their honeymoon schedule and travel plans, may attend this event, but it's not necessary that they be there.

The brunch can be a casual, simple affair to say thank you and one last good bye to out of town friends and family.

Gifts: Giving and Getting

If instead of a gem, or even a flower, we should cast the gift of a loving thought into the heart of a friend, that would be giving as the angels give.

—George MacDonald

WEDDINGS MEAN GIFTS. There are the gifts you receive in the form of shower and wedding gifts, the ones you present to each other and to your attendants, and gratuities to the officiant, the musicians, and the caterers. Because the words "wedding gift," however, bring to mind mostly those white boxes tied with silver ribbon, the envelopes tucked discreetly in a decorative birdcage set up to receive them, and all the boxes and parcels that arrive on your doorstep in the days preceding and following your wedding, we'll talk first about how you should deal with the gifts you receive.

Because we get married at a later age than ever before in history and because we have established our own homes before taking this step, the tradition of gift giving is slowly undergoing a sea of change. Brides and grooms don't need nearly as much these days going into marriage as they did in past decades. Quite often, a couple already has an established household with plenty of dishes, sheets, towels, and maybe even a waffle iron if one of them is a good enough cook.

Whether you fly away to Europe for a two-week wedding tour of the Continent or spend a weekend in a mountain hideaway, you'll probably leave for some sort of wedding trip or honeymoon right after your ceremony. Be sure you ask someone to check your doorstep and mailbox while you're away. It's a simple matter to put a hold on your mail, of course, but with UPS, DHL, FedEx, and personal couriers of all sorts, it's a good idea to take steps to make sure nothing sits on your doorstep for a week or two, subject to rain, snow, sun, and thieves. Ask a friend to check every few days to make sure no packages are sitting beside the garage door advertising your absence to all sorts of rapscallions.

Gift Registries

NOT ONLY DO WE ALREADY OWN some of what we need to maintain our households, we just plain don't use the type of things that were once considered proper wedding gifts. No longer is it considered necessary to have four sets of monogrammed sheets and a full place setting for 12 of sterling silver. You can get along without those items that were once considered necessary items for the brand new household.

On the other hand, think of it this way: At what other time in your life are you going to take the trouble or go to the expense to buy the items needed to display in a china cabinet? Part of the traditional wedding experience is to choose a china pattern, a silver pattern, and crystal stemware. It will forever after be known as "your" pattern, and everyone who dines in your home will recognize it. Sure, it may only come out on special occasions, but special occasions need dinnerware just as much as everyday occasions. If you don't register for anything else, sign up for the dishes. You will be grateful some day that you did.

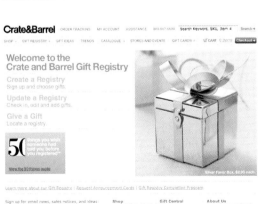

It is thoughtful to register at one or two nationwide or online gift registries. Your out-of-town guests will be able to choose from your list and have their gifts delivered.

If you just can't bring yourself to choose a silver pattern, you can always choose new ski boots.

An elegantly wrapped wedding gift.

Lisa & Chris

We originally said "no gifts." However, we learned that no matter what you say, most people will get you a gift anyway. So we gave in and registered...at REI. Figured we might as well get some stuff we like. We have plenty of toasters and dishes and sheets. We'd much rather get a new camping stove, tent, or bike pump!

Some couples are adamant about not receiving gifts, perhaps in the case of a second wedding or a more mature couple marrying after having households for decades, or as in the case of one recent wedding the couple is quite wealthy and simply do not want or need anything more. In these cases, an altruistic trend has emerged of setting up donations to be made to the couple's favorite charities. This trend allows guests to wish the couple well while helping a worthy cause.

One final note on registering for gifts: It is just a lot of fun to "shop," to admire items, to dream about duvet covers and tablecloths, whole sets of matching linens for the bed and bath, and beautiful crystal and china. Carrying a checklist around Williams-Sonoma, talking to the sales personnel about which wok would best serve your needs or which cookbook you want, browsing, and actually signing up for gifts...it's an exercise in consumer ecstasy that you should have at least once in your life. Enjoy this time together as a couple; many brides are pleasantly surprised by the enthusiasm their grooms show once they get into the spirit of selecting items for their wish list. Along with the dishes, linens, and crystal, be sure to include items that interest him whether it is camping gear, fishing poles, or even an iPod. You never know what someone will want to select for your gift. Give them choices. As you're doing it, though, be sure you make a concentrated effort to list gifts in all price ranges. List the lower priced items to give everyone a chance to get you a gift you really want; list the higher priced ones because some groups of friends, perhaps co-workers, will "go together" to buy one large gift.

Other Gifts

YOU WILL WANT TO GIVE your attendants a special gift to thank them for participating in this day with you. Be as generous as you can afford to be, and make this gift something they will treasure. The bride should present her bridesmaids with a personal gift, either at a bridesmaids' tea or brunch hosted by the bride or at the rehearsal dinner. Picture frames, make-up cases, an item of jewelry—a thoughtful item that will be a keepsake and a memento of your wedding is an appropriate gift. The gift to the maid or matron of honor can be identical or perhaps slightly different; for instance, if you give the bridesmaids a silver photograph frame, you might present a slightly larger one or even one in mother of pearl to the maid of honor.

The groom should gift his groomsmen in the same way, with something to remember the occasion: a money clip, cuff links, tie clip, wallet, or other such accessory. This can be presented at the grooms-men's outing or rehearsal dinner.

It seems almost redundant and has fallen out of practice in recent years, but in the past the bride and groom exchanged gifts on their wedding day. Perhaps because couples pay for at least a part of their own weddings now, this added budget item seems unnecessary to many brides and grooms. After all, the two will presumably be exchanging gifts from now on, and on their wedding day they just have many other details to be concerned with. If you decide to give each other gifts, a piece of jewelry or a watch would be appropriate.

This happy couple takes a private moment amidst all the hubbub to quietly exchange gifts.

Attendants are in a special class when it comes to giving wedding gifts. They are responsible for giving a gift to the couple as individuals, just like every other guest at the wedding, but there is a tradition of joining together to give a gift to the person they are preceding down the aisle—bridesmaids to the bride, groomsmen to the groom. This should be personal and useful and something that will be kept for many years as a memento of the day. Picture frames, serving trays, silver coffee service, or a special piece of china are appropriate for the bride; for the groom, a special tie tack or belt buckle is appropriate as a gift from his attendants.

Wedding Favors and Goody Bags

S MALL TOKEN GIFTS THAT ARE MEANT as a thank you to all the guests at your wedding are a recent addition to the reception, and your guests will be charmed by such thoughtfulness. You may set the gifts on a special "thank you" table or make them part of the place setting. It's another detail and another chance to add a decorative touch to your event.

Heather & Mark

Heather and Mark gave baby fir trees as wedding favors. Packaged in clear tubes, the trees were visible inside the wrapping. They tied ribbons around them in their wedding colors (the retailer had included personalized inserts that had their names and the date on them). They then personally passed them out to all our guests throughout the reception. That way, they were sure to personally thank each guest for coming.

Heather says, "It is so great to visit family and friends and see those trees now. I'm not sure how many actually got planted, but a few friends who could took the extras so they could plant their own personal forests somewhere. The one at my mom's is nearly six feet tall (and it was only about 6–8 inches tall on our wedding day). Plus, we felt like we were doing a great thing for our planet as well.

There are whole web sites devoted to items you can give your guests as a wedding favor...small gifts such as shot glasses, custom printed M&Ms candies in your wedding colors, boxes of chocolates or mints (again, in your own personal color scheme), and innumerable other items. This item is not necessary, and unless you are very careful to keep the cost down, it can contribute hundreds of dollars to your wedding budget. Make it thoughtful if you do it; in the price range of under $2 per item that is usually spent on favors, candy, small candles, or Christmas ornaments are most appropriate.

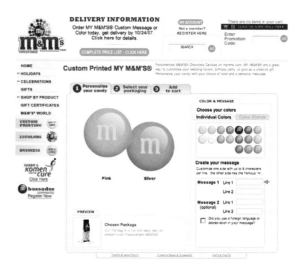

Color coordinated M&Ms printed with your wedding day message is a great favor idea.

Goody bags aren't just for children's birthday parties any more. Another custom that is gaining popularity is that of the hotel room goody bag for out of town wedding guests. What a truly thoughtful thing to do! This is another opportunity to incorporate your wedding colors or theme to demonstrate your eye for detail. The sky is the limit here, too. Include small packages of cookies, candy, chips, gum, bottled water, breath mints, aspirin, or even a bottle of your favorite wine and other snack items to help keep your guests entertained until it is time to start attending the festivities. T-shirts with your names and wedding date imprinted on them are a unique item you can include here, and if your out of town guests are bringing children, some crayons, coloring books, or puzzle books would be most welcome.

Why We Do That

To incorporate something that symbolized their heritage, Michael Douglas and Catherine Zeta-Jones gave their wedding guests love spoons; traditionally, a Welsh man presented a young woman with a love spoon as an invitation to begin courting. Love spoons have become symbols of love, and many believe that the term "spooning" comes from this Welsh tradition.

Courtesy Shutterstock © Ryan Lindberg

Guest favors arrayed on a table at the reception.

Legal Considerations

*Rituals are important.
Nowadays it's hip not to be
married. I'm not interested in
being hip.*

—John Lennon

GETTING MARRIED IS A LEGAL undertaking; you may do it in a church or synagogue; it may be a sacred ritual, a spiritual joining of two souls, a religious rite, or all of these; and, of course, your family, friends, and community will forever after look upon your relationship in a different way, but it is in government and business affairs that your new status will make a great difference to your everyday life. It's possible to live together as a couple, have children, go to work, shop, and have dinner with your neighbors without ever having made your arrangement legal. Goldie Hawn and Kurt Russell have pointedly chosen to conduct their lives without benefit of matrimony, and their household seems to work just fine. Then again, living together is not what sparked your interest in picking up this book; you want to know about planning your wedding and living together happily ever after.

You've probably already given some thought to whether you will change one or both of your surnames after the wedding, and of course, you have "apply for license" on the to do list in your three-ring binder, but there are several other legal and business things you'll need to tidy up. Nothing too onerous, but you do have some phone calls to make and forms to fill out that don't involve caterers and photographers. You may find yourself sitting "on hold" on the phone while your credit card company transfers you to one person after another before you find the one who can send the form you need to fill out or tell you what legal papers you'll need to fax to them. And then there's the matter of the name....

This bride most certainly took her husband's name as her own; brides today have more choices than she did.

Who would have thought it would take so much paperwork to get to this day?

License to Marry

CHECK WITH LOCAL AND STATE authorities well ahead of time to find out what is necessary to obtain a marriage license. Some states require a blood test, some a waiting period of three days from the time the license is issued until the ceremony can take place. Others, known as quickie states, allow you to marry as soon as the license is issued. Just make sure you mark this errand in bold and circle it in red on your list of things to do. Life can get hectic just prior to your wedding day, and this is one matter of paramount importance that could be easily overlooked. And you usually both have to appear in person, with plenty of identification and records of prior marriages and divorces; it's not often that an application can be "mailed in." Go online or call ahead to verify what is required at your local courthouse. Many do not accept checks or credit cards, so be prepared with cash for the fee. Make a date to meet your fiance' at the courthouse and then enjoy a leisurely lunch reveling in the fact that you are almost "official." You may want to bring your camera along and ask a helpful clerk to snap your photo as you fill out your paperwork to recreate your own version of the famous Norman Rockwell painting titled "The Marriage License."

Ask the pastor, priest, or rabbi who will be performing your ceremony for advice. He or she will be familiar with the requirements of your city and state. It can vary according to which city you live in, too. New York City, for instance, has marriage laws that differ from the rest of the state.

Same sex couples continue to fight for their right to be legally wed. Many of them are in more stable relationships than some of the married couples we all know, so it seems as if the state should really have no objection. But, of course, it does. The story of Jackie and Joni is a story of two people united in love to form a family, complete with five children and a puppy. They were legally wed during one of those "windows of opportunity" that arose in Massachusetts in 2004.

Jackie & Joni

Joni tells us: "We had our wedding on a beach in Provincetown with our children and some family and friends in attendance. Some of our guests traveled from Canada, Illinois, and Texas. Jackie and I wore linen slacks and sandals and short sleeve blouses. All of our guests stayed at a B & B in Provincetown, and we had a small catered reception the night before our ceremony. We also invited two other guests at the B & B to join us since they would be there and we practically took over the entire B & B with our wedding party. The day of the ceremony, our Reverend Brenda set up the beach with beautiful flowers. All of our guests walked down to the beach (down the street from the B & B) ahead of Jackie and me and were waiting for us as we walked down the street hand in hand. We had Shania Twain's "From This Moment" playing. Our guests snapped pictures, and there were some tears shed. I had my three sisters there with their husbands and two of my nieces. Jackie's brother was there with his wife. Our three older daughters were there (Colleen, Sarah, and Kelly) and our puppy Chester. We decided for our two youngest children to share it through photos and explanation later. There were also some of Jackie's and my dearest friends.

Our daughters said a few words about how they felt about our marriage and the coming together of our family. They spoke of how their lives have changed since I entered the picture; I was so moved by their sincerity. Our daughter Colleen read the *Bible* passage from the *Book of Ruth*: "Where thou goest, I will go." We found it to be very fitting and appropriate for our ceremony. Jackie and I each wrote our own vows that we said to each other. My family later told me how moved they were by our own words being used in our ceremony. They commented on how beautiful it was and how different from other weddings they had ever attended. Their participation and attendance imprinted the legitimacy and sincerity of our union in all of their minds.

After the ceremony, we walked down the street to a local restaurant and had a wedding dinner with all of our guests, complete with a champagne toast as Jackie and I walked in. We had a beautiful dinner. Our two other guests from the B & B that we invited to our reception the previous night also attended our ceremony and we invited them to join us for dinner. Their names were Matt and John, but we dubbed them our Wedding Crashers. They were such great guys and got along great with everyone and had a great time. We still keep in touch, and they said it made their first trip to Provincetown tough to top. After dinner, we had music and a little dancing. Jackie and I danced our first dance to Joshua Kadison's "Beautiful in My Eyes." It was a beautiful and memorable day spent with all the people we love.

Changing Your Name

TRADITION, OF COURSE, dictates that the bride change her surname to her new husband's surname. Of course, that has changed quite a bit in recent years, and now the sky's the limit. Some women choose to drop their middle name, use their maiden name as their middle name, and take their husband's surname; others hyphenate their maiden and married names, and then some couples opt to both use the hypenated combination. We have "the artist formerly known as Prince," who simply had no name for a while. Of course, he still has a legal name. It's the one he uses to report his earnings to the social security administration. You now have the opportunity to change your legal name if you want to; or you can choose not to change it. If you do change it, you'll need to notify a few people and organizations.

Why We Do That

The idea of a woman keeping her maiden name after marriage arose during the social reforms of the 1960s and '70s. It's a modern concept, right?

Wrong. Amelia Bloomer, the woman who was instrumental in getting us all out of corsets and into...bloomers, and her husband Dexter were among early feminist reformers who argued for changing some of the traditions of marriage, such as the woman taking the man's name. Amelia, it happens, did take Dexter's last name, but she argued in her writings for the right not to. She actually was known as Amelia Jenks Bloomer, incorporating both of their names into her own.

By the way, Amelia didn't invent bloomers, but she did wear them, and she advocated for the change in fashion in her newspaper *The Lily*, the first publication by and for women in America. It was Fanny Wright who invented the bloomer costume. Fanny also bought slaves, freed them, and gave them land to live on, and was an advocate of free love and even more shocking concepts that included socialism and interracial marriage. In the 19th Century, these women, along with the more well known Elizabeth Cady Stanton and Susan B. Anthony, argued for women's rights in and out of marriage... and many other civil rights.

In the 1850s when a woman married, her legal existence was absorbed by her husband. She, in effect, became him. When Lucy Stone married Henry Blackwell in 1855, however, they both signed an agreement which stated that she did not give up her freedom and that she did not have to obey him, as the marriage vows at that time required. Among other things, she retained the right to the "profits of her own industry" (she got to keep any money she made if she worked).

If you decide to change your name when you marry, you must notify your employer and the Social Security Administration. Go to the Social Security web site at www.ssa.gov to find out how to go about this. Of course, if you both change your names to a hyphenated or combined version of your two previous names, you will both need to notify Social Security and your employers.

Find the information you need to change your name and request a new social security card at www.ssa.gov.

Why We Do That

Two women living together in a marriage relationship is another 20th Century development. Same sex couples are able to live together openly now in ways that were not thought possible only 50 years ago. Of course, we all know that is true, right? Wrong again. In a relationship referred to as a *Boston marriage*, a term derived from the novel *The Bostonians* by Henry James, two unmarried women were able to share a household in the mid-19th Century as if they were marriage partners. It is unclear whether these "marriages" involved a sexual relationship or not—probably some did and others were merely arrangements of convenience. After all, it would have been impossible for a single woman to live alone during that era; she needed the protection of a man. By sharing a home, two women dispensed with the need for marriage to a man altogether.

Insurance

YOU'LL NEED TO CONSULT WITH your insurance agent and with the Human Resources departments where you both work to find out what sort of insurance you are eligible for as a married couple. Most companies have an open enrollment period during which their employees can sign up for health insurance. If you don't do it during that enrollment period, the only circumstances under which you can add a new person for coverage is if you are married or a child is born or adopted into your family. Under those circumstances, however, you have a limited amount of time during which you can notify your employer of the need for coverage for a new person. Do not let that deadline slip by. Inquire about this well ahead of time. If you miss the deadline, you will have to wait until the next open enrollment period.

Do some comparison shopping. If one of your employers offers free insurance to a spouse and one charges a monthly fee for it, that might be the best deal. But check the coverage itself. What are the co-payments? Think before you leap at the most obvious choice. It may not be the best choice.

Life insurance is another concern. As a married couple, you have new responsibilities to another person and benefits to offer each other. Now is the best time to address those issues. Set up an appointment with your insurance agent to go over your options soon after you return from your honeymoon. Or even before the wedding date. You'll come away with lots to think about and plan for. Retirement planning is about to get much more important to you, too, because you do want to be able to spend your golden years together living at a leisurely pace, not scratching for pennies and eating canned tuna three times a week.

You will also want to take a look at your life insurance policies. Getting married usually means you will want to change the beneficiaries. You probably had named a parent or sibling originally, but now it's time to make your spouse the recipient of all your worldly goods, including benefits from life insurance policies. Unless, of course, you have children from a previous relationship. In that case, you will need to make necessary arrangements to maintain their rightful portion of your insurance as well as any other assets. If you have a will, you will need to rewrite that too. And if you don't have one, now is a really good time to consider getting that set up too, especially if either of you is coming into the marriage with children. Marriage laws are different in each state, so don't assume that your wishes will be automatically carried out if you do not have a valid will in place.

And, finally, be sure to also notify your car insurance agent of your new status. As a couple, you might qualify for better rates. Married men nearly always have lower premiums than single men. In fact, you might be about to do several things that could affect your insurance rates. If one of you is moving from your urban loft apartment to live in the house the other one owns in the suburbs, call your insurance agent. You are most likely moving to a neighborhood with lower insurance rates. Auto insurance providers are very well informed about crime rates and statistics, and they base their rates on the likelihood that your car will be stolen or damaged. Parking it in a suburban garage makes you much less of a risk than parking it on a busy city street every night. Where you live matters. Being a married person matters. Age matters. Check with the car insurance provider whenever your address or marital status changes.

Checking Accounts, Credit Cards, and Taxes

NOW IS A GOOD TIME to shop for a new bank or to open a joint checking account. Banks have many rules and regulations for adding someone to an account. You should pay a visit to your bank, sit down and discuss your upcoming change of status with an officer of the bank, and then decide what you want to do.

Notify everyone you do business with of your name change, including credit card companies.

There are as many ways of handling finances as there are couples. If one of you loves numbers and is highly organized and the other can't seem to even find the checkbook (or the phone bill), you should probably have a joint checking account and put the accountant in charge of the checkbook. Let one person maintain it, but the other should always be closely involved so that there are no misunderstandings about money. If you are both comfortable with maintaining your separate bank accounts and you've been cohabiting for a while doing just that, there's little need to change how you handle your accounts, although you still will need to notify the bank of any name changes.

One big advantage to being married, of course, is the joint tax return. Just for fun, figure your taxes as if you were single. Then figure them jointly. Then, even try figuring them "married, filing separately." You'll most likely be pleasantly surprised by the results of the joint filing status you're now eligible for. Again, talk to your human resources adviser at work. You may need to change the number of dependents you claim and give yourself a slight weekly raise.

Check out this page at the IRS web site:
Tips for Newly Married or Divorced Taxpayers.

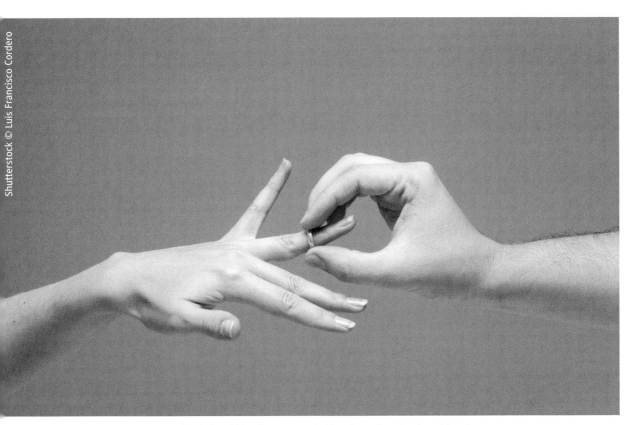

That little gold band is accompanied by a host of new legal considerations.

Planning the Honeymoon

*Love is not affectionate feeling,
but a steady wish for the loved
person's ultimate good as far as
it can be obtained.*

—C. S. Lewis

PLANNING YOUR HONEYMOON started several months prior to the wedding day, of course. It started when you first began to plan a budget for your wedding and decide just how much you had to spend on this once-in-a-lifetime event. So you should know well ahead of time approximately how much you'll have to spend on this trip that will be the beginning of your life together.

Even if you know you both have to be back at work Monday morning and there's only time for a weekend away, you should plan now to make that weekend a special one. Your honeymoon, just like your wedding, is all about the two of you, your personalities, and things you have in common. It may be the first time you compromise on something as big as a vacation. So many big changes in such a short time! Surely you deserve some time to relax and just enjoy each other, and that is what the honeymoon is for. The honeymoon is a time at the beginning of a marriage for learning about each other, spending time together, and not being interrupted by any outside concerns. By definition, it should last a month. Realistically, you're very lucky if you get two weeks in a resort. Whatever the amount of time, the intent remains the same— to learn about each other, to spend time together, and to indulge yourselves in such luxuries as breakfast in bed. It may well be the last time you are able to put so much effort into pleasing each other without outside interruptions.

If you both enjoy golf, a week at a golf resort might be exactly right for you; just be sure to schedule some time off the course as well.

Talk about what this trip means to both of you. Come to an agreement on where you'll go and what you'll do, but remember: it's a time for being alone together. Don't take your dog with you; leave your children with their grandmother or a favorite aunt; and limit the phone calls. This is meant to be alone time, couple time. You'll be caught up soon enough in the busyness of life. Use the honeymoon as it was intended, to make sure your marriage gets off to a good start, a strong bonding between the two of you.

This tranquil waterfall is a perfect place to spend an afternoon alone.

If you are leaving the country, begin early to make sure your passport is updated and you have any required visas. If your destination requires inoculations of any kind, make sure you take care of that well before the wedding. Shots can make you sore, leave you bruised, or cause other adverse reactions, so you want to get them out of the way a few weeks before the wedding.

Tell the hotel clerk, resort representative, or travel agent that this is your honeymoon. They may have special suggestions or offer a special room at a special rate. Tell everyone you encounter that it is your honeymoon. As the saying goes, everyone loves lovers. Restaurant hosts may seat you at waterside tables. Waiters may bring you a complementary drink or dessert. Even flight attendants get into the spirit and, if space is available and you are not traveling with 20 other honeymooners to a popular destination, they may bump you up to first class for the trip. Of course, it is in bad taste to expect preferential treatment, but it doesn't hurt to let people know so they can share in your joy if they wish to.

Your honeymoon can be an adventurous trek to foreign shores if you are the intrepid types. You have a lifetime of travel and fun together to look forward to.

Why We Do That

Early in the history of English society, people began their married life at a much younger age; girls particularly were plucked from their home to be wedded to wealthy merchants and landowners. Not an eyebrow was raised when a dashing young knight in his 20s, or even 30s, was married to a barely-in-her-teens girl child or when two teenagers became husband and wife. Of course, girls of that age were not very well prepared for marriage despite the best efforts of their older female relatives who tried to educate them; in many cases, the boy wasn't either. But married they were, and custom dictated that they begin reproducing right away.

The time allowed for them both to be "trained" in their new duties was one month, or a *moon*, in the parlance of the day. It was customary for the couple to spend this time alone and to spend it partaking of a sweet wine called mead. It was sweet because it was made from honey. And so this period of time, this month at the outset of a marriage, become known as the *honey moon*. Basically, the couple used that honey wine to get a buzz that helped them overcome their shyness about going to bed together for the first time.

Maybe this explains part of why we tell youngsters about "the birds and the bees." At least it explains the bee part.

Destination Wedding and Honeymoon

O F COURSE, IF YOU'RE PLANNING a destination wedding, you will presumably already be in a vacation spot. Your family and friends will be there too, and of course, you'll want to spend time with them. Still, the time after the wedding will be a time reserved for the two of you to spend alone, perhaps continuing your vacation at the site of the wedding, perhaps traveling on to another vacation spot.

You have been on many trips before, ski trips with friends, family vacations and road trips to Aunt Margaret's house, and no doubt you had a great time with your buddies or your brothers and sisters on those trips. But this trip has a purpose. Plan to do some fun things together, but also plan some down time, days when you sit together and stare at the fire, read the newspaper in bed together after ordering room service, or just sit on the porch of your cabin and stare out at the lake. Getting married is a big deal, and you'll need time to come down from all the excitement. You should not make plans to hit the golf course or the hiking trail every morning...although the beach isn't a bad idea.

Time alone is what matters, whether it be camping in the mountains or a private villa in Greece.

Jennifer & Ryan

Jennifer and Ryan had a destination wedding in Maui. Jennifer says:

"We wanted the wedding to feel like a big family vacation and since we were already in Maui, it was the perfect setting. We arranged for everyone to arrive a week before the actual wedding so we could spend time as a group and with designated families. I consider that entire week to be a pre-wedding event."

At the end of the reception, Jennifer and Ryan took a limo back to the hotel where they met everyone outside to continue celebrating and visiting. Plan to do what feels right to you both on your honeymoon. Don't leave your guests until you are ready, especially if they all traveled far to be at your wedding; the event will be over soon, and then your honeymoon will begin.

Courtesy Shutterstock © trialartinfo

Swinging in this hammock overlooking a deserted section of Pacific Ocean beach is a perfect honeymoon plan.

Leave some time every day for relaxing together. Now is the time for long talks about your future.

Part IV

The Wedding Day

YOU'RE ALMOST READY FOR THE CHURCH *bells to chime. This is where all the organization and delegation, the planning and dreaming, come together. Most of the topics we've discussed so far involved the supporting characters in this show business event that is your perfect wedding: caterers, photographers, wedding planners, and florists, all aimed at getting the church or synagogue and the reception hall beautifully ready to delight the senses of your guests. We've discussed inviting those guests, registering for gifts, and throwing the biggest party of your lifetime (and a few smaller parties). Now it's time to talk about the two people most central to this undertaking: the bride and groom.*

It's time to think about what you'll be doing on the day of your wedding and what you can do beforehand to prepare for those tasks; if you think about it, what you really need to do is learn how to put on a good show. Throughout the whole process, don't stop thinking about the vows you'll be taking; consider what they mean, and prepare yourselves for a lifetime of shared living. In short, now that everything is ready, the cake is ordered, and the flower petals are about to be strewn in your path, it's time to talk about the core of the matter—getting and staying married.

Getting Ready for the Big Day

Practice means to perform, over and over again in the face of all obstacles, some act of vision, of faith, of desire. Practice is a means of inviting the perfection desired.

—Martha Graham

WEDDING PLANNING IS something of a long term project. With the average length of engagement in the United States being 17 months, you have plenty of time to get yourselves in shape for the big event. Think about the things that will be central to the big day and the impression you'll make. You'll be smiling and dancing, and you'll need to be gracious and hospitable to all your guests, of course; you'll need to look good doing it all because you'll be followed by at least two people carrying a camera and spotlight throughout the entire day, from the moment you walk into the church with your hair in curlers, carrying your Starbucks cup, until you hop in the fairy tale carriage about 8 hours later to be carried off to "happily ever after" land. By the time this day ends, you'll feel much more sympathetic toward celebrities, who are followed everywhere by *paparazzi*.

All your life, trips to the dentist, the hair stylist, the gym, and the dermatologist have been leading up to this day when you are going to shine for all to see. Perhaps I overstate the purpose of those cosmetic efforts of a lifetime, but not by much. On this day of all days, you need to look really good, be really graceful, and smile no matter how much you want to sit down, kick off your shoes, and rest for a few minutes.

Queen Elizabeth, never considered to be a natural beauty, taught us that all brides are beautiful. All brides and grooms can be gorgeous on the day of their wedding. It helps to do a little cosmetic and fitness work ahead of time though. We must assume that Queen Elizabeth, due to her place in society, was trained in all the social arts. Perhaps you have been, too; then again, if you've been busy learning about nuclear medicine or elementary education and have overlooked a few of life's necessities, such as cutting a fine figure on the dance floor or even shaping up your eyebrows, this is your opportunity. In fact, it is your responsibility to prepare yourselves to be the stars of your own show.

Courtesy Tiffany Webster Larsen and Chad Larsen
© www.aaronlockwoodphotography.com

Looking this well groomed did not just begin this morning.

Preparing Yourself for the Event of a Lifetime

COSMETIC SURGERY, teeth straightening, and massive weight loss are growing in popularity. Everyone has dreams (or nightmares) about being the star of one of those reality shows, like *The Biggest Loser* or *The Swan*, where you undergo radical physical change. If you are considering something along the lines of gastric bypass or nose straightening, you need to start the process long before you begin the wedding planning. If this sort of body change is important to you, it's probably not the best time to be planning a wedding anyway. Engagement periods have no official time period, so if you think you really need rhinoplasty and an eyebrow lift, call *Dr. 90210* first—then start your wedding planning. In fact, if it's important to you to finish your master's degree or spend a year as a missionary before marriage, knock out those major life goals and then get back to me. Life is a growth process, growth is sometimes painful, and you want to be in the midst of only one or two all consuming life changes at once.

You may be thinking you want to lose 50 pounds or have a breast reduction or liposuction so that you will look your best as you walk down the aisle or wait at the altar. You'll want to get anything surgical done well before the wedding date so that you have plenty of time to recover and so that friends, co-workers, and acquaintances have a chance to get used to the "new" you on an everyday basis before they are overwhelmed by the new you in a wedding gown or tux and a Hollywood make-up job with your hair in an unaccustomed up "do." Someone who doesn't see you every day might start checking his invitation to make sure he's at the right ceremony!

Everything works: hair, teeth, skin, all beautiful.

Courtesy Shutterstock © 273472S246

If what you have in mind is more along the lines of some dermabrasion, the removal of a few skin tags or moles, teeth whitening, or even losing up to 20 pounds, you can probably fit those in your wedding planning schedule. You should do any minor surgical procedures early on to give yourself time to heal completely. Cosmetic surgery often takes a few weeks or months to totally heal, so get that out of the way first. Teeth whitening isn't permanent, no matter what they say, so you want to time those types of procedures just a couple of months before the wedding so the effects haven't worn off.

Porcelain veneers are permanent, but they can cost from $500 to $2,000 per tooth. It takes about two to three weeks to complete the process, so allow time if you decide on—and can afford—this option. Of course, getting your teeth cleaned is also important, so make sure that's been done in the month or two before the wedding as well.

Under no circumstances should you buy a wedding dress that is two sizes too small for your current size and plan to lose enough weight so that you will fit into it by your wedding day! Plan to lose weight if you want, but please, do not count on it. Many things can happen, especially during the frenetic period of engagement and wedding planning, that will keep you from that goal.

Alterations work like this: It's easy to decrease the size of an article of clothing; it is virtually impossible to increase it. So shop for the dress, buy it in the size that fits you at the time of purchase, then continue your weight loss efforts. If you lose the desired amount, that's great! The dress can be altered. If you don't reach your goal, the dress still fits! It's a win-win situation. But if you buy a size 6 when you wear a size 12 and plan to lose the weight required to let you fit into that dress before the wedding— well, what if you don't? It's very difficult to add even a few inches to a dress. And you don't want to end up with two wedding dresses—it's not the sort of thing you'll be wearing again someday.

If you've considered doing some cosmetic dentistry or teeth straightening, start that immediately. Teeth straightening takes time, sometimes years, but the sooner you start, the better you'll look in your wedding photos. Ask your dentist about invisible braces if you think you'll still be wearing them in your wedding pictures. They aren't totally invisible, but they almost are. Recovery time from dental surgery takes some time too, and you don't want to be in pain or still not at your best from that on the wedding day. Get these kinds of things done early and get them over with. This is also the time to begin scheduling regular facials—for relaxation as well as to ward off any stress-induced break outs. You should also begin any waxing you or your fiancé may need for the honeymoon—think bikini area and possibly his back if that's your thing.

Pre-Marital Counseling

Counseling may not show in your wedding photos, but it will certainly have an effect on your life together. It really should be at the top of your list of things to do before the wedding. Some churches, or even individual clergymen, require pre-marital counseling for everyone whose weddings they perform. Given the current divorce rate in this country, that's not a bad idea. Even if your officiant does not require it, you should plan to do this for yourselves. You are doing much planning and work to put together an event that will last a day, possibly a weekend. But that event is only the beginning of your lives together. Try to set aside a few hours for an appointment with a couples counselor or spiritual guide just to talk about the purpose of this day. Some religious organizations or spiritual groups offer couples counseling at weekend retreats tailored for couples contemplating marriage. This can be an excellent chance to gather your wits and calm yourselves before you jump back in to the whirlwind of pre-wedding chores and decisions.

The cost for this service can range from free if it is provided by your church or synagogue to about $80 an hour for a certified social worker, $400 for a weekend getaway at a cozy B&B type retreat, or all the way up to $2,000 for a five-day intensive couple-focused spa and retreat with planned exercises in learning how to handle the formidable job of *being* married for the rest of your lives after you've finished the all-consuming months-long job of *getting* married. You should do as much as you can afford; consider it taking out divorce insurance. Some states even give you a discount on your license if you participate in pre-marital counseling.

Dancing Lessons

Even if you are a sought after dance partner in all the clubs you frequent, chances are what you do there is not the same sort of dancing that will be required of you on your wedding day. Hip-hop, boogie, and country line dances are certainly likely to be aspects of the dancing at your reception, but before the crowd hits the dance floor, you're going to have to participate in some special dances. There is an order of events at the reception. Your photographer and the catering director or your wedding planner will, no doubt, guide you through them. Let me just tell you now though: there will be a spotlight. It will be on just the two of you for a good three minutes, and you will be dancing alone to a waltz or some sort of sweeping ballroom type of dance.

Picture yourself being the center of attention and being comfortable about it. Picture yourself sweeping around the dance floor, just the two of you, looking and feeling relaxed and professional. How can you get to that point? Practice. Practice and a few dance lessons. Some dance studios give free introductory lessons, and many offer packages. Please, for your own comfort, if you are not already a practiced ballroom dancer, take a few lessons. You will be so proud of yourselves.

The spotlight is on you!

Courtesy Shutterstock © Matt Antonino

After the two of you perform to "your song" on the dance floor, the DJ or bandleader will invite some others to join you. First, the groom is joined by his mother and the bride by her father, and the dancing continues. This, too, is a special spotlighted dance. If you think your parents will be uncomfortable or unpracticed, take them along for your dance lessons. Or take the time to teach them what you've learned. Going out dancing with your parents could be another fun excursion as you prepare for your wedding.

Hair Styles

Have you always dreamed of an up "do" for your hair on your wedding day, a perfect style that shows off your veil, your hairpiece, and your beautifully made up face? Always dreamed of it, but you currently have a nice bob or shorter style? Get started working with your hair stylist right away. Tell him what your goal is. You still have some time to grow some hair—and it's much easier to do than losing 20 pounds. Even if you don't manage to grow it out in time, there are extensions, weaves, and all sorts of ways to give yourself just the look you want.

Start working with your hair stylist months ahead of time to achieve the look you want. If experimentation is needed, start early so that you can settle on a look and work to attain it. Don't forget highlights or color; those too may need some experimentation to get just right.

Practice your wedding day hairstyle before the day; it will make getting ready much less stressful.

Every ringlet is in place to show off this beautiful Victorian hairpiece.

Toning Your Body

Of course, another place you should be visiting on a regular basis anyway is the gym, but if you haven't been doing that regularly, the time of your engagement is the time to start. A good fitness routine not only makes you look good in your clothes, it also improves your posture and skin tone, and it puts a sparkle in your eyes. It is much more beneficial than cosmetic surgery to make you a picture perfect bride. Nothing is more beautiful than health. Work out. Eat right. Get plenty of sleep. Now is the time to turn over a new leaf. It will make a difference in how you look and feel on your wedding day.

You may want to visit a tanning salon for a spray tan to achieve a golden glow without skin damage or a nasty burn before the wedding. After all, wouldn't a nice tan show off your beautiful new whitened teeth and perfect hair? Just remember two things. Don't over do it, and don't over do it. Some tan is good, especially if you are very pale. Too much tan looks like you're trying too hard. Don't do it at all when your wedding is less than two weeks away. Experiment several weeks in advance to find your preferred depth of tan. Some brides like a slight glow while others prefer a more bronze look. Make absolutely certain that your tanning salon's spray tan formula does not rub off on clothing when you perspire! Your white wedding gown is not the place to discover this nasty result of some tanning formulas.

About a week before the wedding, try to work in some relaxing times for just the two of you. Massages, an overnight trip, or just a private cuddle with a good movie and a bowl of popcorn can work wonders for your stress level after all the details you've been keeping track of. Things should be starting to come together now, so an evening of non-wedding-centered activities is an excellent idea for decompression and stress relief.

A healthy, happy, beautiful bride.

Courtesy Priscilla Webster Mellette © Cameron H Photography

The Day Before the Wedding

THIS IS AN EXCITING TIME, a time of final preparations. There are unbelievable numbers of errands to run and stress-inducing problems coming at you from all directions. The word of the day is delegate. If you have a professional wedding planner, he should have your life under control. If you don't have a professional, nothing beats a reliable, highly organized friend, your mother, and your maid of honor. If you're lucky, you'll have many assistants you can depend upon.

With so many helpers and willing hands, you should be able to take the day before your wedding to prepare yourself for your big event. Schedule this as a spa day with your bridesmaids. Get a manicure, a pedicure, and a relaxing massage. Of course, you have been working on your make-up plan for weeks now. Start early in the day, then take a nap before the rehearsal dinner so you'll be fresh and rested before the excitement begins.

Put a friend in charge of getting any necessary items to the rehearsal dinner. These might include:

Stereo and CDs or preloaded iPod (if needed for appropriate background music)

Camera and extra film (presumably you won't have a professional photographer at the rehearsal or the rehearsal dinner)

Toasting glasses

Attendant gifts (if you didn't present them on an earlier occasion)

Flowers, candles, or other centerpieces if not included by the caterer

Place cards and menu cards if you have them

Kudos to the behind-the-scenes event manager this bride was lucky enough to have. A PR professional and graphic designer by trade, this close friend made invaluable contributions from designing the save the date cards and wedding programs to overseeing the set up and sequence of events at the reception so the bride could enjoy her day.

Make a note also to be sure these items are gathered and brought back home. Make sure there is gas in any vehicles you will be using tomorrow.

Go to the rehearsal, pay attention, make sure all your attendants and all participants in the ceremony pay attention and everyone knows his part. This is truly a rehearsal, not a social occasion. Then go to the rehearsal dinner, relax, and enjoy your friends and family. Have a drink. Have two. But no more than that. You should feel free to leave the party early and go home to continue your preparations for the big day tomorrow and try to relax and get a bit of sleep. Rest is the keyword of the day today.

The Morning of the Wedding

EAT A LIGHT BREAKFAST before you leave for the ceremony. If you aren't hungry at all, nibble on a cracker or two and sip some juice. Don't forget your morning coffee or soft drink if that's a routine for you. Have some light snacks available in the dressing rooms, bagels, fruit, even a Danish. After you know all the details are handled and every person and thing is in place for the ceremony to begin, you might suddenly experience that delayed hunger. Make sure you eat something, even just a few bites; the last thing you want is to stand at the altar and hear a rumble coming from your stomach as it reacts to a lack of food.

If you plan to get dressed at the ceremony site, have a list of essential items to take with you to the ceremony. This will include the obvious, necessary items for dressing:

Foundation garments (bra, underwear, slip, pantyhose)

Dress (okay, you probably don't have to have this on a list, but why not—every item you will need for the ceremony should be on this list)

Accessories (gloves, fans, hair pieces, jewelry)

Veil

Shoes

Bouquets (keep these refrigerated as long as possible)

Plan to get to the ceremony at least half an hour before you know you need to be there. Allow for traffic and forgotten items and anything that might go wrong.

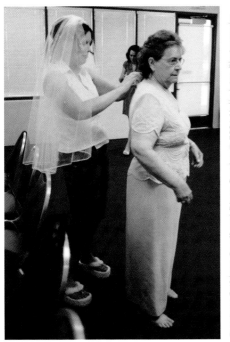

The bride may not be the only one who needs a helping hand getting dressed today.

No detail is too small to be overlooked on your wedding day. A makeup diagram is a wonderful guide.

Put together an emergency kit for the bride and bridesmaids, but entrust it to a good friend to bring to the ceremony. Here's a sample of such a list from one of our brides:

Emergency Bag Checklist

Health

Tums

Benadryl (good for hives that can result from nerves and is a mild anxiety reliever)

Prescription drugs

Nasal spray

Eye drops

Smelling salts

Breath spray/mints

Advil

Band-Aids

Hard candy

Tampons, pads, and liners

Beauty/Grooming

Hand lotion

Handi-wipes

Kleenex

Make-up

    Lipstick

    Mascara

    Eyelash curler

    Blush

    Powder

    Eyeliner

    Eye makeup remover with cotton pads and Q-tips

Baby powder (works great for spills on your white dress—just dab with water and then sprinkle with powder)

Lint remover (can be used to remove makeup from tuxes)

Deodorant

Perfume

Nail polish in shade worn

Nail polish remover

Nail file

Nail clippers

Clear nail polish for runs in pantyhose

Small hand towel (put these around your neck while doing your makeup to avoid stains)

Hair dryer (for hair but also dries clothing after stain removal)

Hair gel

Hairspray (good for runs in pantyhose, too)

Hair brush

Water mister

Barrettes and bobby pins

Hand mirrors

Toothbrush and toothpaste

Attire

Extra earring backs

Emergency buttons (for tuxes)

Collar extenders (for tuxes)

Flat shoes

Iron

Pantyhose (extras just in case)

Safety pins

Sewing kit with thread in color of bridesmaids' dresses, white, and black

Duct tape or sewing tape for last minute ripped hems

Black electrical tape for emergency repairs to tuxes

Miscellaneous

Directions to reception—bring extra copies

Phone numbers of all vendors (bring your three-ring binder) and the important people responsible for helping get everyone where they need to be on time

Cell phone (don't forget to charge it the night before)

Cooler containing:

Juice

Sodas (include club soda for stain removal)

Champagne

Crackers

Cups

Here are some chores you can hand over to a trusted friend:

Call ahead to the reception site to tell them you're on your way

Pay clergy and organist

And then it's time to get ready to march down the aisle.

Let's go, girls!

After you have your hair and makeup done, after you put on every article of underwear you will be wearing, just before you don the dress, the veil, the train, and other finishing touches—go to the bathroom. Go whether you need to go or not. As soon as you get completely dressed, when you're standing there waiting, unable to sit for fear of wrinkling your dress, ready for the walk of a lifetime—you are going to suddenly "have to go." Try to head that one simple bodily emergency off. Go before you finish dressing.

You might need some assistance getting into position to begin the march.

The Ceremony

*Marriage is the perfection of
what love aimed at, ignorant
of what it sought.*

—Ralph Waldo Emerson

T HE MUSIC—USUALLY PIANO, organ, or violin, but sometimes a three-piece string ensemble—is quietly playing in the background. Everyone is seated. The groom and his best man enter from a side door and stand patiently at the altar. The bride is poised on the arm of her escort.

If it's a Jewish ceremony, everyone enters in the procession together, including all parents and grandparents; no one has to stand waiting at the altar. The groom enters ahead of the bride, escorted by both his parents. The bride follows last, making her entrance escorted by both her parents. Music accompanies every step of any wedding, and the choice of what you play at your wedding is entirely up to you. You can use music to honor your heritage, your religious beliefs, and simply your taste in music. Some whimsy is appropriate, and so is a lot of tradition.

It's considered traditional for a bride to be escorted down the aisle by her father, but that's only one option. You may be escorted by both parents, by your mother, your stepfather, or any other significant person in your life. Some brides even choose to make the trip alone because they feel they've gotten to this point on their own. Some couples, especially if they have dated or lived together for several years, prefer to walk down the aisle together to symbolize their mutual decision to marry. If tradition works for you, that's great, but if you want to change things a bit and walk down the aisle with another male family member, a female family member, or one or two of each, that is perfectly acceptable. It's what makes this *your* perfect wedding.

This bride chose to walk down the aisle accompanied by her mother.

Music for the Ceremony

MUSIC IS PERSONAL AND IT SPEAKS to people at a level words cannot often reach. You've probably given plenty of thought to "your song" and what you'd like the music to be for your first dance. Consider also what you want to hear playing in the background as your guests are seated and as you take your places at the altar.

> If you are not familiar with the music listed here, you can go to www.amazon.com, do a search for wedding music, and click on any album that strikes your fancy. Then click on Listen to Samples beneath the album cover that appears on the left of your screen. You have probably heard most of this music many times—you just never knew each piece had a name!

Some of the music that might be playing while your guests wait during a Christian ceremony:

Arioso	Bach
Gavotte	Bach
Jesu, Joy of Man's Desiring	Bach
O' Perfect Love	Barnby
Selections from *Fiddler on the Roof*	Bock
Polovetsian Dances	Borodin
Ode to Joy	Beethoven
Trumpet Voluntary	Clarke

Oh, Promise Me	Dekoven
Love's Greeting	Elgar
I Love Thee	Grieg
Water Music	Handel
Royal Fireworks Music	Handel
Liebestraum	Liszt
Wedding March	Mendelssohn
Kanon	Pachelbel
Trumpet Tune	Purcell
Ave Maria	Schubert
Love Theme from *Romeo and Juliet*	Tschaikovsky
Bridal Chorus	Wagner
Danny Boy	Weatherly
Selections from *Phantom of the Opera*	A.L. Webber

Some of the music often played during a Jewish ceremony includes:

Hevenu Shalom Aleichem	Dodi Li
Erev Shel Shoshanim	Hava Nagila
Erev Ba	Sunrise, Sunset
Hana' Ava Babanot	Jerusalem of Gold
To Life	Miserlou
Patch Tanz	Bei Mir Bistu Shein
Ose Shalom	Mazel Tov

Many more selections are available. Give this some thought. You want every aspect of your wedding to be memorable and touch the hearts of your guests. Music is a fantastic way to set a mood.

The Wedding as Entertainment

A WEDDING IS PART CIVIL SERVICE and part sacred ritual. It can be religious and personal, and it certainly should be a celebration; but in addition to all those uplifting, soulful, and legal qualities, it should be entertaining. Everyone is dressed formally, even your grandfather who you've never seen wearing anything except his old gardening hat and a pair of work pants. You could just walk down the aisle, get married, sigh in relief that it's over, and walk back up the aisle to shake everyone's hand and head off to the party. As long as you're doing this, though, and because it means so much, you should probably put some effort into making it "just right." Use your imagination, do some research, and figure out a way to make the ceremony itself a real event.

Of course, if what you want is the minimum, then that is exactly what you should do. Get married and then go party. It's your wedding and it should reflect your wishes and values.

Tiffany & Chad

In keeping with their Victorian style wedding, the flower girl wore a beautiful gold vintage gown and she pushed a vintage pram filled and decorated with flowers down the aisle of the church. The ring bearer and all grooms-men wore black tuxes with tails. They each wore a top hat and white gloves. The brides-maids entered the church from the back and the groomsmen from the front. They met at a special point and did a beautiful curtsy and bow to one another; they then walked up to the front of the church, on stage, and did another curtsy and bow and parted. It was very formal and beautiful, and again gave the bridesmaids and groomsmen time to feel special.

Priscilla & Josh

As the bridesmaids and groomsmen walked down the aisle, they stopped halfway and did a dance spin together. This was a way of giving each bridesmaid and groomsman a special time for them to shine. The song used was very appropriate for not only the time of year but for the dance moves the attendants used.

The Vows

THE VOWS YOU MAKE TO your spouse on your wedding day can be the time-honored ones:

You may promise to "love, honor, cherish, and protect, forsaking all others and holding only unto..."

Or perhaps, "...to have and to hold, in sickness and in health, for richer for poorer, for better or worse..."

You may also choose some combination of those. Essentially, you are making a promise to place the person facing you first in your life, to stick by him or her no matter what misfortune may befall either of you, and to do it all with good grace and love. No wonder people cry at weddings! This a serious lifetime commitment you've asked them to witness.

Look into each other's eyes as you exchange vows.

A few decades ago, it was common for women to promise to "obey and serve." We don't make that sort of promise any more. And the discovery that the vows could be changed from those that had been in use for quite some time taught us that it was possible to write our own vows. And many of us began to do just that. You can write your own vows, you can use the ones prepared for you by your faith, or the ones suggested by any number of priests, rabbis, pastors, and judges, who are all in the business of marrying people. Many officiants will offer you some choice of vows or ask if you want to say something on your own. You can even use the vows provided for you and then add something if you want. The vows can be highly personalized and personal. Say what you think, what you believe, and only what you are happy to promise.

This groom waits patiently as his bride approaches.

Why We Do That

Throughout history, the wedding ceremony has gone through many changes, not the least of which is that we can't seem to decide whether it's a religious rite or a legal contract. It is both, but depending on the culture, the government, and the social mores of the time, it is sometimes more one than the other. Early Romans (prior to Christendom) rejected religion as a whole and along with it, some of the religious rituals that were observed, including marriage rites.

Until the 16th Century, weddings continued to be secular. A couple was married if they swore to be married in the presence of witnesses. Then the Roman Catholic Church issued an edict making marriage a sacred rite of the church, and slowly people turned to the church as the preferred place to exchange their vows. Then in 1791 the French Revolution tossed religion out along with the monarchy and declared a civil service to be the only way to become husband and wife.

Couples in the United States, of course, have the right to be married in any way they wish, and most opt for a religious ceremony of some sort. Still, they need a license from the state to make it legal.

The wedding ceremony contains many rituals and blessings, readings, and remarks by the officiant, but the core of the entire ritual is this:

The two of you:

1. Declare your intent

2. Exchange wedding vows

3. Exchange rings

4. Kiss

And, of course, many people have been married without benefit of a ring exchange. Perhaps some have even been married without the ending kiss.

So the act of becoming a married couple can be honed down to about three minutes worth of words and actions. The rest is added window dressing, albeit highly appropriate and meaningful window dressing. There may be opening and closing comments by the priest, pastor, or rabbi; there may be candle lighting, glass breaking, and sand blending. There will, in any religious ceremony, be prayers, blessings, and instructions...and more candle lighting...there may even be communion. You might want to add handfasting, broom jumping, and any number of ethnic or cultural traditions that have actually stood the test of time along with newer traditions such as unity candles.

Most states require two witnesses to a marriage, but seldom does a wedding take place with fewer than 30 guests, and usually that number is more like 200.

It's all your decision and you can keep it very simple or make it as sumptuous and complicated as you want. Some churches have their own rituals and rites; some are optional and some are required; your officiant will lead you through the requirements if you are having a religious ceremony.

Interspersed among those simple exchanges can be as much ritual as you want. A typical Christian ceremony might consist of the following:

1. Entrance, processional, and music

2. Introduction

3. Readings, songs, candle lighting, and prayers (this part often involves other family members)

4. Questions and declaration of intent

5. More readings, songs, and prayers; perhaps some sand blending

6. Wedding vows (I plight thee my troth…)

7. Music, prayers, and possibly more readings

8. Exchange of rings

9. Lifting of veil and first kiss

10. Introduction of the couple and recessional

You may choose to exchange traditional vows or write your own, very personal ones.

Courtesy Sarah O'Donnell Panella and Jason Panella © Elizabeth Woodhouse

The declaration of intent is the part where you answer the question, "Will you have this man…?" and "Will you have this woman…?" The vows consist of "I promise to love, honor, and cherish…." The exchange of rings and the kiss come last, and then you are pronounced husband and wife. Usually the officiant says something like, "Ladies and gentlemen, may I present Mr. and Mrs. Suze and Tobias Jones." And you turn around and greet your guests and walk, beaming at the world, back up the aisle and out of the room.

If you want to use truly traditional wedding vows, The Book of Common Prayer, The Solemnization of Matrimony (1662) is the place to find them. The language is that of Shakespeare or The King James Bible, elegant, flowing, poetic:

> "Dearly beloved, we are gathered together here in the sight of God, and in the face of this congregation, to join together this Man and this Woman in holy Matrimony...."

> "I N take thee M to my wedded husband, to have and to hold from this day forward, for better for worse, for richer for poorer, in sickness and in health, to love, cherish, and to obey, till death us do part, according to God's holy ordinance; and thereto I give thee my troth."

(Modern brides tend to object to the word "obey," so just cut that from the vows. This was written in 1662, and custom has changed a bit since then.) The man promises only to love and cherish his wife, and uses the words "I plight thee my troth."

And the ceremony continues:

> "Wilt thou have this Woman to thy wedded wife, to live together after God's ordinance in the holy estate of Matrimony? Wilt thou love her, comfort her, honour, and keep her in sickness and in health; and, forsaking all other, keep thee only unto her, so long as ye both shall live?

> With this Ring I thee wed, with my body I thee worship, and with all my worldly goods I thee endow."

And it ends with the charge to the world:

> "Those whom God hath joined together let no man put asunder."

Just what does "plight thee my troth" mean? *Plight* means to pledge. *Troth* means truthfulness; it's the word from which our present day word *truth* is derived. So "Plight thee my troth" means "I promise to always be truthful." "Give thee my troth," the version spoken by the bride, means "I give you my truth." The word *betrothed* is a form of the root word *troth*, or truth, and means, virtually, "united in truth."

If you *plight your troth* or *pledge your troth* or *give your troth*, it means that you are promising to always be truthful. And you're promising to do it for the rest of your life. These vows really are not to be taken lightly.

The exchange of rings is a highlight of the ceremony.

According to www.WeddingDetails.com, a Jewish ceremony, too, can be broken down into some very essential core activities:

1. The bride accepts an object worth more than a dime from the groom (usually a wedding ring).

2. The groom recites a ritual formula of acquisition and consecration.

3. There must be witnesses to these two acts.

Make it This bride and groom return a basin of water to the Earth after using it in a ritual hand cleansing ceremony. You can incorporate many such rituals in your ceremony to make it special for your wedding.

Everything else is merely custom: the chuppah, the seven wedding blessings, the breaking of a glass, even the presence of a rabbi are not religious requirements for a Jewish wedding. A typical wedding, however, might go in this order:

1. Blowing the Shofar

2. The processional

3. Encircling the groom (the bride circles around the groom seven times)

4. Entrance under the wedding canopy

5. The seven betrothal blessings

6. Havdalah (a ceremony marking the end of the Sabbath)

7. Kiddush (blessing of the cup)

8. Exchanging vows

9. Ring ceremony

10. Tallit covering (prayer shawl)

11. Blessing

12. Presentation of bride and groom

13. Breaking of the glass

14. Recessional

15. Cheder Yichud (bride and groom are secluded in a room together for a few minutes)

Lisa & Joe

"Because Joe and I are of different faiths, we got married outside by a judge. We were married under the chuppah (the marriage canopy under which the bride and groom stand during traditional Jewish wedding ceremonies). We also did the breaking of the glass and the lighting of the unity candle to represent the different religions of our families.

One of my brothers sang during the ceremony, and my other brother did a Jewish blessing at the end."

A couple marrying in a nonreligious ceremony often incorporates many aspects of the wedding ceremony that we think of as religious. The line blurs, but the religious parts, of course, include blessings, prayers, and communion. A pretty ritual that has been incorporated into many Roman Catholic Church ceremonies is the traditional presentation of flowers before the shrine of Mary that is found in most Catholic churches. The flowers may be a small bouquet similar to the wedding flowers or three roses (symbolic of the Holy Trinity). Some Catholic brides actually lay their wedding bouquets before the shrine of Mary after the wedding ceremony. It is tradition for the bride or couple to say a prayer at the shrine for a blessing on their marriage.

All eyes are on the bride and groom as they exchange their vows.

Communion is a part of the mass celebrated during a Roman Catholic or Anglican wedding.

Cathleen & Chris

We were married by a business-forms sales-man who happens to be a Universal Life Minister. He let us write our own ceremony and vows, which was a nice touch. Instead of a traditional ceremony, we told a very short version of how we met, since our meeting and courtship were a little unusual and many guests didn't know the full story.

We wrote our own vows, which were half silly, half sappy. We both laughed and cried through the whole ceremony and had most of the audience in tears, too. Several people told us afterward that it was the most touching ceremony they'd ever been to. I think because we were just so happy! I hate speaking in front of people (though, as a teacher, I do it), but I wasn't nervous at all because Chris was literally the only person in that rose garden with me. When I got up there, I literally forgot about every other per-son there...except my bridesmaid, who was standing behind me sniffling away! It was a short ceremony, but it was beautiful, if I do say so myself. It encapsulated who we are—it was offbeat, humorous, and touching all at the same time, which is what we wanted. Our ceremony wasn't really religious. Neither Chris nor I practice any religion, so we just left it as a celebration of our relationship and love, more than about religion.

Some rain may fall, but your wedding day will always be a perfect memory.

There are many rituals, new and old, that you can weave into your ceremony to make it your own. The lighting of a unity candle is a recent addition to the "traditions" involved in a wedding ceremony. Variations on this theme have the parents of the couple going onstage together to light a candle, then the couple themselves each one taking his or her respective candle and lighting another "unity" candle.

Another is the sand ceremony, the blending of two different colors of sand by pouring them into a new container, where the colors blend together. If you have children, this is also something they might participate in so that they can have a role in the wedding ceremony. The blending of the sand symbolizes the blending of two adults and any number of children to form a new family unit. Another thoughtful and touching way to include children in the ceremony is to present each child with a special piece of jewelry after the ring ceremony. Some families present girls with symbolic pendants, lockets, or bracelets, while boys may receive a lapel pin or ID-style bracelet.

Sand mixing is becoming a popular ritual in the wedding ceremony.

Readings are also a part of the service, and only your imagination, your religious beliefs, and your time to find them or write them limit the uniqueness of yours. Typical sources for reading material are The Book of Solomon, Ecclesiastes, and The Rubaiyat of Omar Khayyam, and there are many others.

Karen & Joe

In Karen's and Joe's Cherokee nuptials, the wedding place was blessed for seven consecutive days prior to the ceremony. The bride and groom each chose four elders to be their confidantes throughout their marriage. In the traditional ceremony, the bride and groom arrive separately, each wrapped in a blue blanket. When they are proclaimed to be husband and wife, they are covered in one white blanket.

In Native American tradition, the bride and groom give gifts to their guests rather than receiving them. When food is served, none can be wasted and must be given to all.

Another Native American tradition is the Indian wedding vessel with two spouts. The bride drinks from one spout while the groom drinks from the other. Some couples break the vessel after the service; some do not. Karen's and Joe's was presented to them by a Cherokee man named John Cucumber.

They also exchanged marriage sticks. Theirs were made by Lloyd Owl. These sticks are wrapped in leather with feathers and fringe hanging from them.

Jennifer & Ryan

There was a part of the ceremony where the officiant took our rings before we put them on and walked them around to our guests asking the guests to blow on the rings as a symbol to bless the rings. There was also another moment in the ceremony where my husband and I were asked to look out at the ocean. The officiant told us to continue looking at one spot and then close our eyes. He told us to remember that image when times get tough—close your eyes and remember this moment. We also had a ukulele player who played us our first song and asked us to have our first dance during the ceremony. Also the blowing of the conch shell when we were pronounced husband and wife is one of my favorite memories.

Here's a tip from Michie, the mother of two of the brides whose wedding stories are pictured in this book: One of the most important elements of both weddings was to keep the flow smooth and continuous throughout the entire wedding, especially during the ceremony. We've all gone to weddings and sat through times where nothing was going on. For a few seconds, the room is quiet and kind of uncomfortable. Maybe during a transition period from one event, such as a prayer or candle lighting to vows or some other planned time.

It takes some planning and coordination to keep this from happening, but it doesn't cost a dime. Just plan each moment as if you were the director of a play. For instance, have a vocalist begin to sing while some necessary movement is taking place or candles are being lit. Plan each moment so that something special is always taking place. And for the overall planning of the wedding, make it your own. Use the things that are important in the bride's and groom's lives to make your day truly reflect who you are. This way the day is as special and as perfect as it can possibly be.

Courtesy Nicole and Will Robertson © Mick Pederson

This gorgeous couple walks back up the aisle as husband and wife.

After the Vows

AFTER YOU EXCHANGE YOUR VOWS, exchange rings, kiss, and are introduced as husband and wife, the recessional takes place. This is the two of you walking back up the aisle as a newly married couple.

After the recessional, there may be a receiving line at the ceremony site. Some couples choose to forego that and greet their guests individually at the reception, but the receiving line is considered a traditional part of the service. After the receiving line, the bride and groom depart for the reception site. There is a tradition of throwing rice, bird seed, flower petals, and all sorts of interesting things at the departing couple.

This groom expresses his joy by scooping his bride up in his arms and carrying her away.

Tiffany & Chad

"In the foyer of the church we put the programs in an old vintage trunk. We also made a scroll for the guests to sign as they entered the wedding. I got a piece of canvas from a paint supply store and cut it to the size I wanted to use, (about 2' wide by 6–8' long). I used tea and coffee to die the fabric and left it scrunched up until it dried. We rolled both ends of the fabric around a curtain rod which had the Fleur-De-lies symbol on each end. We had the calligrapher personalize the top of the scroll with the bride and groom's names and wedding date. We now hang that scroll on our bedroom wall, and we have a daily reminder of our special day and the guests that made it special."

Photo Sessions

Most couples feel some residual superstition about seeing each other before the ceremony on the day of the wedding, and that makes it rather inconvenient to take many formal pictures early in the day. Many photojournalistic-type photos can be taken of the bride and groom, their attendants, and their parents dressing and preparing, but any pictures that are taken of the bride and groom together will necessarily have to wait until after the ceremony. The result of this minor logistics problem is that guests are often left cooling their heels at the reception waiting for the bride and groom to finish their photo session, get to the reception, and make their grand entrance so they can host their first social affair as a married couple.

Hors d'oeuvres and drinks passed by waiters before you arrive help to keep everyone entertained and mingling.

Why We Do That

Even in cultures that are most unlike ours, the things that are required at a wedding ceremony are to intend to be married, to exchange vows, exchange rings, and kiss. During the Communist reign in the USSR, religious weddings were declared null; the only weddings recognized by the state were civil ones, and couples were discouraged from seeking out a religious ceremony under the atheist Soviet government. In today's Russia, after the wedding, a couple travels to a World War II memorial and lays flowers on the monument there. Cars are important in the Russian ceremony, too, the bigger, the better, and getting in the car to drive somewhere after the ceremony is important. (During the Soviet reign, only high government officials could afford big black sedans, so these are a big status symbol to everyday Russians now.)

The couple then proceeds to a restaurant where their families await them. Instead of a wedding cake, they each must take a bite from a large loaf of bread. Tradition has it that the one taking the biggest bite is the one who will rule the home.

Couples in Russia today still must apply to the ZAG, the department of registration, which keeps track of all births, marriages, and deaths, as they did during Soviet rule. There is usually no engagement period and no engagement ring; couples who register are required to wait one month before they report back to the ZAG for their ceremony. Brides do wear wedding gowns, which they often make themselves. Two witnesses are required at the ceremony, and there is a reception with a big meal and lots of drinking later in the day. In fact, the measure of success of a wedding in Russia is the amount of liquor consumed.

The couple exchange wedding rings during the ceremony, and these are worn on their right hand, not the left as is common in the United States. Church weddings are allowed now that Soviet rule has ended, but they still are not considered legal; the couple still must go through the civil ceremony at ZAG.

There are some things you can do to ease the boredom for your guests and to make this a fairly seamless part of the day. First, have something for your guests to do while they wait. They will arrive at the reception site hungry and in need of some sort of libation. Provide that for them in the form of a bar with instructions that it be open as soon as the first guest arrives. Make sure your caterer understands this. Wait staff have been known to think it proper to wait until the guests of honor arrive to begin serving food or drink. You don't want any misunderstandings about this, so be very clear. Guests should be served as soon as they arrive.

> **Keep the receiving line to a minimum. It's best if just the two of you greet all your guests. You are probably the only members of your wedding party who know everyone, and if only the two of you are in the formal receiving line, there's no need to take the time for introductions at this point. Your parents and close family members can stand unobtrusively nearby and greet anyone they know. Then if you really think it necessary that your mother and stepfather be introduced to Sally from Accounting, handle that social amenity later at the reception.**

Immediately following the ceremony, you'll be on a tight time schedule for a couple of hours. Rely on your supporting cast to see you through; in fact, remind them that you are expecting their help in keeping the program moving along, especially the formal picture taking which will begin as soon as your guests have left for the reception. You may choose to have a receiving line at the ceremony site or wait until you reach the reception and informally visit each table to greet all your guests. Usually, the receiving line takes place in the entry or foyer of the ceremony site after the recessional and as your guests are filing past you on their way out. At this time, you should enlist the aid of some nieces and nephews to pass out bubbles, rose petals, bird seed, or anything you plan to have guests toss at you for good luck as you exit the church. After everyone has been greeted and has assembled outside, you should leave. Make a quick getaway to your waiting vehicle and just go. You may circle the block or go for a short drive, savoring each other's company for a moment of alone time during a hectic day. Give your guests time to get to their cars; then return to the church or synagogue for the formal wedding photographs.

Making a getaway has never been so luxurious.

Before you arrive to make your grand entrance, your guests might appreciate some light entertainment, such as strolling violins, classical guitarist, a barbershop quartet, or ethnic music, such as an Italian accordion player or a reggae performer. A balloon animal artist for the children is also a hit. Use your imagination to create a festive mood as soon as the guests arrive at the reception site; even though you aren't there yet, they'll know you are thinking of them. Make sure the DJ or band is playing some upbeat background music that will have everyone's toe's tapping in anticipation of the dancing to come later.

Meanwhile, you'll be getting all those formal photographs taken, as many as you want. You should have already worked out a plan with your photographer to make this go as quickly as possible. Make sure your bridal party and both sets of parents are aware of the critical need for speed and efficiency. You need to get the pictures taken, and get to the reception, but there's less urgency to do this if you know your guests are being well cared for until you arrive. You'll walk into a room full of happy people who are ready to party.

Many things have been thrown at departing brides and grooms through the years. Several years ago, it was almost always rice. Then there were objections to that, so it was replaced with bird seed. Both were considered a liability hazard because both are slick and can cause people to slip and fall. Couples then started passing out small bottles of bubbles with wands. The latest trend is sparklers. Everyone gets a lit sparkler and waves it at the departing couple. Waves it...not throws it at you, we hope.

Some couples replace the confetti or rice throwing with a release of doves, a way of expressing love and peace to the world on their special day.

In the midst of the receiving line, the leaving and returning, the bubbles and sparklers, the well wishes and congratulations, don't forget to take a quiet moment to visit with your officiant for the signing of the marriage license. This is a legal requirement. You don't want to forget, so give someone the assignment to remind you to do it. The priest or rabbi or pastor should remember, but just in case—find a way to remember this important act.

16

The Reception

Ah, fill the Cup: what boots it to repeat

How Time is slipping underneath our Feet:

Unborn Tomorrow, and dead Yesterday,

Why fret about them if Today be sweet?

—The Rubaiyat of Omar Khayyam

THE CEREMONY WAS PERFECT, the music was beautiful, the flowers were gorgeous, no one fainted, and now you are husband and wife—it is time to make your way to the wonderful party that awaits you.

After the pictures are taken and you arrive at the reception site to make your grand entrance, there are a few more photo sessions you'll have to pose for and then you'll be free to celebrate and enjoy your party and your guests. Your responsibilities are coming to an end now, and you can relax. While your guests were waiting for you to arrive, they were nibbling on hors d'oeuvres and partaking of refreshments, perhaps even being amused by the entertainment you thoughtfully provided for them.

When your guests arrive at the reception hall, a guest book or a presentation with table cards should greet them. They'll stop to sign the guest book and retrieve their table cards for directions to their tables. If you're working to keep a theme going throughout your wedding, the table card is a fantastic opportunity to be creative. Instead of directing guests to their table by number, keep your theme in mind. If you're having, for instance, a Christmas wedding, you might give the tables reindeer names. You could name the tables for milestones in your courtship or for anything that's important to the two of you.

Cathleen & Chris

Cathleen's and Chris's table naming scheme was based on places they would be visiting on their honeymoon. Their tables were called The Tower of London, the Canterbury Cathedral, the London Eye, and so forth. They bought inexpensive stand-up 5×7 frames and printed out the table name with a picture of the location on it for each table. A board near the entrance of the venue instructed guests which London tourist site they'd be sitting at.

Courtesy Sara O'Donnell Panella and Jason Panella © Elizabeth Furbish

She's a Red Sox fan; he's a Yankees fan, so their tables were named for sports legends from both teams. Their table cards included baseball quotes (which were also applicable to marriage) too.

When you do arrive, the wedding party will make a grand entrance and be announced by the DJ or bandleader; the bride and groom will enter after their attendants and their parents have been introduced to the waiting guests. Again, music is a central part of the reception. Something upbeat should be playing before you arrive; and then something a bit more soothing during dinner.

This bride and groom make a joyful entrance to their reception.

Courtesy of Michael and Marni Migliaccio

Heather & Mark

"We bought a wooden bound scrapbook, and all of our guests passed it around during the reception and wrote notes and poems, drew pictures, or just signed it. We liked that idea more than just a guest book with limited room for people to express themselves, and all of our friends and family wrote such wonderful things. Then I put all of the "paper" from the wedding in it, copies of the invitations, a program, a copy of the ceremony, the list of music we used for the ceremony and reception, and the large-format photos of the wedding that we printed for ourselves.

Through the years I've added the cards we give to each other on our anniversary and the like. It even has the reservation confirmation for the place we stayed on our honeymoon, and the card I signed there with my new, married name, the first time I signed it that way."

Guests turn to greet the bride and groom as they enter.

Food and Drink

FTER YOU'VE MADE YOUR GRAND entrance and stepped into the already ongoing party, it is your responsibility to make your way through the crowd of people waiting to greet you and, as quickly as possible, make your way to your head table so that you can be served dinner. A prayer before dinner is appropriate if it's something you want to do, especially following a religious ceremony. If you've invited your clergy-man to the reception, ask him to say grace. If dinner is a buffet, you need to go through the line immediately after you are seated and get settled—because no one else can eat until you are served, and people are getting hungry. As a matter of fact, you should stop, rest, and enjoy dinner and give your guests time to do the same. You've had a long, busy day and not one chance to eat since before the ceremony. This is also your first chance to sit down and enjoy each other's company for a moment. Take your time with dinner, and make sure you stay hydrated as well. You'll confer with a headwait-er or server who will help you with this process, but the sooner you eat, the happier everyone will be. After dinner, you can make your way around to visit with all your guests for a brief period of time before you move on to a few other activities.

Reception meals can be anything from a formal sit down dinner served by white-gloved waiters to a buffet of Italian, Greek, or other ethnic favorites, an early afternoon brunch, or even a wedding break-fast. An alternative to a buffet line is the concept of food stations scattered here and there throughout the room so that guests can choose from a carving station with roast beef and ham and then move on to a table where various salads are offered.

An array of light but taste-temping foods is appropriate for a wedding supper and can be served throughout the evening rather than having a complete dinner service that's over in an hour—this type of food service can contributes to the festive atmosphere by allowing your guests to snack, dance, rest, and nibble some more.

Not everyone can enjoy the sugar-laden confection that is the wedding cake. Serve some fruit during the cake cutting ceremony to provide a healthy option for those who need it or a light accompaniment to the cake for everyone.

Take a break from the hectic round of events and enjoy your first meal as husband and wife!

If you are providing a complete bar for your guests, you'll want to have some idea of what sort of liquor to have on hand. We've seen lists that tell you exactly how much you'll need. Those are general lists and they can't be accurate for everyone everywhere. If your reception is being held in a large hotel or banquet facility, and if you are paying by the drink, this won't be such a concern. Presumably, the site has a virtually never ending supply of liquor and can meet the demands of your guests. If you are paying by the bottle in the same sort of facility, this is also true.

If your reception is being held in a private club or residence and you need to predict what your bar needs will be, we suggest you seek the advice of your caterer or a bartender in your city. Drinking habits are different from one region to another; for instance, you might expect to use a lot more tequila than scotch if you live in Texas. In any southern state, bourbon probably is more in demand than gin. Vodka is typically a Midwestern or northern libation. The weather, the time of day, and the length of your reception all have an effect on what and how much your guests will want to

Whether yours is a do-it-yourself reception with family and close friends pitching in to supply the food or a formal affair in a hotel ballroom, you should provide the food and beverages for your guests; don't ask them to pay for their own liquor, even if that means not having any liquor. Do not, under any circumstances, set up a cash bar. There is no shame in being unable to provide a complete open bar for a reception that runs late into the night either. Pay for what you can afford. If that's a never-ending flow of martinis and fancy liqueurs, that's wonderful. If you can't afford to have an open bar, have the caterer set up a bar that serves just beer, wine, and soft drinks. If that is too expensive, just serve enough sparkling wine for everyone to toast with.

Even a tip jar on an open bar is crass. It should be assumed that you, as the hosts, will be taking care of the cost of all liquor, including the bartender's gratuity.

The bridal couple precedes their guests through the buffet line.

drink—chilled white wine is more popular in the summer, but if you're serving prime rib in December, the red wine to white wine ratio will probably increase. There is no formula that can accurately predict how much liquor you will need, and several factors go into making the determination. You should also investigate:

- ℭ Whether you must pay for any unopened bottles.

- ℭ Whether the laws of your state will allow you to transport opened bottles of liquor (if you pay for it, it's yours, but some states have laws against "open containers").

- ℭ Liquor liability laws (also known as host laws) in your state.

Decorative champagne glasses await the bride, groom, best man, and maid of honor for the toasting ceremony.

This couple stops a moment to savor the day, cake cut and toasting glasses in hand, they are ready to relax and enjoy the rest of the evening.

Lisa & Chris

Lisa and Chris got married on the beach in Tofino, British Columbia. The wedding was small, only 21 guests. The reception for 75 guests was two days later, back home in Seattle at a local beach house, Alki Bathhouse in West Seattle, which is pretty much a "do-it-yourself" kind of place.

Lisa says, "It's a small building right on the beach, looking out to downtown Seattle. We wanted something casual, fun, and right on the water. Both of us love West Seattle. We've spent hours running up and down the paths along the beach, getting ready for one of our many races. We wanted a place that meant something to us, and the bathhouse in West Seattle seemed to fit perfectly."

You will mingle a bit after dinner and then it will be time to cut the cake. Your DJ or bandleader and the head server should be your guides at this point, but if your reception is more casual and you don't have this sort of staff available to you, just keep the action moving and head to the cake table. You will need a small plate, a cake knife, a cake server, and toasting glasses. This is the time also for the best man to toast the happy couple. The maid of honor may also offer a toast if she wants. Toasting should be kept short and clean. Encourage anyone who will be speaking to practice a bit before the reception. Practice is the only way to make sure you get any kind of public speaking right.

Raising his glass, the best man toasts the bride and groom as the sun casts long shadows over Maui.

Why We Do That

Most of the customs, traditions, and superstitions associated with wedding celebrations today have their roots in fertility rites. In much earlier days, before we had access to fertility drugs (not to mention birth control), people who wanted to ensure that they'd start reproducing right away, rather than just wishing that it were so, devised some traditions that were rumored to ensure they'd have lots of happy, healthy children. Grain, in the form of rice and wheat (depending on what grew nearby) was often thrown at the couple in the hope that the seed would have an effect on their reproductive efforts. Eventually, loaves of bread were crumbled over their heads in a further effort to ensure fertility. It was even considered lucky to eat a piece of that bread, so wedding guests often scrabbled about on the ground after the bride and groom had passed by in the hopes of eating a crumb that had dropped off one of them.

The next step, of course, was to try to end some of the rowdiness, so the bride and groom began handing out the bread to their guests. After fine flour milling became common, the bread was replaced by cake, and over the course of time, those rough cakes of the past became the sugar-coated small architectural triumphs that are symbolic of weddings today.

The brother of the groom knows just what to say
as he toasts the happy couple.

Your wedding cake can be as elegant
or as whimsical as you like it.

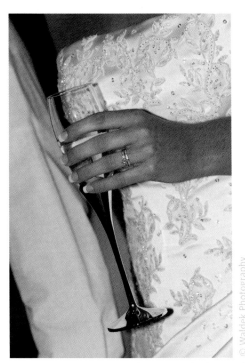

The bride stands ready while the best man makes his speech.

These whimsical hand-painted glasses are personalized with the couple's names and the date. They'll be used for toasting many anniversaries to come.

This couple put their dancing classes to good use at their reception.

The DJ or bandleader will take over now and guide you through the rest of the activities. The dancing will start, and again, you must be first. One of the most touching moments of your life together, one you will remember on anniversaries for years to come, is this first dance together.

This couple begins dancing as their parents and attendants await their turn to join in.

After the two of you enjoy your first dance together, which by the way, doesn't have to last through an entire song—unless you want it to—the DJ will invite some special people to cut in. The groom will dance with his mother and the bride with her father. After a few minutes, their escorts should join in, and all should go back to dancing with their own spouses. At this point, the wedding party should come to the dance floor, and shortly thereafter, all the guests should be encouraged to join in the fun. The party just got started! You are free now to do as you please. Dance a few more dances, but if you aren't the dancing kind, relax and mingle. Try to speak to all your guests, if only for a moment.

At some point later in the evening, after everyone has had a chance to relax and wind down a bit, the DJ will call you both to the dance floor again for the last two activities that will be required of you today: the bouquet toss and the garter toss. That is, if you choose to participate in either of these traditions, which some couples today forgo entirely.

This innocent item of apparel has caused many scuffles on the dance floor as single men vie for the bridal trophy.

Why We Do That

Tossing the garter has long been a part of weddings, but why do we do that? In 14th Century France, it was considered lucky to snatch a piece of clothing from a bride. In much the same way that people at concerts today like to retrieve a sweaty bandana from a rock star, people at weddings in those days liked to win a trophy from the bride. Brides, understandably wanting to keep their clothing intact, began the practice of tossing small articles to the assembled company, including garters.

In England it was common for wedding guests to escort a newlywed couple to their bedchamber. As the mead flowed and guests became more and more rowdy, some of them wanted to participate in the fun of disrobing the bride. To distract them, it is said the groom often tossed them a garter.

The garter is symbolic of the bride's virginity, and when the groom removes it from her during the wedding celebration, he is making a public demonstration of his new rights as her husband. It has long been considered lucky to catch it, although in days past, that luck meant the fellow who caught it could present it to his own lady love, thereby ensuring her fidelity. Nowadays, we've translated that to "he'll be the next to wed."

Most brides invest in a "tossable," or throwaway, bouquet—one that is smaller and less elaborate or expensive as the one they carry during the ceremony. They use this for tossing and keep the real one as a table centerpiece. Using the flowers from the bouquet you carry on your wedding day to make a pressed flower wall hanging is a way of preserving your beautiful bouquet as a memento of the day and a decorative item for your home. Frame and mat the pressed arrangement and place it under glass, and you have a beautiful item to use for decorating.

Cathleen & Chris

Like many brides today, Cathleen didn't like the idea of humiliating all the single women by asking them to line up and scramble for a tossed bouquet. It seems to say something that is counter to the beliefs of most women today: "I'm not okay with being single and I'll do anything to get this bouquet, which supposedly means that I'll get married soon and end this awful spinsterhood!"

Cathleen had also made her own bouquet, so she wasn't about to just toss it away. She had heard of a new custom where you give the bouquet to the woman who has had the biggest impact on your life. For her, that was her mother, so she surprised her by making a speech about her and giving her the bouquet.

Another replacement for the bouquet toss/scramble is to give the bouquet to the longest-married woman in the crowd in exchange for that woman's best piece of advice about marriage.

There are many ethnic traditions regarding dancing at this point in the ceremony; one that is becoming quite popular is the "dollar dance." Guests line up to dance with either the bride or the groom and hand them money for the privilege. Probably stemming from Italian or Polish immigrants, this was a way to ensure that the couple started their lives with a few extra dollars. It is more popular in some parts of the country than in others, but it's fun, and if you want to include it, you should. Choose a somewhat slow song that is fun for everyone to dance to, such as "Friends" by Elton John or "You've Got a Friend" by James Taylor, have the DJ announce that this is everyone's chance to dance with the lucky couple, start dancing together, and wait for your guests to break in. Usually, they will line up for the privilege, so you'll need to assign your best man and maid of honor, or perhaps the DJ's assistant, to keep the line moving by escorting new partners to join you every few minutes. This custom provides you with a chance to spend quality time with several guests in one small timeframe.

As the party gets underway, many women will begin kicking off their shoes. A thoughtful gesture is to provide several pairs of nice sport socks or anklets. It will provide your guests with protection for their feet and pantyhose and encourage lots of lively dancing.

Music

ONE THING THAT HAS BEEN continuous throughout the day, sometimes more noticeable than others, is music. Music can be used to lull, to entertain, to fill in empty spaces, to get a party started, and in fact, to end the festivities. It is often used as a cue, for instance, when the wedding march begins to play, all eyes turn to catch sight of the bride. Skillfully planning the music is your best bet for keeping your wedding festivities going the way you want them to go throughout the entire day. At the reception, this responsibility falls to the DJ. Your DJ, the person in charge of food service, and your photographer should work together to see that events flow smoothly throughout the evening.

Music in particular should be well thought out in advance. You may have particular songs and artists that you know you and your friends will want to dance to later in the evening. Earlier though, before dinner, during dinner, and during the cake cutting and garter tossing, you should take into account the makeup of your crowd. There will most likely be many older family members and children at your wedding, and you don't want to interrupt their conversation early in the evening. Later, after the plates have been cleared and the mood changes, is time enough for the band or DJ to crank up the hip-hop and boogie music.

Music is a highly personal thing, and you probably have definite tunes in mind for your first dance and for dances with your parents, but just in case you have trouble deciding, here are a few possibilities:

For your grand entrance
Theme from Rocky
Chariots of Fire Theme
Mission Impossible Theme

Cake cutting songs
Happy Together (The Turtles)
Recipe for Love (Harry Connick, Jr.)
Pour Some Sugar on Me (Def Leppard)

For your first dance together
A Moment Like This (Kelly Clarkson)
Dance With Me
At Last (Etta James)
It's Your Love (Tim McGraw)

Father/daughter dance
I Hope You Dance (Lee Ann Womack)
Sunrise Sunset
Butterfly Kisses (Bob Carlisle)
You Are So Beautiful (Joe Cocker)

Mother/son songs
I Wish You Love (Natalie Cole)
Sunrise Sunset

Bouquet Toss Music
Girls Just Wanna Have Fun (Cyndi Lauper)
It's Raining Men (The Weather Girls)
Girls Night Out (The Judds)

Garter Toss
You Sexy Thing (Hot Chocolate)
Theme from Jaws
Macho Man (The Village People)
I'm Too Sexy (Right Said Fred)

These are just some ideas to get your creative juices flowing. Choosing the music for your reception is a fun project that can occupy your leisure thought for weeks before the wedding. Make sure your DJ has a list of your preferences. You can listen to samples of most music at amazon.com and at itunes.com. This is such a great way to express who you are and what you want to say to all your guests on this one special day. Think it through and choose wisely; there's so much to choose from, but you have several hours to fill with music so you will be able to fit everything in. Just keep in mind that you will want to address the various moods as the evening progresses.

Courtesy Mitzi and John Koontz
© Waldek Photography

© James Karney capaphoto.com

Your guests will find many ways to amuse themselves with dancing at your reception.
Here, at a late October wedding, guests don Halloween masks to celebrate the upcoming holiday.
At another wedding, they hold their candles aloft in surprise tribute to the Led Zeppelin song the couple chose for their first dance.
And, of course, children and teenagers are a natural for the dance floor at a wedding reception.
The bride joins in the fun during a folk dance.

Lighting

Lighting is a developing phenomenon in the spectacular event that is your wedding reception. It started with lighted cake tables, dance floor light balls in the '80s, and has grown to the precise laser light shows of today. You can do as much or as little with lighting as you please, but it certainly can be used to set a mood. Just turning down the overhead lights and lighting some candles makes a big difference in the ambience of a room. Spotlights, colored lights, and washes of light provide drama, get people's attention, and set a mood in a distinct way. Lights combined with music can turn your reception into a show business spectacular.

And that's it. Party as long as you want and then leave. In past decades, the bride and groom made a dramatic exit from the reception shortly after the garter throwing and left their guests to continue the party without them. Today's couples usually prefer to stay and not miss out on any of the fun. The choice is yours, but you are free to leave when you want once you've spoken to all your guests and danced all you want. It's your perfect day, so you get to decide when it ends.

Priscilla & Josh

This couple had a lighting person during the ceremony as well as the reception to create the illusion of snow flakes dancing all around the room at just the right time and in all the right places, including on the bottom of Priscilla's gown as she and her father walked down the aisle.

For the first dance the lighting expert played an intricate part of the "show." He used lighted snowflakes on the dance floor, which was covered in the initials of the bride and groom, and at just the right moment during the dance he lightly dusted the bride and groom with artificial snowflakes. The song Priscilla and Josh used for the first dance was the one Josh had used on the night he proposed to Priscilla.

The Honeymoon and Beyond

There is nothing more lovely in life than the union of two people whose love for one another has grown through the years, from the small acorn of passion, into a great rooted tree.

—Vita Sackville-West

So you did it. You pulled off the event of a lifetime. And everything was perfect.

Now it's time to begin your honeymoon. You planned that well in advance too, and this special time will be the perfect way to start your new life as a married couple.

This book, like your wedding, is about much more than finding the perfect cake knife, or making sure the favor boxes are aligned neatly above the charger, or finding just the right tiara to hold your veil in place. Of course you want to put your very best effort into making sure everything is perfect on your wedding day, from the music played during the processional to the last dance of the evening and limo ride to the hotel where you spend your wedding night. Tomorrow starts a new day—your honeymoon—and even more importantly, your marriage.

May you always have walls for the winds,
A roof for the rain, tea beside the fire,
Laughter to cheer you, those you love near you,
And all your heart might desire.

—Irish blessing

May your life be long and happy and filled with love.

The Beginning…

Sample Forms and Checklists

Here are some samples of one bride's checklists, a quiz, and some forms you might want to use as you plan your wedding. Remember: Keep all these lists in your three-ring binder.

Budget Sample

THE FIRST ITEM ON YOUR LIST of necessary paperwork is the budget. See Chapter 4, "Dream, Plan, Realize," for links to some great budget planning software to get you started. Also, there are many free downloadable checklist and budgeting templates available on the Internet. Here's one bride's partially completed budget and recordkeeping spreadsheet for the paper items for her wedding:

Paper Items

Item	Quantity	Estimated Cost	Actual Cost
Wedding Invitations	(140)	$300	$347
Response Cards	(75)	$80	$72
Directions/Map Insert	(50)	$5	(free – printed them on computer)
Travel/Hotel Block Insert	(50)	$5	(free – printed them on computer)
Postage – Invitations	(120)	$100	$96
Postage – Response Cards	(100)	$40	$40
Rehearsal Dinner Invitations	(20)	$50	$43
Postage – Rehearsal Invitations	(20)	$10	$8
Thank You Cards	(120)	$80	$80
Postage – Thank You Cards	(120)	$50	$48
Wedding Programs	(80)	$150	$132
Table Cards	(80)	$45	$40
Printed Reception Napkins	(200)	$100	$70
Cake Boxes	(50)	$50	$32
Hotel Welcome Cards	(30)	$20	$20
Calligraphy – Invitations	(120)	$200	$225
Calligraphy – Table Cards	(80)	$75	$80
TOTAL		**$1,360**	**$1,333**

Discussion Questions for Couples

HERE'S AN INTERESTING EXERCISE for the bride and groom to do. You can go to the web site at www.courseptr.com, enter *Picture Yourself Planning Your Perfect Wedding*, and click the Downloads link to print these sample forms and quizzes. Try this as a couple, and see where these discussion topics lead you—just some food for thought.

The object of these questions is to discuss your beliefs and improve your understanding of your expectations prior to marriage. Each of you should take a separate piece of paper and answer the questions in private, giving thoughtful (and truthful) answers. Then, bring your answers to each other and discuss them to figure out how to improve the areas that need work. Don't worry, there will—and should—be some!

Exercise A

1. Why are you considering marriage? Briefly, what does marriage mean to you?

2. Do you trust this person you want to spend your life with? Will you be trustworthy to your spouse? How? Why?

3. What are your goals in marriage?

4. What, in your opinion, constitutes a "good marriage"?

5. Are you prepared to make this new family unit first (before friends and relatives) in your life from now on?

6. How do you make decisions? How will you make decisions after you are married?

7. What do you think you, as a couple, agree most on? (Name at least 5 things.)

8. What do you disagree most about? (Name at least 3 things.)

9. What happens when you disagree?

10. What is your definition of compromise?

11. How do you feel about compromising?

12. What kinds of things are you willing to compromise about?

13. What kinds of things will you NOT compromise about? Why? (Really think on this one.)

14. What happens if you don't compromise?

Exercise B

1. In what ways are you alike?

2. In what ways are you different?

3. Name one thing you like to do together. Why?

4. Name one thing you do not like to do together. Why?

5. How's your temper? What happens when you lose your temper? Why?

6. When you were growing up, how was anger handled in your home?

7. What were a couple of pluses or minuses about how anger was handled in your family?

8. How could you improve on how anger is handled in your own home?

9. Do you feel that you and your partner resolve differences and discuss relationship issues well?

10. Do you feel that you carry an unfair burden in resolving differences and discussing relationship issues? What would you like to change about the way you do this?

Exercise C

1. What are your expectations for the next 5 years? 10 years? 20 years? Be as specific as possible. Do you expect to have kids, buy a house, change career paths?

2. How many children do you want to have?

3. Do you agree that being parents means being there and raising the children, not leaving their care and training to a sitter or caregiver? Do you think that both parents should share the parenting responsibilities or only one parent? Which responsibilities do you think will be yours? Your partner's? Do you agree with that division? Is it fair or acceptable to you?

4. Will one of you stay home with the children? For how long? How do you feel about daycare?

5. Do you both plan to work to support the family?

6. Who will care for the children and house? Will the division of labor change if one of you stays at home with the children? Is that acceptable to both of you? How will that parent get a break or time to him/herself?

7. How will finances and budgets change if only one partner is working outside the home?

8. How will disciplining the children be handled? Should both parents determine the appropriate discipline? Under what circumstances can one parent decide alone? Will you use corporal punishment or other methods of discipline? Under what circumstances, if any, is it okay to spank?

9. Have you thought about the care and discipline of your children as they reach the "trying teens"?

10. Will you both be involved in the children's schooling by being in regular contact with teachers, helping with homework, and so on?

11. Will they be allowed to watch TV? How much? What other activities could you do together to create family time?

12. Do you have ideas about what kinds of foods kids should eat? Do you agree that the family should share meals together? How often?

Exercise D

1. If your partner got transferred to another city, what would you do?

2. In what parts of the country/world are you willing to live? Not willing to live?

3. Do you want to live in a small town? City? Suburb? Country? House? What size? For how long? New construction? 20 year old construction? 80 year old construction? Ranch? Two-story? Big master bedroom? Lots of entertaining space? Big yard?

4. How did your parents handle the division of labor in your home when you were growing up?

5. How do you plan to handle the division of labor in your home?

6. Is a "clean" house important to you? How clean? How often? What are the minimum standards you are willing to live with? Who decides what is most important?

7. Are pets in the house acceptable? If so, which ones? How many? Are there any pets that are not acceptable to you?

8. Under what conditions would you ask for financial help from others either inside or outside of the family?

Exercise E

1. Did you and your family attend church as a child?

2. How has this influenced your life?

3. Do you attend church now? How important is that to you?

4. Do you intend to attend church together as a couple? How important is that to you?

5. Do you intend to attend church together as a family? How important is that to you?

6. Do you think it is important for your children to attend church or have some form of religious instruction?

7. Is it important that your children attend parochial school? Do you agree on this?

8. Do you think spirituality helps develop moral character? What aspects of your partner's character would you like to see passed on to your children? What changes do you wish to see in your partner to ensure strong character in your children?

9. Do you want your kids to be raised in your religion/culture? Is it important to you to celebrate holidays in your traditions? How? Which ones are most important to you?

10. Do you want to visit family for holidays or stay home? Will this change when you have kids? Which holidays are important for you to spend with your family?

Exercise F

1. What kind of food do you like to eat on a daily basis? Do you like to just catch some meals for yourself, even when your partner's home, or do you always want to eat together when possible? Does the way your partner eats bother you? How can you help each other to develop healthier eating habits?

2. Is it okay to have a "night out" alone? If so, will you be sure to always remember family responsibilities and not do anything to endanger family solidarity? Under what circumstances would a night out be unacceptable? How will you agree on the limits?

3. What about jealousy? Is it okay for you or your partner to have friendships with members of the opposite sex? Touch them? How? What do you consider flirting? How will you handle jealousy?

4. Is it okay for you or your partner to go out alone with members of the opposite sex to a restaurant? For lunch? Dinner? To a movie? Concert? Ride in a vehicle? Go to their place? In what circumstances? If not, how can you both best avoid these circumstances?

5. Can you discuss sexual needs openly? How about other physical compatibility? Do you like sleeping curled up together or with space between you? Do you think frequent affection (holding hands, snuggling, hugs, kisses) is important? Can you make it a practice to show affection to your partner at least once a day? How do you feel about displaying affection in public?

6. Do you like to watch TV in bed? Read in bed? Does having someone watching TV or reading in bed keep you from sleeping? Do you have objections on other grounds to TV or books in bed? How will you find a compromise?

Exercise G

1. What kind of financial arrangements do you think would work best for you and your partner? All joint accounts? Separate accounts? Joint and separate accounts? If you're using some variant on separate accounts, will you each pay a proportional share of joint expenses? An equal share? Pool everything, but each get spending money to put into individual accounts? How will you allocate "mad money"? Equally or proportional? How do you feel about the options that aren't your first choice?

2. Do you agree that financial commitments (debt) made prior to this marriage must be honored?

3. Do you agree that you will do everything you can to contribute whatever support is needed to meet your prior commitments and current and future financial responsibilities? (This may mean you both work more than one job to pay off old bills, and not taking on new debts, including having children, in the meantime!)

4. Will you agree to set up a workable budget and stick to it?

5. As soon as old bills are taken care of, will you work together to build a bank account and start a retirement fund so that you can protect your family in times of need?

6. Can each of you agree not to take on debt without the knowledge and agreement of the other partner? In what amounts? Anything over $100? $250?

7. How much do you expect to spend on your relatives as gifts?

8. Is it important to you to save for your children's college education? To save enough to pay for all of it? Is it more important to save for their education than to buy them nice clothes in elementary school?

9. How about saving for retirement?

Exercise H

1. Under what conditions would you consider divorce? (If he/she converts to a religion you disagree with? If he/she has an affair? If he/she loses his/her sex drive? If he/she stops taking care of his/her body? What does it mean to "stop taking care of his/her body"? If he/she won't help out with the household chores or caring for the children?) What can you do to prevent that from happening?

2. Do you agree that marriage is a sacred, lifelong commitment to each other and to God?

3. In your opinion, what is "abuse"? Has anyone ever accused you of being abusive? Do you think you are ever abusive? If yes, why? Name three better ways to respond.

4. Will you commit to getting marital counseling before getting a divorce?

5. Do you take care of your personal health—not abuse alcohol or drugs, visit your doctor at least once a year, and so on? Will you commit to this?

6. Can you envision "growing old" and sharing a life and family with this person? Does this appeal to you?

Exercise I

1. How much private time/space do you need? What kind of private time do you need? Are there any of your belongings that you don't want your partner to disturb?

2. What do you expect your evenings and weekends to be like after you are married? Is that okay with both of you? How often do you expect to go out together? Alone? With friends?

3. What do you like to do with your partner?

4. Where do you want to go/what do you want to do on vacation? How frequently do you want to go? For how long? Are you a three-day weekend person or a two-week vacation person?

5. When you get together with other people as a couple, do you feel that your partner treats you well in public? How do you wish you were treated differently?

6. Do you have a lot of common friends? Do you think it's okay for couples to argue in public, or should they only argue in private? Is it okay to argue about some things publicly, but not others? If so, which things? Is it okay to disagree, but not to argue?

7. How often do you like to go to parties? What kind of parties do you like to go to? Is it okay for you to attend parties alone?

8. Do you like to host your own parties? What kind? How often? What are your entertaining expectations after you are married?

9. How about hosting more casual get-togethers? How often do you expect to do these things?

The Master To Do List

ERE IT IS! The master to do list. A step-by-step plan to planning and enjoying *your* perfect wedding!

Announce Your Plans

- ❧ Choose your rings.

- ❧ Tell your parents and your children, if you have them.

- ❧ Tell other close friends and family.

- ❧ Announce your engagement in the press—alumni magazines or websites, and newspapers in couple's current city, hometowns, and each set of parents' current cities of residence.

Planning Phase

- ❧ Decide on the degree of formality and the number of guests you'll invite.

- ❧ Hire a wedding planner if you want one to oversee the entire affair. If not, ask a reliable, organized friend not in the wedding party to oversee the wedding day details for you.

- ❧ Choose preferred dates and times for the wedding—your final decision will be based on the availability of your church or synagogue, officiant, and preferred reception site.

- ❧ Reserve the venue for the wedding and rehearsal, and make certain the officiant is available.

- ❧ Set a time to meet with the officiant, especially if you're having a religious ceremony.

- ❧ Plan church/synagogue arrangements. Determine whether any premarital counseling or classes are required, and schedule that as early as possible.

- ❧ Reserve the reception site.

- ❧ Start working on your guest list.

- ❧ Send "save the date" cards if you are using them.

Choose Your Attendants

- ❧ Invite the bridesmaids, maid or matron of honor, best man, groomsmen, ushers, and others to participate in your wedding.

- ❧ Give each attendant a list of his or her responsibilities.

- ❧ Copy all wedding party names, addresses, phone numbers, faxes and e-mail addresses into your three-ring binder. Keep an electronic file of everything too.

- ❧ Create a detailed calendar for the months preceding your wedding date.

Choose Your Service Providers

- ❧ Hire a caterer, call your Aunt Mary, or get food service recommendations from your reception site.

- ❧ Interview and hire florist—view samples/photos of work of at least three, contact recent clients for references, and request estimates.

- Interview and hire photographer and videographer—view samples/photos of their work, contact recent clients for references, and request estimates.

- Interview and hire (or ask if you have talented friends or family) musicians for the ceremony—make sure the site allows the music you plan for.

- Hire a band or DJ for the reception.

- Reserve block of hotel rooms for out-of-town-guests, including hospitality suite if needed.

Leading Up to the Big Day

- If the reception is to be at a home, begin planning logistics, consider the current decor when making your color selections, and begin any necessary refurbishing as well as reserving any rental items needed.

- Shop for your gown, veil, and other attire.

- Select and purchase wedding shoes.

- Schedule initial consultation with stylist for your wedding day hairstyle and makeup. Begin growing out hair if necessary and experimenting with highlights or color if you choose. Select hair accessories to match your hairstyle.

- Schedule any desired cosmetic procedures with dentist, orthodontist, dermatologist, esthetician, etc.

- Choose dresses for bridesmaids and flower girl; advise them about shoes, jewelry, make-up, and accessories.

- Advise the mothers on attendants' dress colors so they may make their selections. (MOB first, then MOG and stepmothers).

- Choose attire for groom, groomsmen, ushers, FOB, FOG, stepfathers, and ring bearers; schedule fittings and reserve tuxedos.

- Whether hiring limousines or using friends, contract (or arrange) all wedding party transportation to the ceremony and from the ceremony to the reception. Consider arranging transportation for out-of-town relatives as well.

- Register for gifts. Especially choose silver, china, and crystal patterns in addition to useful daily items.

- Schedule fittings for attendants.

- Have a blood test if required.

- Order invitations, thank you notes, and all stationery.

- Mail invitations six to eight weeks before the wedding.

- Decide upon the particulars of your wedding reception.

- Schedule bridal gown fittings as necessary.

- Coordinate dates with hosts and hostesses for bridal or couples' shower, bachelor, and bachelorette party. Provide hosts and hostesses with guest lists.

- Coordinate other parties—bridesmaids' tea/brunch/spa party, groomsmen's outing, welcome BBQ for out-of-town guests, etc.

- Send a schedule of shower and party dates to the bridal party.

- Keep a record of all your wedding gifts, item, date received, and who the gift was from. Send out thank you notes within one week of receipt of gifts.

- Select the groom's ring if it is to be a double-ring ceremony, and have it engraved.

- Select wedding gifts for each other if you are exchanging gifts.

- Order thank-you (hostess) gifts or flowers for those who entertain for you.

- Select gifts for the maid/matron of honor, bridesmaids, flower girl, ringbearer, ushers, groomsmen, and best man.

- Make plans for the honeymoon, including passports, visas, and inoculations if needed.

- Change your name(s) on all important business papers (insurance, credit cards, bank accounts, legal documents, driver's license), if applicable.

- See your attorney about making a will.

- Schedule manicure and pedicure for the day before the wedding.

- Schedule hair and makeup appointments for bride and bridesmaids the day of the wedding.

- If you are announcing your wedding in any newspapers, check for requirements.

- Keep the groom's family up to date on the guest list and wedding gifts received.

- Confirm that space will be available for the bride and bridesmaids to dress on the wedding day.

- Set a date to go with the groom to get a marriage license. (Take cash for license fee, results of blood test, driver's license, or any other required documents. Call ahead to confirm what you'll need.)

- Save some ribbons from gift and shower packages for your bridesmaids to make into mock bouquets to use at the wedding rehearsal.

- Make arrangements for the rehearsal dinner.

- Select a responsible person to handle the guest book at the wedding and bring it to the reception.

- Design your wedding program and have it printed.

- Plan for something old, something new, something borrowed and something blue, a penny in your shoe, and any other tradition or superstition that's important to you.

- One week before the wedding, confirm all vendors by phone or fax, including caterer, florist, photographer, videographer, musicians, limo service, parking attendants, last minute gown alterations, time you can get into the ceremony site, and cake delivery.

- Prepare checks for all outstanding balances due to vendors, ceremony and reception musicians, the officiant's honorarium or fee, etc. Be sure to have your checkbook on hand the day of the wedding to cover any forgotten items or amount discrepencies that crop up.

The Week Prior to the Wedding

- Pack for honeymoon. Carry all legal and travel documents, cameras or camcorders, and travelers checks in a purse, travel bag, or other small carry on bag.

- Confirm all honeymoon plans[md]flight schedules, hotel reservations, directions, etc.

- Confirm wedding night arrangements or reservations, including your transportation from the reception to your wedding night suite and delivery of your luggage to the suite if departing for the honeymoon the next day.

- Make arrangements for someone to take the bride's gown to be cleaned and preserved and return the groom's tuxedo following the wedding.

ধ Write thank you notes to your parents for their love and support. Have them delivered while you are on your honeymoon.

ধ Have any necessary hair removal procedures performed—eyebrow shaping, bikini line for honeymoon, back waxing for finance', etc.

ধ Plan activities for out-of-town attendees.

ধ Prepare your home for house guests.

ধ Confirm any last minute changes and guest count for the rehearsal dinner.

ধ Count acceptances for the reception and estimate the number of late responses; notify the caterer (check their "guarantee" requirement times).

ধ Create and organize table and menu cards for the reception.

ধ Gather in one place everything you will need to dress for the wedding. Refer to the emergency checklist in Chapter 14.

The Day Before

ধ Make sure all vehicles used are fueled, clean, and ready for passengers.

ধ Deliver goody bags to hotels where out-of-town guests will stay.

ধ Pick up wedding gown and veil.

ধ Pick up tuxes—try them on at the shop!

ধ Take favors, disposable cameras, decorations, cake knife and server, and toasting glasses to reception site. Make arrangements for someone to gather items for you following the ceremony and at the end of the reception.

ধ Nail appointment for manicure and pedicure and relaxing massage.

ধ Rehearsal and rehearsal dinner.

Day of Wedding

ধ Bride's hair and make up appointment.

ধ Give payment envelopes with checks to a trusted friend or family member to distribute to vendors, musicians, and officiant on the wedding day.

ধ Give groom's wedding band to maid/matron of honor and bride's wedding band to best man prior to ceremony.

ধ Eat something.

ধ Delegate all event management duties to someone else.

ধ Get married.

ধ Enjoy the party!

Sample Verification Letter/Fax

HERE'S A SAMPLE CONFIRMATION letter to verify the menu and bar requirements for the rehearsal dinner. You can use this as a template to write your own such letters for every vendor you deal with. Put your requirements in writing and get the vendor to sign the agreement so you have every communication in writing.

To: Mary Kelly, Oktoberfest Restaurant

Date 10/25/07

Re: Rehearsal Dinner—Sat., 11/03/07

From: Sam & Sarah

Phone: (321) 555-1234 (work) (321) 555-4321 (home)

Hi Mary,

We really enjoyed having dinner at the Oktoberfest Restaurant a few weeks ago to select the menu for our rehearsal dinner. We would like to make the following changes to the sample menu that you originally provided for our consideration.

Event Time:

Start time: 8:00 p.m.

Dinner: 8:15 p.m.

End time: 10:00 p.m.

Increase Quantity of Beers:

Domestic Beer (Coors Light, Budweiser): 50 units

Premium Beer: 60 units

Increase Quantity / Reduce Selections of Wine:

Wine (merlot & chardonnay):

10 bottles total (5 of each)

Non-alcoholic beverages:

Offer water, coffee, & iced tea only (no sodas)

Add non-alcoholic bottled beer: 10 units

Dinner Menu:

Tossed Salad with Ranch or Vinaigrette Dressings

Warm Rolls & Butter with Soft Bavarian Pretzels

Mixed Wurst over Sauerkraut

Schnitzel

Lemon Pepper Chicken over Wild Rice

German Potato Salad

Fresh Vegetable Medley

Mini Apple Strudel ala Mode

Please fax a price estimate based on this new menu to me at 555-1211. Also, is there a beer and wine list that we can use to select which premium beers and wines we would like to serve?

If you have any questions, please feel free to contact me at 555-1234 (W) or 555-4321 (H). Thank you.

Event Manager Master To-Do List—Rehearsal

Décor/Set Up:

Place guest place cards and buffet item menu cards on tables.

Set up portable stereo with German CDs for background music during dinner.

Place guest favors at each place setting (Oktoberfest German mustard with personalized labels)

Table decorations:

—moss

—white and ivory pillar candles in hurricane glass

—cranberries

—white gourds

—grape vine

—kissing balls

—white holiday lights

—German steins

Schedule of To Do Items:

At Rehearsal:

Camera and extra film

Distribute wedding day itinerary for attendants and families

Give marriage license to Fr. Thomas

Carry ribbon bouquet from showers—church rehearsal

7:45 – Rehearsal Dinner:

Stereo —background music during dinner

Camera and extra film

Toasting glasses

Distribute attendants' gifts

Gather all items to take home (steins, toasting glasses, camera)

Event Manager Master To-Do List
—Wedding Day

Ceremony

Wedding programs

Guest book and pen

Check envelopes for vendors, musicians, and officiant honorarium

Extra maps to reception

Reception

Table cards

Table menus and numbers

Votive candles

Cake knife

Wet wipes

Toasting goblets

Bird cage (for card and gift envelopes)

Table favors

Disposable cameras w/guest instruction notes

Basket for disposable cameras and sign (place in foyer near door)

Restroom courtesy items

Luminaries (w/sand and tea lights)

Long butane lighter (for luminaries and pumpkins)

Carved monogrammed pumpkins (w/candles – place at entrance)

Mums (place with pumpkins)

Ceremony Music Outline for Musicians

Pre-Ceremony Music:

Adagio	Albinoni
Air on G String	Bach
Jesu, Joy of Man's Desiring	Bach
Air – Water Music Suite No. 1	Handel

Lighting of Candles:

O' Perfect Love	Barnby

Note: The 3 candle lighters will enter together, light the altar candles, and return to their pews.

Seating of the Families:

Arioso	Bach

Note: Seating order will be 1 grandmother with escort, the groom's parents, and the bride's parents.

Processional:

Canon in D	Pachelbel

Note: There are five pairs of attendants.

Bride and Groom Processional:

Trumpet Voluntary	Clarke

Note: Bride will enter alone to walk to the groom at the pew break. Bride and groom will proceed to the altar together.

Responsorial Psalm:

The Lord is Compassionate	Psalm 145:8-9, 10, 15, 17-18

Note: The Psalm will be read.

Gospel Acclamation:

Celtic Alleluia

Note: The cantor will sing the acclamation.

Holy Communion:

Panis Angelicus	Franck

Note: The cantor will sing this.

Presentation of Flowers:

Ave Maria	Schubert

Note: Bridesmaid #3 will sing this.

Recessional:

Wedding March	Mendelssohn
La Rejouissance, Royal Fireworks Music	Handel
Ode to Joy	Beethoven

A Sample Wedding Program

The Sacrament of Holy Matrimony Uniting

Sarah Marie Harper
and
Samuel Parkhurst Adams

November 3, 2007
All Saints Catholic Church
Boston, Massachusetts

The Order of Service

Prelude

"Adagio"	*Albinoni*
"Air on G String"	*Bach*
"Jesu, Joy of Man's Desiring"	*Bach*
"Air, Water Music"	*Handel*

Lighting of Candles	*Marie Harper & Peter Adams*
"O' Perfect Love"	*Barnby*

Seating of the Families

"Arioso"	*Bach*

Processional

"Canon in D"	*Pachelbel*
"Trumpet Voluntary"	*Clarke*

Greeting and Opening Prayer

Old Testament Reading ....*Mark Adams*

Love is Strong as Death................*Song of Songs 2:8-10, 14, 16a; 8:6-7a*

Responsorial Psalm

The Lord is Compassionate ....*Psalm 145:8-9, 10, 15, 17-18*

New Testament Reading ....*Ashley Adams*

Live in Love and Thanksgiving...................................*Colossians 3:12-17*

Gospel Acclamation ....*"Celtic Alleluia"*

The Holy Gospel..*Father Thomas Doyle*

Remain in My Love...*John 15:9-12*

Exchange of Vows

Blessing of Rings

Prayer of the Faithful

Nuptial Blessing

Preparation of the Gifts

Lord's Prayer

Sign of Peace

Holy Communion

"Panis Angelicus"..*Franck*

Presentation of Flowers

"Ave Maria"...*Schubert*

Final Blessing

Recessional

"Wedding March"...*Mendelssohn*

"La Rejouissance from the Royal Fireworks Music"....................*Handel*

"Ode to Joy"..*Beethoven*

The Wedding Party

Parents of the Bride .... Gordon & Lynn Harper

Grandmother of the Bride .... Judith Walker

Parents of the Groom .... Frank & Nancy Adams

Edward & Lila Fayette

Matron of Honor .... Catherine Baranay

Best Man .... Kevin Jones

Bridesmaids .... Tammy Gates

Melissa Wells

Sara Wyneken

Susan Wyneken

Groomsmen .... Scott Reid

Bill Rosenstihl

Forrest Young

Rick Lancaster

Scripture Readers .... Mark Adams, Ashley Adams

Greeters .... Nikki Howard

Ashley Howard

Candle Lighters .... Marie Harper, Peter Adams

Celebrant .... Father Thomas Doyle

Organist/Pianist .... David Kinson

Violinist .... Ginny Romaro

Trumpeter .... Michael Golbright

Vocalists .... Terry Curtis, Susan Wyneken

Eucharistic Ministers .... Greg Goodyear, Chris Etzler

The altar Memorial Candle is lit in loving memory of those we miss:
Grandmother Lilly McCabe
Grandpa & Grandma Adams
Aunt Anita Petto

You cannot be with us in person, but we feel your loving spirit as we carry your memory in our hearts today and always. During your time with us, you were extraordinary examples of how to live and love. We will strive to honor your memory by committing ourselves to our marriage as you committed yourselves to your own families.

We love and miss you all very much.

To our parents, your unconditional love and caring have comforted us all the days of our lives. As we begin our life together as husband and wife, we look forward to the day when we will have children of our own so that we may pass the lessons of love, compassion, and respect that we have learned through your example to the next generation.

To our friends and family, we are truly honored by your presence here today. The friendship, laughter, support, and love each of you has provided has enriched our lives beyond measure. We look forward to sharing our lives with you for many, many years to come. You are always welcome in our new home:

11233 North Oak Street
Boston, Massachusetts 02210

May God bless and keep you all.

With our love and thanks,
Sarah & Sam

They are no longer two, but one flesh.
Therefore what God has united, man must not divide.
Mark 10:8-9

Photographer's Guide

HERE'S A SAMPLE LIST of the formal photographs you might want to include in your photography session. Your photographer will no doubt have other suggestions, and your family arrangement may be different from this one. Use this as a guideline and create a list of the shots you want to be sure to get. And don't forget: candid shots are needed, too. Find a photographer who specializes in "capturing the moment."

Bride's Formal Photos:

Photo 1—Three Generations of Bride's Mother's Family
Bride
Mother
Grandmother

Photo 2—Bride's Mother's Family
Bride
Mother
Stepfather

Photo 3—Bride and Father
Bride
Father

Photo 4—Bride and Father's Family
Bride
Father
Aunt #1
Aunt #2
Uncle #1
Cousins

Groom's Formal Photos:

Photo 1—Groom with Parents
Groom
Father
Mother

Photo 2—Groom with Immediate Family
Groom
Father
Mother
Brother #1
Brother #2
Sister

Photo 3—Groom with Extended Family
Groom
Father
Mother
Brother #1
Sister-in-law
Brother #2
Sister
Brother-in-law
Nieces and nephews

Photo 4—Groom with Siblings
Groom
Brother #1
Brother #2
Sister

Bride & Groom's Formal Photos:

Photo 1—Bride and Groom with Bride's Mother's
Family
Bride
Groom
Mother
Stepfather
Grandmother

Photo 2—Bride and Groom with Bride's Father's
Family
Bride
Groom
Father
Aunt #1
Aunt #2
Uncle #1
Cousins

Photo 3—Bride and Groom with Groom's Family
Bride
Groom
Father
Mother
Sister
Brother-In-Law
Brother #1
Brother #2
Sister-in-Law
Nieces & Nephews

Pre-Ceremony & Ceremony Photos:

Church (exterior)
Church exterior sign
Church doors
Church (interior)
Church alter
Ceremony Musicians
Greeters
Groomsmen seating guests
Groom & Groomsmen Entering
Seating of Grandmother & Mothers
Bridesmaids' Processional
Bride and Father—outside church
Bride and Father's entrance
Bride and Groom's processional

Informal Photos

Wedding gown on hanger
Bride getting ready
Bridesmaids getting ready
Bride and bridesmaids toasting
Groom and groomsmen getting dressed

Master List for Reception DJ

NOTICE THE HELPFUL PHONETIC spelling of names—information the DJ absolutely needs.

Greetings & Introductions:

[The coordinator will notify you when the bridal party has arrived.]

DJ: Invite all guests to gather in the lower atrium to welcome the wedding party. When everyone has congregated in the atrium, begin the introductions. Wedding party will enter from the foyer and will gather to the right and left of the atrium staircase.

[music: "Are You Ready for This?"—Space Jam]

Best Man	Kevin Jones
Groomsmen	Rick Lancaster
	Scott Reid
	Bill Rosenstihl [rosen-still]
	Forest Young

[music: "More, More, More (How Do You Like It?)"—Andrea True Connection]

Matron of Honor	Catherine Baranay [baron-a]
Bridesmaids	Melissa Wells
	Tammy Gates
	Sara Wyneken [win-i-ken]
	Susan Wyneken [win-i-ken]

[music: opening prelude of "Bawitdabaw"—Kid Rock]

"Ladies and gentleman, it is my distinct pleasure to welcome, for the first time, Mr. and Mrs. Samuel Adams."

Cake Cutting:

Immediately following the introduction of the bridal party, the bride and groom will cut the cake.

Dinner:

Prayer by Father Thomas Doyle

Welcome Comments from Groom

Toasts: Best Man, Father of Bride, etc.

Dances:

First Dance: "Let's Stay Together"—Al Green

Father/Daughter Dance: "You Are So Beautiful"—Joe Cocker

Invite wedding party and all guests to join us on the dance floor.

All Fast Dance: "Get Down, Boogie-Oogie-Oogie"—A Taste of Honey

Last Dance of the Night: "Last Dance"—Donna Summer

Index

A

A Diamond is Forever Web site, 21
accessories
    fans, 121
    gloves, 120
    handbags, 121
    handkerchiefs, 121
    hosiery, 121
    lingerie, 121
    shoes, 122–123
    slips, 121
    tiaras, 120
    trains, 118
    undergarments, 121
    veils, 119
air-conditioning/heating concerns, reception location considerations, 85
albums, photo, 147
alcohol
    liquor liability laws, 224
    at reception, 223–224
    regulation, 84
Alfred Angelo custom designer, 113
Alfred Sung custom designer, 113
A-line style dresses, 109
altar flowers, 135
alumni magazine announcements, 40
amateur photographers, 147
American Bridal Web site, 101
American Gem Society Laboratories (Diamond Quality Document), 26
Amsale custom designer, 113
Angelo, Alfred (custom designer), 113
Anglican churches, reading the banns tradition, 39
announcements, engagement
    alumni magazines, 40
    bride's family, 33
    children first, 35–36
    effects on family, 32

    by e-mail, 34
    engagement parties, 41
    groom's family, 33
    newspaper announcements, 38–40
    by phone, 34
    when to tell, 34
    by written letter, 34
arranged marriages, 12–13
Artzproducts Web site, 147
attendants
    best man
    best man responsibilities, 104–105
    bridesmaids
        dresses, 124–125
        flowers, 133
        responsibilities of, 104
    flower girls
        ages, 104
        dresses, 125
        flowers, 134
    gifts, 167
    groomsmen
        attire/tuxedos, 126
        responsibilities of, 104–105
    how many, 102
    how to choose, 103
    junior bridesmaids, 104, 125
    maid/matron of honor
        gifts, 167
        responsibilities of, 104
    non-gender specific tradition, 102
    responsibilities of, 104–105
    ring bearers, 103, 127
    ushers, 104–105
    Victorian time tradition, 102
Austen, Jane, 12–13
authentication, diamond rings, 26
auto insurance, legal considerations, 177

B

baby's breath, 133
bachelorette parties, 156–157
Badgley Mischka custom designer, 113
ball gown dresses, 109
ballerina dress length, 111
balloons, 136
band selection, rings
    gold bands, 28
    matching bands, 29
    platinum bands, 28
    Scott Kay style sample, 27
    white gold bands, 28
bands/DJ selection, 50
    contracts with, 89
    dance floor availability, 88
    master list for, 260
    reception location considerations, 88
bargain basement shopping, 116
bateau neckline, 109
Beautiful wedding invitations Web site, 97
beauty/grooming items, 198
Bessette and Kennedy wedding, 5
best man responsibilities, 104–105
betrothal, 14, 49
bids, 89
bird seed, 217
black, emotions associated with, 95
Blissweddings Web site, 65
Bluenile Web site, 21
blusher veils, 119
bouquet, bride, 227
bouquet toss, 227
boutonnieres, 135
Bouvier and Kennedy wedding, 5
bras, strapless, 121
breath mints, 198
bridal show and expo shopping, dresses, 117
bridal showers
    bachelorette parties and, 156
    couple, 155
    linen, 155
    modern, 156
    registries, 156
    themed/specialty, 155
    traditional, 155
    who should give, 156

bride
    average age to wed, 60
    bouquet, 227
    escort, 202
    family of
        financial responsibilities, 61–63
        groom family introductions, 36
        telling about engagement, 33
    father of, tuxedos/attribute, 129
    father/daughter dance, 230
    flowers, 133–134
    gift to groom, 167
    mother of, dress selection, 126
    name changes, 70
Brides Web site, 96
bridesmaids
    dresses, 124
    flowers, 133
    gifts, 167
    junior, 104, 125
    responsibilities of, 104
brocade dress fabric, 112
brown, emotions associated with, 95
brunches, post wedding, 161
bubbles, 217
budget plans, 45–47
    averages/percentages, 65
    Blissweddings Web site, 65
    calculations, 64–66
    elagala Web site, 46
    Eventageous Web site, 65–66
    example of, 64
    head count considerations, 66
    online wedding calculators, 65–66
    Outoftheordinary Web site, 66
    sample spreadsheet, 236
    who pays for what, 61–63
buffet lines, receptions, 222
business agreements, 70
business arranged marriages, 12–13
bustling, 118

C

cake
    for bridesmaids' tea, 158
    as centerpiece, 141
    cutting, music for, 230

cutting the cake tradition, 225

flavors, 141

freezing, 141

leftover, 141

smearing in face, 143

storage, 141

table decoration, 141

taste tests, 138, 141

traditions, 142

when to reserve, 138

camera and film, 196

candles

as decoration, 136

unity candle lighting, 211

cap sleeve style, 110

car decoration, 103

car insurance, legal considerations, 177

carat weight, diamond rings, 24

catalog and online shopping, dress choices, 115

caterers, hiring, 84

Catholic churches

flower presentation tradition, 210

reading the banns tradition, 39

celebrity weddings, 4–6

Celtic joining ceremony tradition, 19

centerpieces, 135

certifications, diamond rings, 26

chain store bridal boutiques, shopping for dresses, 113

chapel train length, 118

charitable donations, as wedding gifts, 166

checking accounts, legal considerations, 178

checklists. *See* **sample forms and checklists**

children, telling about engagement, 35–36

Christian ceremonies, 78

music suggestions, 202

vows, 207

clarity levels of diamonds, 23

clergyman availability, 80

colors

combinations, how to mix, 95–96

diamond grades, 24

emotions associated with, 94–95

fall, 92

honoring your heritage, 93

pastel, 95

personal taste and preference, 92

primary, 94

secondary, 94

spring, 92

summer, 92

Web site resources, 96

winter, 92

common law *versus* community property states, 68–69

communion, 210

comparison shopping (planning), 48

confetti, 217

conflict diamonds, 21

consignment shops, shopping for dress, 116

contracts, band/DJ, 89

coordination, documentation as, 82

corsages, 135

cosmetic surgery, 191

cosmetics, 198

costs

average wedding costs, 18

bids, 89

budget planning, 45–47

costume designer (Rose Helen), 5

cotton dress fabric, 112

counseling, premarital, 192–193

couples gifts, 167

couples showers, 155

court train length, 118

credit cards, legal considerations, 178

crepe dress fabric, 112

cuff links, 127

cummerbunds, 126

custom designers, dress choices, 113

cut of diamonds, 22–23

D

dance floor availability, 88

dancing

dollar dance, 229

first dance, 227

lessons, 193

song selections, 230–231

David's Bridal, 108, 114, 118, 120

day before wedding activities, 196

day of wedding to do list, 252

day of week selection, 53–54

declaration intent, vows, 207

dentistry work, 192

department stores, shopping for dress, 115

dermabrasion, 191

designer trunk shows, shopping for dress, 116

destination wedding, 184

diamond rings
    American Gem Society Laboratories, 26
    authentication, 26
    band selection, 27
    Bluenile Web site, 21
    carat weight, 24
    certifications for, 26
    clarity levels, 23
    color grades, 24
    common settings, 29
    conflict diamonds, 21
    cut of, 22 23
    Diamond Dossier document, 26
    diamond fact Web sites, 21
    A Diamond is Forever Web site, 21
    Diamond Quality Document, 26
    flawless, 23, 25
    GIA (Gemological Institute of America) grading report, 26
    gold bands, 28
    as hardest known mineral, 21
    how to choose, 21–26
    loose stones, 29
    platinum bands, 28
    shape of, 25
    solitaire setting, 29
    stone size considerations, 24
    symbolization, 21
    with three stone settings, 29
    Tiffany Web site, 21
    value of, 25
    white gold bands, 28
    yearly inspections, 29
diet and exercise, 195
discussion topics for couples, 239–245
divorce rates, 68
DJ/band selection, 50
    contracts with, 89
    dance floor availability, 88
    master list for, 260
    reception location considerations, 88
dollar dance, 229
dolman sleeve style, 110
doubts about marriage, 6
dresses
    A-line, 109
    ball gown, 109
    bargain basement shopping, 116
    bridal show and expo shopping, 117

    bridesmaid, 124–125
    chain store bridal boutique shopping, 113
    consignment shop shopping, 116
    department store shopping, 115
    designer trunk show shopping, 116
    empire, 109
    fabric choices, 112
    fittings/measurements, 125
    flower girls, 125
    general types, 109
    lengths, 111
    local bridal salon shopping, 114
    magazine shopping, 117
    mermaid, 109
    mother of bride, 126
    mother of groom, 126
    neckline choices, 109
    online and catalog shopping, 115
    sheath, 109
    sleeve styles, 110
    style considerations, 108
    thrift store shopping, 116
    where to find, 113–117
    white gown tradition, 4, 108
    white, shades of, 112

E

elbow length veils, 119
elegala Web site, 46
e-mail, as engagement announcements, 34
emergency backup items, 198
Emily Post's Etiquette, **61–63**
emotions, color associated, 94–95
empire style dresses, 109
engagement
    announcements
        alumni magazines, 40
        bride's family, 33
        children first, 35–36
        effects on family, 32
        by e-mail, 34
        engagement parties, 41
        groom's family, 33
        newspaper announcements, 38–40
        by phone, 34
        when to tell, 34
        by written letter, 34

average length of, 14, 190

betrothal, 14

discussing financial agreements during, 15

parties, 41

engagement rings. *See* rings

entertainment, wedding as, 204

Estes, Clarissa Pinkola *(Women Who Run with the Wolves)*, 157

etiquette, who pays for what, 61–63

Etsy Web site, 123

European medieval times, arrange marriages, 12

Eventageous Web site, 65–66

evergreen boughs, 136

exercise and diet, 195

expenses. *See* budget plans; costs

expo and bridal show shopping, dresses, 117

F

fabric of dress choices, 112

facials

as bachelorette party, 157

before wedding day, 192

fall colors, 92

fall weddings, 52

fans, 121

father/daughter dance, 230

fathers of the bride/groom, tuxedos, 129

favorfavor Web site, 101

favorideas Web site, 101

favors, 168–169

Filenes Bargain Basement, 116

financial agreements. *See also* budget plans

business agreements, 70

discussing before marriage, 15

prenuptial agreements, 15

financial responsibilities, who pays for what, 61–63

fingertip veils, 119

first dance song selection, 230

fishing trips, as grooms' special gathering, 158

fitness routines, 195

Flagler, Caroline (David's Bridal), 108, 114, 118, 120

flawless diamond rings, 23, 25

floor length dresses, 111

flower girls

ages, 103

dresses, 125

flowers, 134

flowers

altar, 135

baby's breath, 133

boutonnieres, 135

bride's, 133–134

bridesmaid, 133

centerpieces, 135

corsages, 135

florists, when to contact, 96

flower girls, 134

pew pieces, 135

traditions, 133

food sampling

reception location considerations, 83

special dietary food considerations, 86

food/buffet line, receptions, 222

footwear, 122–123

formality considerations, wedding location selection, 75

forms. *See* sample forms and checklists

frugalbride Web site, 48

G

garter toss, 227

Georgette dress fabric, 112

GIA (Gemological Institute of America) grading report, 26

gifts

attendant, 167

charitable donations as, 166

couples, 167

for guests, 100–101

registries, 165–166

shower, 156

gloves, 120

Godey's Lady's Book, 110

gold bands, 28

golf outings, as grooms' special gathering, 158

goody bags for guests, 168–169

gowns. *See* dresses

grand entrance, music for, 230

gray, emotions associated with, 95

Greek joining ceremony tradition, 20

green, emotions associated with, 94

greenery, 136

groom
    attire/tuxes, 126
    family of
        bride family introductions, 36
        financial responsibilities, 61–63
        telling about engagement, 33
    father of, tuxedos/attire, 129
    gift to bride, 167
    mother of, dress selection, 126
groomsmen
    attire/tuxes, 126
    gifts, 167
    responsibilities of, 104–105
guest books, 220
guest lists
    budget planning and, 66
    size of, wedding location considerations, 79
    special dietary food considerations, 86
guests
    gifts for, 100–101
    wedding favors for, 168–169

H

hair styles, 119, 194
halter neckline, 109
handbags, 121
handfasting, 19–20, 33
handkerchiefs, 121
hats, 123
head count, budget planning and, 66
health items, morning of wedding planning, 198
heating/air-conditioning concerns, reception location considerations, 85
Here Comes the Bride (The Bridal Chorus), 45
honeymoon, 182–184
hosiery, 121

I

insurance, legal considerations, 177
introductions, bride and groom families, 36
invitations
    12th Century England traditions, 98
    as formality level of wedding, 97
    peel and stick bows, 100
    save the date cards, 99
    Web site resources, 97
IRS Web site, 178

J

jersey dress fabric, 112
jewel neckline, 109
Jewish weddings, 55
    music suggestions, 202
    vows, 209
joint checking accounts, 178
junior bridesmaids, 104, 125

K

karat, gold purity, 28
Kay, Scott (wedding band styles), 27
Kennedy and Bessette wedding, 5
Kennedy and Bouvier wedding, 5
knee length dresses, 111

L

lace dress fabric, 112
laws, on who performs ceremony, 76
Leathercraftsmen Web site, 147
legal considerations
    checking accounts, 178
    credit cards, 178
    insurance, 177
    marriage licenses, 173
    name change, 174–175
    overview, 172
    same sex couples, 173–174
    taxes, 178
licenses to marry, 76, 173, 217
life insurance, legal considerations, 177
lighting considerations, receptions, 87, 232
lighting of unity candle, 211
limousines, 149–150
linen dress fabric, 112
linen showers, 155
lingerie
    as shower gift, 155
    wedding day attire, 121
liquor
    liquor liability laws, 224
    at reception, 223–224
    regulation, 84
local bridal salons, shopping for dress, 114

location of wedding selection, 50
    formality considerations, 75
    guest list size considerations, 79
    religious affiliation considerations, 75–76
    site restrictions, 79
    sites, list of, 78
long, fitted sleeve style, 110
Longoria and Parker wedding, 4
Longworth and Roosevelt wedding, 4
losing weight, 191
love spoons, 169
Lutheran churches, 78

M

magazine shopping, dresses, 117
maid/matron of honor
    gifts, 167
    responsibilities of, 104
make-up, 198
manicures, 196
mantilla veils, 119
marriage licenses, 76, 173, 217
marriage sticks, 212
massages
    as bachelorette party, 157
    as non-wedding-centered activity, 195
master to do lists, 246–249
matchbooks, 100
matron/maid of honor
    gifts, 167
    responsibilities of, 104
menu/place cards, 100
mermaid style dresses, 109
Middle Eastern traditions, 119
mini dress length, 111
Mischka, Badgley (custom designer), 113
modern bridal showers, 156
monarch train length, 118
month of wedding, popular months for, 53
morning of wedding activities, 197–199
mother of bride/groom dress selection, 126
mother/son dance, 230
music
    band or DJ selection, 50
    for bouquet toss, 230
    for cake cutting, 230
    for Christian ceremonies, 202
    for father/daughter dance, 230
    for first dance together, 230
    for garter toss, 230
    for grand entrance, 230
    for Jewish ceremonies, 202
    mother/son dance, 230
    organist/pianist availability, 81
    outline, sample form, 253
    reserving, 81

N

name changes, 70, 175
napkins, 100
Native American traditions, 212
neckline choices, dresses, 109
newspaper announcements, 38–40
nonreligious ceremonies, 210–211
note pads, engraved, 100
note taking (planning), 48

O

off-the-shoulder sleeve style, 110
online and catalog shopping, dress choices, 115
online registries, 165
orange, emotions associated with, 95
organist/pianist availability, 81
outdoor weddings, 50–51
Outoftheordinary Web site, 66

P

Parker and Longoria wedding, 4
parking space considerations, reception location selection, 87
participants of wedding. *See* attendants
parties
    engagement, 41
    pre-wedding
        bachelorette parties, 156–157
        bridesmaids' tea, 158
        grooms' special gathering, 158
        post wedding brunches, 161
        rehearsal and rehearsal dinner, 159–160
        scheduling, 154
        showers, 155–156
passports, 183
pastel colors, 95
pedicures, 196

peel and stick bows, invitations, 100
pew cards, 100
photo sessions
    after the wedding, 214
    at the reception, 220
photographers
    albums, 147
    amateur, 147
    formal (posed) photos, 145
    informal photos, 145
    interviewing, 144
    professional, 144–147
    sample guide, 258–259
    scenic/agricultural-type photos, 146
pianist/organist availability, 81
pillbox hat, 123
place/menu cards, 100
platinum bands, 28
porcelain veneers, 192
portrait neckline, 109
post wedding brunches, 161
premarital counseling, 192–193
prenuptial agreements
    community property *versus* common law states, 68–69
    discussed, 67
    discussing before marriage, 15
    divorce rates, 68
    reason why people want, 68
pre-wedding parties
    bachelorette parties, 156–157
    bridesmaids' tea, 158
    grooms' special gathering, 158
    rehearsal and rehearsal dinner, 159–160
    scheduling, 154
    showers, 155–156
pre-World War II wedding days, 7
Pride and Prejudice, 12
primary colors, 94
Prince Albert and Queen Victoria wedding, 4, 19
Prince Charles and Diana Spencer wedding, 4
professional photographers, 144–147
professional wedding planners, 44
program example, 254–257
proposals
    creative ways to propose, 9–10
    surprise, 9
    traditional, 9
    with/without rings, 11
purple, emotions associated with, 95

Q

Queen Victoria and Prince Albert wedding, 4, 19
questions, discussion questions for couples, 239–245

R

reading the banns, 39
receiving line, 214, 216
receiving lines, reception location considerations, 84
reception location selection, 50
receptions
    air-conditioning/heating concerns, 85
    alcohol beverages, 223–224
    all-inclusive sites, 83–84
    bouquet toss, 227
    cake cutting, 225
    caterers, hiring, 84
    ceremony to site driving route considerations, 84
    dance floor availability, 88
    dollar dance, 229
    first dance, 227
    food sampling considerations, 83
    food/buffet line, 222
    garter toss, 227
    grand entrances, 221
    guest books at, 220
    lighting considerations, 87, 232
    liquor regulation, 84
    parking space considerations, 87
    photo sessions, 220
    receiving lines, 84
    reserving, 83–88
    space concerns, 85–87
    special dietary food considerations, 86
    table cards, 220
    time allowance, 87–88
    toasting, 225
    visiting with guests, 222
record keeping, planning and, 52
red, emotions associated with, 95
Reem Acra custom designer, 113
registries
    online, 165
    shower, 156
    wedding gift, 165–166
rehearsal and rehearsal dinner, 159–160, 250–251
religious affiliation
    changing religions, 80–81
    wedding location considerations, 75–76

religious restrictions, 55
remembrance gifts, 101
ribbons, 136
rice throwing, 217
ring bearers, 103, 127
rings
    circle representation, 20
    diamond
        American Gem Society Laboratories, 26
        authentication, 26
        band selection, 27
        Bluenile Web site, 21
        carat weight, 24
        certifications for, 26
        clarity levels, 23
        color grades, 24
        common settings, 29
        conflict diamonds, 21
        cut of, 22–23
        Diamond Dossier document, 26
        diamond fact Web sites, 21
        A Diamond is Forever Web site, 21
        Diamond Quality Document, 26
        flawless, 23, 25
        GIA (Gemological Institute of America) grading report, 26
        gold bands, 28
        as hardest known mineral, 21
        how to choose, 21–26
        loose stones, 29
        platinum bands, 28
        shape of, 25
        solitaire setting, 29
        stone size considerations, 24
        symbolization, 21
        with three stone settings, 29
        Tiffany Web site, 21
        value of, 25
        white gold bands, 28
    exchange of, 206
    history and traditions, 19–20
    with matching bands, 29
    origin of, 18
    proposals with/without, 11
    as symbol of love and commitment, 18
    yearly inspections, 29
Roman joining ceremony tradition, 20
Roosevelt and Longworth wedding, 4
Rose, Helen (costume designer), 5
Russian weddings, 215

S

Sabrina neckline, 109
same sex couples, marriage licenses and, 173–174
sample forms and checklists
    budget, 236
    couples discussion questions, 237–245
    music outline, 253
    photographer's guide, 258–259
    program example, 254–257
    rehearsal dinner confirmation, sample verification letter/fax, 250
    to-do lists
        day of wedding, 252
        DJ master list, 260
        master, 246–249
        rehearsal/rehearsal dinner, 251
sand ceremony, 212
satin dress fabric, 112
save the date cards, 99
scoop neckline, 109
season of wedding considerations, 52
secondary colors, 94
self written vows, 205
shantung dress fabric, 112
shape of diamond rings, 25
sheath style dresses, 109
shoes, 122–123
showers
    bachelorette parties and, 156
    couples, 155
    gift registries, 156
    linen, 155
    modern, 156
    themed/specialty, 155
    traditional, 155
    who should give, 156
silk dress fabric, 112
sites. *See* Web sites
sleeve styles, dresses, 110
slips, 121
Social Security Administration, name change requests, 176
solitaire setting, diamond rings, 29
space concerns, reception location, 85–86
specialty showers, 155
Spencer and Prince Charles wedding, 4
spreadsheets. *See* sample forms and checklists
spring colors, 92

stationery
    invitations, 97–100
    menu/place cards, 100
    note pads, engraved, 100
    pew cards, 100
    save the date cards, 99
    thank you notes, 100
stone size considerations, diamond rings, 24
strapless bras, 121
strapless neckline, 109
summer colors, 92
summer weddings, 52
Sung, Alfred (custom designer), 113
surgical procedures, 191
surname change, 174–175
surprise proposals, 9
suspenders, 126
sweep train length, 118
sweetheart neckline, 109

T

table cards, at reception, 220
taffeta dress fabric, 112
tanning salons, 195
taxes, legal considerations, 178
taxis, 150
tea length dresses, 111
teeth straightening, 192
teeth whitening, 191–192
telling everyone. *See* announcements, engagement
thank you notes, 100
The Bridal Chorus (Here Comes the Bride), 45
Theknot Web site, 48
three-quarters sleeve style, 110
thrift stores, shopping for dress, 116
tiaras, 120
Tiffany Web site, 21
time of day selection, 54
toasting, 225
toasting glasses, 196
to-do lists
    day of wedding, 252
    DJ master list, 260
    master, 246–249
    planning and, 50
    rehearsal/rehearsal dinner, 251
  toning your body, 195

traditional proposals, 9
traditional vows, 205, 208
traditions
    bride escort, 202
    bridesmaids' tea, 158
    cake, 142
    Celtic joining ceremony, 19
    cutting the cake, 225
    flower selection, 133
    Greek joining ceremony, 20
    handfasting, 19–20
    Middle Eastern, 119
    name change, 175
    Native American, 212
    receiving line, 214
    ring, 19–20
    Roman joining ceremony, 20
    unity candle lighting, 211
    Victorian times, number of attendants, 102
    white gowns, 4, 108
    women and pre-wedding parties, 157
trains, 118
transportation, 149–150
travel plans, honeymoon, 183
T-shirt sleeve style, 110
tulle dress fabric, 112
tuxedos, 126
    for afternoon weddings, 127
    fathers of the bride/groom, 129
    fittings/measurements, 128
    mismatched, 128
    for morning weddings, 127
    personalization, 127
    for ring bearers, 127
    styles, 127

U

undergarments, 121, 197
unity candle lighting, 211
US Marriage Laws Web site, 76
ushers, 104–105

V

value of diamonds, 25
veils, 14, 119
Vera Wang custom designer, 113

Victorian times tradition, number of attendants, 102
videographers, 148
visas, passports, 183
V-neck neckline, 109
vows
    after the, 214, 216–217
    The Book of Common Prayer, The Solemnization of Matrimony, 208
    Christian ceremonies, 207
    cultural traditions, 206
    declaration intent, 207
    Jewish ceremonies, 209
    nonreligous ceremonies, 210–211
    sand ceremony, 212
    self written, 205
    traditional, 205, 208
    with/without ring exchange, 206

W

Wagner, Richard, 45
Wang, Vera (custom designer), 113
Web sites
    1st-class-wedding-invitations, 97
    American Bridal, 101
    Artzproducts, 147
    Beautiful wedding invitations, 97
    Blissweddings, 65
    Brides, 96
    budget planning, 65–66
    for color resources, 96
    diamond fact, 21
    A Diamond is Forever, 21
    elegala, 46
    Etsy, 123
    Eventageous, 65–66
    favorfavor, 101
    favorideas, 101
    frugalbride, 48
    for invitations, 97
    IRS, 178
    Leathercraftsmen, 147
    Outoftheordinary, 66
    Theknot, 48
    Tiffany, 21
    US Marriage Laws, 76
    wedding favor, 101
    Wedding paper divas, 97
    Weddingbasics, 96
    WeddingChannel, 49
    wrapwithus, 101
    Your wedding company, 96
    Zookbinders, 147
wedding favors, 101
Wedding paper divas Web site, 97
Weddingbasics Web site, 96
weight loss, 191
white, emotions associated with, 95
white gold bands, 28
white gown tradition, 4, 108
winter colors, 92
winter weddings, 52
***Women Who Run with the Wolves* (Estes), 157**
wrapwithus Web site, 101

Y

yellow, emotions associated with, 94
Your Wedding Company Web site, 96

Z

ZAG department of registration, Russian weddings, 215
Zookbinders Web site, 147

What do you PICTURE YOURSELF Learning?

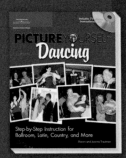
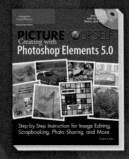

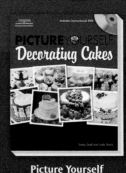